兴义民族师范学院英语一流专业（2019年一流专业建设项目）资助项目成果

中小学英语文学阅读教学引论

Introduction to English Literature Reading Teaching in Primary and Secondary Schools

何泽　著

WUHAN UNIVERSITY PRESS
武汉大学出版社

图书在版编目(CIP)数据

中小学英语文学阅读教学引论/何泽著. —武汉：武汉大学出版社，2021.3

ISBN 978-7-307-22056-0

Ⅰ.中…　Ⅱ.何…　Ⅲ.英语—阅读教学—教学研究—中小学
Ⅳ.G633.412

中国版本图书馆 CIP 数据核字(2020)第 272895 号

责任编辑:邓　喆　　责任校对:汪欣怡　　版式设计:韩闻锦

出版发行：**武汉大学出版社**　(430072　武昌　珞珈山)
(电子邮箱：cbs22@ whu.edu.cn　网址：www.wdp. com.cn)
印刷：武汉邮科印务有限公司
开本:720×1000　1/16　印张:16.75　字数:249 千字　插页:1
版次:2021 年 3 月第 1 版　2021 年 3 月第 1 次印刷
ISBN 978-7-307-22056-0　定价:50. 00 元

目　录

第一部分　中小学英语文学阅读教学课程建构：四种课型①

第一节　引　　言

有报道称在亚洲区域的十二个国家和地区中，新加坡和马来西亚是英语熟练程度最高的国家，中国排名靠后，仅高于泰国。中国英语学习者的人数远远超出世界上其他国家，有十万英语为母语者正在中国各地教授英语，中国已经成为全球最重要的外语培训市场。我国中小学生从小学三年级就开始学习英语，一些城市的家庭甚至从幼儿园就开始就让孩子到各种培训机构去学习英语，而且英语在中考，高考，大学四、六级考试，研究生考试，以及部分职称考试中都是必考科目，但这并没有确保我国公民的英语熟练水平。②

多年来中小学英语教学费时多、效果差造成的投入和产出严重不平衡的局面备受人们诟病，这也促使英语教学工作者反思我国的英语教学到底哪里出现了问题。笔者作为一名有二十年英语教学经历的教师，深切感到虽然我们的英语教学在对外开放和经济发展的反拨下出现了交际教学法、任务教学法等旨在培养学生语言能力的新做法，但面对高考的指挥棒，英语教学大多依然采取“灌输方式”，重视语言知识教学，让学生死记硬背以应付考试。这种被应试教育绑架的语言教育模式严重阻

---

① 本部分是2013年度宁波市教育科学规划课题“英文原著在高中英语教学中的应用研究”(项目编号：2013YGH43)的结题报告，略有修改。

② 新民晚报. 2013-8-14. 原文标题为《中国英语亚洲排名垫底男性水平更差》

碍了学生语言运用能力的综合发展。

《普通高中英语课程标准(实验)》明确把培养文化意识作为基础教育阶段英语课程的总体目标之一。新课程也倡导一种具有文化视野的英语教育，但《普通高中英语课程标准(实验)》对文化意识的界定只限于跨文化交际意识以及相关知识和能力的培养，对文化之精华的文学教育则没有提及。事实上，文学教育在我国中小学英语教育中几乎是一个空白地带。这一缺憾也许与我们接受的英语文化研究中对于文化的理解偏失有关。顾嘉祖先生早就指出："跨文化交际学界近年来比较重视对语言与非语言符号的研究，但却忽略了文学文本的作用。"实际上，语言的文化性不单单体现在外语国家的人文地理、风俗习惯等，还体现在其文学上。文学作品是了解异域文化的一面镜子，能更生动具体地反映异域文化。不仅如此，经典文学以独特的话语方式凝聚了人类对真善美的文化精神追求。因此，文学教育可以说是英语文化教育的生命所在，没有丰富文学滋养的英语文化教育是跛脚的，难以从根本上改变"文化"沦为语言知识传递、语用技能训练附庸的命运。

第二节 国内外有关文学阅读的研究简述

在西方，传统外语教学的目标是培养学生通过阅读来学习目标语文学作品和使用目标语的能力。国外论述文学作品在外语教学中的地位和作用的代表性学者有 Marckwardt, A. H.（著作 *The Place of Literature in Teaching English as a Second or Foreign Language*），以及 C. J. Brumfit 和 R. A. Carter(著作 *Literature and Language Teaching*)，他们从文学在英语教学中的地位以及如何利用文学阅读进行语言教学等角度进行阐述。美国 1999 年出版了主要针对中小学外语教学的《21 世纪外语学习目标》，其学习目标可以归纳为"5C"：Communication(交际)、Cultures(文化)、Connections(连贯)、Comparisons(比较)和 Communities(社区)。具体来说，就是"运用外语交际、体认多元文化、贯连其他学科、比较语言文化特性、应用于国外多元社区"。其中文化内容明确规定，学生必须接触该语言丰富的文化内涵，阅读具有重要意义的文艺作品(陆效用，

2001)。Makay(2001)认为学习语言与文学阅读是相互构建的过程，语言学习目标应当与文学教学进行有意义的对接，他还认为英语课堂教学借助文学作品能带给学生三方面益处：首先，它展现了作者为了取得特定的交际目标而选择的语言形式；其次，它是语言综合运用能力的理想资源；再次，它能提高跨文化意识和培养语感。这些专家和学者都分别从不同的角度阐述和强调了文学作品在外语教学中的重要性：Ess(2002)极力倡导通过文学教学形成语言共同体，促进交际活动和跨文化交际，启发批判性和分析性思维；Hall(2005)呼吁阅读英语经典作品，通过文学阅读掌握语言技能、理解英语文化、提高思想能力；Tomlison(2008)认为英语文学阅读在培养学生跨文化知识和意识方面具有其他任何阅读无可比拟的优势。

在国内，刘润清(1996)认为："正式的外语教学与其他学科教学一样，要想真正掌握一门外语，需要大量的阅读，有独立的思维过程和分析总结过程"；胡春洞(1996)在《英语学习论》一书中指出："离开文学的英语学习路线是一种以实用主义哲学思想为主的路线，是近视而无远视的路线，是抄近路反而绕远路的路线。"黄远振(2009)以个案分析详细论证了文学阅读在中学英语教学中的可行性，介绍了推动文学阅读的策略和方法；曹敏(2010)认为现有中学英语教材中文学作品、经典美文较少；熊金霞(2010)从语言、文化、情感、教学等方面阐述了阅读经典美文和文学作品的重要性；傅云山(2012年)探讨了高中进行文学欣赏课的可行性和必要性，并提出了高中文学作品的选用原则以及文学欣赏课的具体教学模式。

第三节 研究设计

一、研究的理论基础

1. 国家政策

教育部2003年颁布的《普通高中英语课程标准(实验)》明确指出，高中英语课程的总目标是使学生在义务教育阶段英语学习的基础上，进一步明确英语学习的目的，发展学生自主学习和合作学习的能力；形成有效的英语学习策略；培养学生的综合语言运用能力。有效地学习语言需要大量地听和读，没有听和读的海量输入，说和写的语言综合运用能力就无从谈起。因此英语教学既要传播信息，又要培养学生摄取信息、处理信息的能力，而阅读教学的目的就在于培养交际性阅读能力——有效地获取书面信息，并对此信息进行分析、推理和评价，以实现交际的目的。同时，《普通高中英语课程标准(实验)》中对高中毕业生的阅读能力(八级)提出了具体的要求，即：(1)能理解阅读材料中不同的观点和态度；(2)能识别不同文体的特征；(3)能通过分析句子结构理解难句和长句；(4)能在教师的帮助下欣赏浅显的文学作品；(5)能根据学习任务的需要从电子读物或网络中获取信息并进行加工处理；(6)除教材外，课外阅读量应累计达到36万词以上。

2. 教育理论：阅读教学理论

阅读教学理论涉及心理学、语言学、教学法等多个领域，因此不同角度下的阅读教学实践着不同的理论。心理学家们就阅读提出过几种假说。最有影响的是Goodman（1967）提出的"心理语言的猜测游戏"。Goodman是这样解释的："阅读过程是读者用字符的表现方式进行编码信息的重新构思。"与"阅读是被动接受知识的过程"这一传统观念正相反，Goodman认为，阅读是一个主动思考的过程。

Goodman(1967)和Smith（1971)提出了另一个心理语言学的阅读模式，称为"自上而下"模式。该模式以概念理论为基础，提出"在阅读过程中，阅读者根据大脑中已有的句法和语义知识对阅读材料进行预测，并在阅读过程中加以证实和修正"。根据这一模式，阅读活动实际上是一种语言知识的实践和实现。

Rumelhart提出了交互作用模式。此模式建立在Carroll模式和Goodman模式的基础上，它是两者的结合，能全面解释阅读理解中的一些现象。交互作用模式认为，在阅读过程中，人们运用两种方式进行信息处理：一种是"自下而上"的方式，一种是"自上而下"的方式。"自下而上"的方式指学习者从语言的最小单位——字母和单词识别开始，逐步弄懂较大的语言单位，即短语、分句、句子及语篇的意义。“自上而下”的方式强调学习者在阅读过程中是主动参与者，他们不是逐字逐句地去理解文章，而是运用背景知识并结合自己的预测在上下文中找出有关信息。

从以上诸多观点可以看出，阅读并不是一个简单的认字活动，而是一个复杂的、积极的、语言和思维相互作用的心理过程。阅读材料、背景知识、阅读策略，以及读者的动机等非智力因素都能对阅读理解的效果产生影响。

二、概念界定

本研究中所选的英文名著指的是未经过加工处理的原汁原味的经典名著。这些作品符合高中生的认知特点，略高于学生的知识水平，兼具可读性、趣味性和教育性。所选的文学名著大多以经典英语小说为主，因为小说以其巧妙的构思、细腻的文笔和优美的情怀为学生展现了英语国家的社会文化和风土人情。

三、研究目标

1. 落实英文名著阅读在高中英语教学中的实践应用，让学生获得审美快乐、丰富人生经验，同时提高人文素养。

2. 通过行动研究，构建英文名著应用于高中英语课堂教学中的主要课型及相应教学策略。

3. 英文名著走进高中英语课堂是可行和有效的，并且具有特殊的思想、人文等诸方面的课程价值。它作为重要的课程资源，既能帮助学生提升英文素养，培养文化意识(课程目标之一)，又能改进课堂质量，促进学生精神的成长，从而实现英语教学到英语教育的转变。

四、研究方法

1. 行动研究法

通过和教育专家的沟通，作为行动者的我们在本次研究中尝试用科学的方法对自己的教学行为进行研究。以文学作品作为课堂教学的资源为研究内容，通过发现问题、分析问题、解决问题，不断改进自己的教学行为。

2. 经验总结法

及时积累研究案例，反思、体会，总结、筛选课题研究中的做法。在已有的客观现实材料及思想理论材料基础上，运用各种逻辑和非逻辑方式进行加工整理，以理性思维的形式反映教育的客观规律。

第四节　研究过程

一、理论探索：英文名著应用于高中英语教学中的价值认识

阅读是人们获得信息、汲取知识的一个重要途径。拥有良好的阅读能力不仅能培养语感、体会语境，而且有助于提高语言综合运用能力。对于高中生而言，培养阅读习惯、掌握阅读技巧、增加阅读实践，是实现阅读能力飞跃、提升个人语言素养的有效方法。原版文学名著是学习语言的绝佳材料。一方面，文学是语言的艺术，是语言最完美、最崇高的形式，语言依赖文学展现它的美；另一方面，语言又是文学的载体，文学依赖语言来表达它的含义。

《普通高中英语课程标准（实验）》在欣赏类选修课里把英语文学欣赏课列为可供参考开设的选修课程。这表明了文学对英语教学有着极其重要的意义。英美文学课为学生提供了一些了解英美国家的生动的、全面的、深刻的语言素材，是学生熟悉与了解西方文化的直接通道。从这个意义上看，没有任何其他材料可以代替文学作品。这是因为，学习英语的理想方式是亲临英语语言环境、感受其文化氛围，然后不断地运用英语与以英语为母语的人交流。但是，这样的机会目前对于大多数学生来说不易得到，我们只能给学生提供文字资料或录像资料来进行学习，所以文学课可起到弥补这一不足的作用，文学作品也自然成了一种最理想的学习语言与文化的材料。由于文学与文化之间存在着密不可分的联

系，通过学习文学作品，学生可以从深层次上体验英美国家的思想发展轨迹和风俗习惯的形成，以及不同历史时期的不同社会状况，从而在整体上客观了解西方文化，缩短英汉语言因文化造成的差距。可以说，文学作品中的世界是西方现实社会的真正缩影，它们穿越了时空与文化的差异，在与学生进行直接的对话。

英美文学作品中的语言是英语中的精华，阅读英美文学作品有助于提高学生的英语语言能力，这既包括对文学作品语言的感受能力，又包括对文学作品内容的欣赏能力。由于文学语言是语言应用的最高层次，所以阅读文学作品时，学生不再是单调乏味地学习单词或句型，而是在作者基于现实生活、经艺术加工所创造的世界里，亲临语言环境，感受不同场合中不同语言的运用，这是语言学习的一大挑战。毋庸置疑，不同流派的作家、不同风格的语言有助于学生掌握语言的多样性和丰富性。尽管文学作品中有些语言显得古旧陈腐，但是其语言的丰富和精练以及具有的感染力，仍不失为学习书面语言和文体知识的可靠材料。同时，英美文学教学有利于陶冶性情、开阔眼界、充实心灵、启迪智慧，可以培养与提高学生的文学修养与人文素质。从语言学习的角度看，文学欣赏能力的高低能反映出学生语言能力的强弱。同时，从人文教育的角度看，文学作品又通常包含某种深刻的哲理，这有利于拓宽学生的思维与认识空间，启迪审美意识，陶冶人生情操，以达到培养健全人格的目的。

二、现实分析：宁波经济社会发展需求与现实英语教育的冲突

宁波作为沿海开放城市，其英语教育在教育理念和教学方法上一直走在全省的前列。近几年随着宁波人民经济生活水平的大幅提高，其对优质教育的需求越来越强烈。近年来，宁波有多所高中相继引进国外的优质教育资源（如宁波效实中学的国际文凭课程，宁波外国语学校的AP课程，等等），以及大批学生选择出国留学，这也从另一方面说明人们对现行教育状况的不满足。为了满足广大人民对教育的新的需求，特别是对国外优质教育资源的需求，我们英语教育者承担的责任更加重

大。我们的英语课堂应该率先引进国外优质的教育资源，而英语文学名著就是语言学习的优质资源。

笔者任教的宁波效实中学和宁波外国语学校(笔者从2012学年至2015学年在宁波外国语学校支教)有良好的英语教学传统，两所学校近年来在英语教学中引进国外原版教材《环球英语》《联想英语》《典范英语》等，但这些教育资源大多以教材文本和简写本的形式出现。随着时代的发展，学生英语水平的提高，英语教育改革的步子应该更大些，引进英文名著的时机也已经成熟。笔者从2012学年就开始在宁波外国语学校高中英语课堂教学中尝试补充文学名著的教学，迄今为止已经完成英语原著《夏洛的网》、《相约星期二》、《老人与海》、《傲慢与偏见》(第一部共二十三章)、《了不起的盖茨比》的阅读和教学任务。从实验的教学效果看，此项举措深受学生欢迎，学生的阅读质量、词汇量、听说能力都有大幅度提升，部分学生甚至自觉阅读其他英文名著，这说明将英文名著引入高中英语教学是可行的。

现行高中学段仍在采用人民教育出版社2007年版的高中英语教材，教材的更新速度较慢，缺乏经典、完整的文学语篇，从模块一到模块八只有 *The Million Pound Bank Note* 和 *Pygmalion* 两篇课文涉及文学名著，且均以剧本的形式出现，学生接触原汁原味的文学名著的机会少之又少，一定程度影响了学生人文素养的提高，也不符合英语课程具有工具性和人文性双重性质的理念。为高中英语课堂教学注入新鲜血液，拓展高中英语课程资源势在必行。

三、名著选择

近两年的教学实践证明，将合适的英文名著应用于高中英语课堂教学是可行的。两年的教学实践中，我们已经完成了《夏洛的网》、《相约星期二》、《老人与海》、《傲慢与偏见》(第一部共二十三章)、《了不起的盖茨比》的阅读教学任务。在教学过程中，教学内容始终是核心，决定教什么比怎么教更加重要。所以在教学实践中，文学作品的选择是关键。所选的文学作品要符合学生的语言认知水平，力求语言优美、地道，同时作品的内容要具有吸引力、主题要积极向上，这样既能保证学生浸润在原汁原味的语言中学习地道的语言，又能保证教学内容对青少年的心理成长和思维发展起到积极的推动作用。

1. 选择原则

(1)参考国外中小学的文学阅读教学实践以及国外一些主流媒体的推荐

笔者在教学实践中和国外一线的文学老师保持频繁的沟通。美国的Mr. Glen先生和宁波外国语学校国际部的几位文学老师通过邮件或当面交流的方式商讨名著的选择，他们一致认为第一本文学名著的选择很关键，选择的原则应该是可接受、有趣味，所以实践中笔者选的第一本英文名著是《夏洛的网》。该书是一部儿童文学名著，是傲居“美国最伟大的十部儿童文学名著”首位的童话，风行世界五十年，发行千万册，大多学生已经阅读过该书的中文版本。在国外，该书是被推荐给小学四年级的学生阅读的。考虑到这本书难度不大，学生也了解一定的背景知识，所以选择该书。从实践来看，学生完全能够接受这本书。《老人与海》和《傲慢与偏见》是两部经典名著，其中《老人与海》是海明威的一篇中篇小说，是他最著名的作品之一。它奠定了海明威在世界文学中的突出地位，相继获得了1953年美国普利策奖和1954年诺贝尔文学奖。《傲慢与偏见》是简·奥斯丁的代表作，也是一部经典的小说，在英国广播公司(BBC)的“大阅读”(Big Read)“有史以来最受读者喜爱的小说”调查活动中名列第二名，仅次于小说《指环王》(“大阅读”活动由BBC以电视系列专题片的形式介绍多部优秀文学作品，再由观众投票选出一部“有史以来最受读者喜爱的小说”)。《了不起的盖茨比》在美国“现代文库”的20世纪百大英文小说中名列第二。

(2) 现实成功经验的验证

第一本文学名著阅读实践成功后，笔者得知宁波外国语学校国际部高一文学课上也在阅读英文原著，在征得文学老师Mr. Richard的同意后，笔者深入他的课堂观摩学习。经过两周的课堂观摩，笔者不仅学习了国外教师的英文原著阅读课的教学经验，还借鉴了其教学资源——第二本书即选用当时国际部阅读的《相约星期二》。Mr. Richard 提供了教学参考资料，在实践中，笔者仍然就这本书中的某些话题和 Mr. Richard 保持频繁的交流。实践证明，学生也特别喜欢这本书。

(3) 国外成功教材的引入

例如笔者所教班级选择阅读的原著《了不起的盖茨比》。这本书出版于 1925 年，是美国作家弗朗西斯·斯科特·基·菲茨杰拉德创作的一部以 20 世纪 20 年代的纽约市及长岛为背景的短篇小说，被视为美国文学“爵士时代”的象征。其后的数十年它更成为国外高中、大学文学课的经典阅读素材。

2. 学生的心理需求和成长需要

(1) 高一学生的心理需求分析

《夏洛的网》是一首关于生命、友情、爱与忠诚的赞歌。高一学生刚刚踏入高中的校门，在新的环境中学习，迫切需要适应新的学习环境，希望结交新的朋友。这本童话的主题是友谊和爱，刚好符合高一学生当时的心理需求。另外，其语言难度也不大，具有童趣，大多学生在小学时候已经阅读了这本书的中文版本，所以将其作为第一本阅读的原著，不论是从主题还是内容难度上，都是符合当时学生需求的。

(2) 学生成长需求分析

《相约星期二》是一个真实的故事：年逾七旬的社会学教授莫里在 1994 年罹患肌萎性侧索硬化症，一年以后与世长辞。作为莫里早年的得意门生，米奇在老教授缠绵病榻的十四周里，每周二都上门与他相伴，聆听他最后的教诲，并在老师去世后将其醒世箴言缀珠成链，冠名《相约星期二》。这是一本进行人生教育和生命教育的绝佳教材。高中学生逐渐步入成年期，对生活中关于家庭、情感、金钱、死亡等一些重大问题开始有自己的思考，《相约星期二》正是人生教育和生命教育的绝佳教材。这本书直视青少年成长过程中遇到的困惑和烦恼，在学生中引起了强烈的共鸣。

3. 教育价值引领

《老人与海》讲述了一位古巴老年渔夫与一条巨大的马林鱼在离岸

很远的湾流中搏斗的故事。这本书篇幅适中，大多学生也阅读过中文版本或看过相关介绍，对该书内容较熟悉，并且该书还是一本很好的励志教材。《傲慢与偏见》和《了不起的盖茨比》都以爱情和金钱为主题。在这个物欲横流的社会里，应该养成怎样的金钱观和爱情是青年学子无法回避的现实问题。这两本名著的阅读有利于培养学生正确的爱情观和金钱观，为他们的健康成长奠基。

4. 现实教育基础分析

课题实践中所选的文学名著都有中文译本，而且大多有几种经典的、广为流传的中文译本(《傲慢与偏见》就有四种以上权威的中文译本)，这样学生在阅读过程中遇到困难的时候可以参考中文版本。除了中文版本以外，所选文学名著都被改编成电影、电视剧等形式，其中《傲慢与偏见》和《了不起的盖茨比》有不同时代的电影版本，BBC拍摄了《傲慢与偏见》的电视剧版本。另外，这些文学名著还有音频，学生在不同的时间和场合可以听这些英文名著。这几本英文名著在国外的中小学文学阅读课堂也经常被阅读，所以很容易通过网络找到这些文学名著英文版的阅读指导，这也给教学提供了很大的便利和可行性。

四、英文名著教学

英文名著教学实践中摸索出的几种课型有：任务展示课、读写实践课、综合分析课、欣赏表演课，等等。

1. 任务展示课(Presentation)

教学策略：阅读前把阅读任务分配给各小组（通常是周末或假期前，以确保学生有充足的阅读时间)，这些任务包括小说的情节(plot)(案例1)、人物分析(character analysis)(案例2)、精彩语句或段落赏析(good paragraphs)(案例3)等，每个小组可以选择一个主题做好展示作业(大多是PPT形式)发送到指定邮箱，在学生展示前老师会批阅学生的作业，提出修改意见，然后集中在某个教学时段让学生展示作业，其他同学可以根据同学的展示做好笔记，提出问题。

教学效果：任务展示课能激发学生阅读的兴趣，充分发挥学生学习的主动性，既能培养学生的团队合作精神和资料搜集整合能力，又能发展学生的自主学习和终身学习的能力。

☞ 案例 1

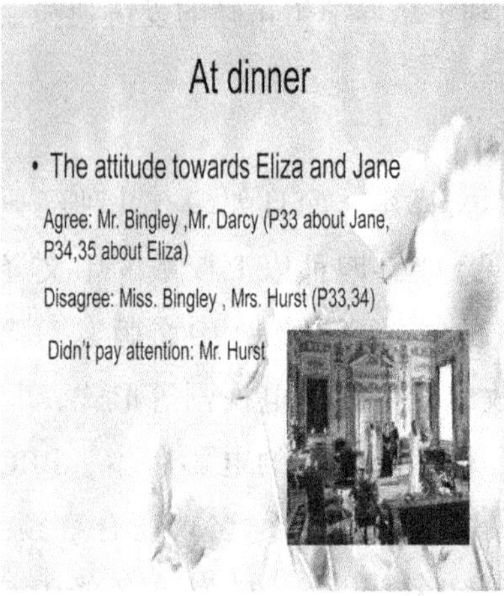

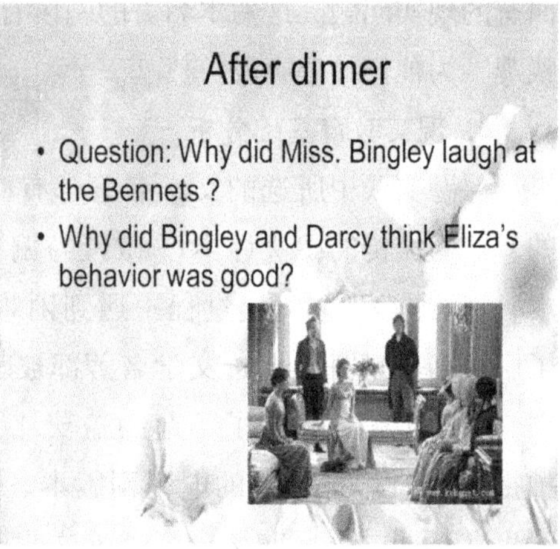

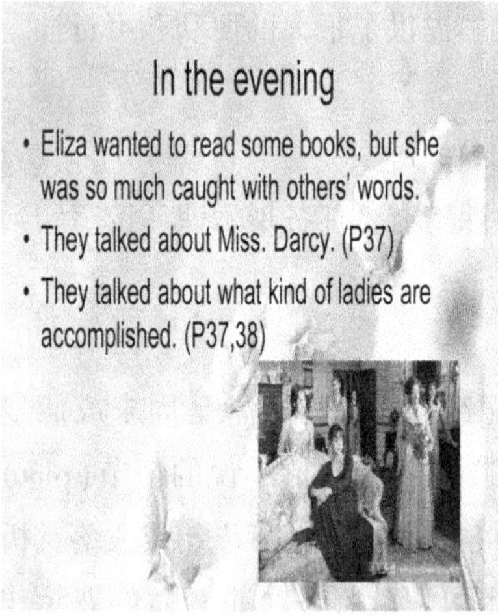

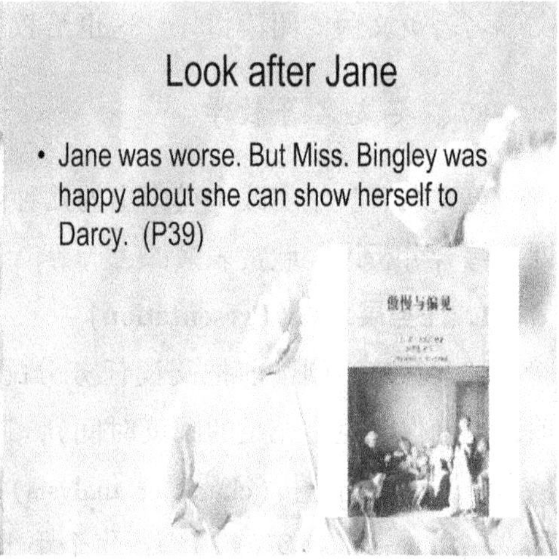

【**点评**】该课件展示的是小说《傲慢与偏见》第八章的情节。课件紧紧抓住了“时间”这一线索(用餐中、餐后、晚上)，清晰明了地介绍了该章的主要情节，情节中还穿插个别问题让同学们思考，这种生生互动

的模式提高了课堂的学习效率，活跃了课堂气氛。课件中还嵌入了电影中与该情节对应的图片，显得生动活泼。

☞ 案例 2

``The indirect boast; -- for you are really proud of your defects in writing, because you consider them as proceeding from a rapidity of thought and carelessness of execution, which if not estimable, you think at least highly interesting. The power of doing any thing with quickness is always much prized by the possessor, and often without any attention to the imperfection of the performance. When you told Mrs. Bennet this morning that if you ever resolved on quitting Netherfield you should be gone in five minutes, you meant it to be a sort of panegyric, of compliment to yourself -- and yet what is there so very laudable in a precipitance which must leave very necessary business undone, and can be of no real advantage to yourself or any one else?"(P46)

From this sentence，we can see that Mr Darcy is a very proud man .He thinks you meant it to be a sort of panegyric, of compliment to yourself ,that's too direct without thinking.

``You write uncommonly fast."
``You are mistaken. I write rather slowly."
``How many letters you must have occasion to write in the course of the year! Letters of business too! How odious I should think them!"
``It is fortunate, then, that they fall to my lot instead of to yours."
``Pray tell your sister that I long to see her."
``I have already told her so once, by your desire."
``I am afraid you do not like your pen. Let me mend it for you. I mend pens remarkably well."
``Thank you -- but I always mend my own."（P45）

This conversation tells us that Miss.Bingley want to develop a great relationship with Mr.Darcy. She doesn't want Mr.Darcy to have an opportunity to approach Elizabath. To sum up，we can see Miss.Bingley is a girl who is scheming.

Mr. Darcy smiled; but Elizabeth thought she could perceive that he was rather offended; and therefore checked her laugh. Miss Bingley warmly resented the indignity he had received, in an expostulation with her brother for talking such nonsense. （P49）

This paragraph belongs to the psychological description of characters , and it also reflects_Elizabeth's education. Elizabeth is good at observation , and she knows when she should express her emotions.

【点评】该案例是小组围绕小说《傲慢与偏见》第十章中的人物性格这一主题完成的展示任务，该小组能紧扣文本中的材料，通过分析得出达西骄傲、宾利小姐工于心计、伊丽莎白善于观察等性格特征的结论，有理有据，令人信服，充分体现出了同学们严谨求学的态度。

☞ 案例 3

loneliness

- **For a while he stood gloomily indoors.**
- **Suddenly Wilbur felt lonely and friendless.**
- **He groaned (叹息), "I'm young, I have no real friend here in barn."**
- **Wilbur was crying again, for the second time in two days.**
- **Wilbur didn't want food, he wanted love. He wanted a friend ---someone who would play with him.**
- **Sadly, Wilbur lay down and listened to the rain.**
- **Friendless, dejected, and hungry, he threw himself down in the manure and sobbed.**
- **This was certainly the worst day of his life. He didn't know whether he could endure the awful loneliness any more.**

【点评】该案例是小组围绕小说《夏洛的网》的精彩语句完成的展示

作业。教师要求学生找出描写小猪威尔伯孤独的语句，然后对这些语句进行赏析。该作业能利用一根主线串起该章的精彩语句，这些语句描写生动、形象，能让学生领悟语言的魅力，增强对语言的感悟能力。

2. 读写实践课(Reading and Writing)

教学策略：学生在课外的阅读时间是有限的，教师在课堂上要保证学生一定的阅读时间和阅读量。课堂上的阅读形式以精读和出声朗读为主，主要是让学生阅读一些重点章节和段落，让学生一起品读分享。要给学生读出声的机会，让学生展示自己的语音语调，诵读出经典文学作品的魅力。还可以结合一些主题来读，比如让学生读人物对话(案例4)、读人物描写(案例5)、读景物描写(案例6)、读心情描写(案例7)、读最喜欢的段落(案例8)等。读的地点也会做适当的变动，除了在教室读外，还可以去图书馆读；读的形式除了出声朗读外，还可以默读、分角色朗读、朗读接龙(popcorn reading)，读后偶尔穿插一些写的活动。目前普遍尝试的写的活动有阅读后回答问题，这个活动每个章节都有，每个章节会以"Reading Comprehension Check"的形式设置4~5个经典问题来检查学生的理解(案例9)，读完后可让学生选取一个角度写小书评(book review)(案例10)。

教学效果：朗读有助于熟记(memorize)语言材料，加深理解。阅读过程中，单词、短语和句子都会在脑海里留下清晰的印记。通过朗读，学生会把单词的搭配形式、句子的结构模式、上下文的联系(cohesion)方式，语音、语调、重音等都潜移默化地掌握起来。读是输入的过程，写是输出的过程，有了足够的输入，输出就自然丰富了，读后穿插适当的写作练习既可以检测读的效果，又在一定的语境中灵活运用了读的过程中输入的语言材料，这样就形成了输入有效、输出优质的良性循环。

☞ 案例4

"Where's Papa going with the ax?" said Fern to her mother as they were setting the table for breakfast.

"Out to the hoghouse," replied Mrs. Arable, "Some pigs were born last night."

"I don't see why he needs an ax," continued Fern, who was only eight.

"Well," said her mother, "One of the pigs is a runt. It's very small and weak, and it will never amount to anything. So your father has decided to do away with it."

"Do away with it?" shrieked Fern, "You mean kill it? Just because it's smaller than the others?"

Mrs. Arable put a pitcher of cream on the table. "Don't yell, Fern!" she said, "Your father is right. The pig would probably die anyway."

Fern pushed a chair out of the way and ran outdoors. The grass was wet and the earth smelled of springtime. Fern's sneakers were sopping by the time she caught up with her father.

"Please don't kill it!" she sobbed, "It's unfair."

【点评】这是小说《夏洛的网》第一章中阿拉布尔和女儿弗恩的对话，细读对话可以深深地体会到女儿弗恩焦虑和生气的心情。

☞ 案例5

They were strange shoulders, still powerful although very old, and the neck was still strong too and the creases did not show so much when the old man was asleep and his head fallen forward. His shirt had been patched so many times that it was like the sail and the patches were faded to many different shades by the sun. The old man's head was very old though and with his eyes closed there was no life in his face. The newspaper lay across his knees and the weight of his arm held it there in the evening breeze. He was barefooted.

【点评】这段英文节选自小说《老人与海》，朗读后仿佛看到一个饱经风霜但精神饱满的老人浮现在眼前。

☞ 案例 6

About half way between West Egg and New York the motor-road hastily joins the railroad and runs beside it for a quarter of a mile, so as to shrink away from a certain desolate area of land. This is a valley of ashes—a fantastic farm where ashes grow like wheat into ridges and hills and grotesque gardens where ashes take the forms of houses and chimneys and rising smoke and finally, with a transcendent effort, of men who move dimly and already crumbling through the powdery air. Occasionally a line of grey cars crawls along an invisible track, gives out a ghastly creak and comes to rest, and immediately the ash-grey men swarm up with leaden spades and stir up an impenetrable cloud which screens their obscure operations from your sight.

【点评】这段英文选自《了不起的盖茨比》，是对灰谷的情景描写，朗读中可以体会到灰谷一派灰暗但忙碌的景象。这里也是威尔逊一家生活的地方，通过环境描写可以体会到下层阶级生活的艰辛。

☞ 案例 7

In the dark the old man could feel the morning coming and as he rowed he heard the trembling sound as flying fish left the water and the hissing that their stiff set wings made as they soared away in the darkness. He was very fond of flying fish as they were his principal friends on the ocean. He was sorry for the birds, especially the small delicate dark terns that were always flying and looking and almost never finding, and he thought, the birds have a harder life than we do except for the robber birds and the heavy strong ones.

【点评】这段英文选自小说《老人与海》，描写了老人的心理活动，可以让读者充分体会到老人对大自然的敬畏和尊重。

☞ 案例 8

It is a truth universally acknowledged, that a single man in possession of a good fortune must be in want of a wife. However little known the feelings or views of such a man may be on his first entering a neighbourhood, this truth is so well fixed in the minds of the surrounding families, that he is considered as the rightful property of someone or other of their daughters.

【点评】该段英文选自小说《傲慢与偏见》的开篇，作者的语言诙谐幽默，特别是第一句“一个家财万贯的单身汉，必定需要一位太太，这是一条举世公认的真理”已经成为名言。这样的段落可要求学生背诵。

☞ 案例 9

Reading Comprehension Check 1 for *Pride and Prejudice*

Chapter 1-Chapter 2

1. Which central themes and narrative characteristics of the novel are introduced in the famous opening sentence of *Pride and Prejudice*? What is your understanding of it?
2. Why does Mrs. Bennet state that it is impossible for her and her daughters to visit Mr. Bingley if Mr. Bennet does not visit him first?
3. Why does Mr. Bennet prefer Elizabeth over his other daughters?
4. How do Mr. Bennet's comment on his wife's nerves provide a clue to his overall opinion of his wife?
5. Choose one of the Bennets' daughters and talk about the character by using some evidence.
6. Write a short summary of the first two chapters. (about 50 words)

【点评】这六个问题是针对小说《傲慢与偏见》第一章和第二章设计的，这些问题既有细节的找寻，也有评价和归纳等开放性问题，既有助于加强学生对文本的理解，也有利于培养学生的创新意识和创新能力。

3. 综合分析课（Comprehensive Analysis）

教学策略：综合分析课以讨论、分享为主。讨论是针对所读作品某一问题或信息，小组成员发表意见，同伴间交流看法、交换意见，讨论是交互影响、相互启发的小组合作学习。分享是个体与群体的互动，分享的内容包括人物分析、情节分析、解析难懂的语句和段落、谈论阅读心得体会和经验、换位思考、预测下章。综合分析课的课堂组织形式有师生互动式分析(案例10)、生生互动式分析(案例11)、小组互动式分析(案例12)等形式。综合分析课是文学阅读教学活动中的重要教学形式，教师要充分发挥自己的引导作用，从宏观处把握好作品的主旨，把握好作品的主线，并结合青少年的特点，充分挖掘作品中的积极元素来激发学生对文学的热爱、对生活的热爱，并充分尊重学生对文学作品的个性解读，激发他们的探究精神和创新能力。

教学效果：综合分析课能培养学生的语言综合运用能力，激发学生对作品的探究，促使学生从不同角度去解读作品。课堂上经常会撞出思想的火花，年轻的头脑往往能另辟蹊径，提出很多让人眼睛一亮的观点。

☞ 案例10

师生互动式分析。课堂上笔者经常和学生分享的几个问题是：

1. Which character do you think is the most impressive?
2. What is the most interesting sentence/paragraph/chapter in the story?
3. Suppose the story occurs at present, what do you think is the most possible ending/result?
4. If you can continue writing the story, how do you develop the story?

【点评】综合分析课是为了加深学生对文学作品的理解，可以就一些问题达成共识，也可以抛砖引玉，激发同学的思考。

☞ 案例11

生生互动式分析。课堂教学不仅仅局限于师生的互动，有效的生生互动能够和谐课堂气氛、增强同学间的凝聚力。本案例是某同学在读完小说《老人与海》的第12至16页后和同班同学的互动。

P.12　The friendship between the old man and the boy

The old man went out the door and the boy came after him. He was sleepy and the old man put his arm across his shoulders and said, "I am sorry."

"Que va," the boy said, "It is what a man must do."

What kind of friendship is it in your eyes?

老人走出门外后，男孩跟着出来，他还很想打瞌睡，老人把手臂搭在他的肩膀上说："对不起。"

"怎么会！"男孩说："这是男子汉应该做的事。"

P.14　His attitude towards the sea.

But the old man always thought of her as feminine and as something that gave or withheld great favors, and if she did wild or wicked things it was because she could not help them.

What is the old man's attitude towards the sea?

可是，老人总认为海洋是女性，有时带来恩惠，有时带来恶运，而当海洋变得蛮横狂暴或是邪恶时，那是因为她没有办法控制。

P.16

But, he thought, I keep them with precision. Only I have no luck any more. But who knows? Maybe today. Every day is a new day. It is better to be lucky. But I would rather be exact. Then when luck comes you are ready.

What is the old man's personality like from this passage?

然而他却认为，我就是要保持精确。只可惜我的运气不再了。可是，谁知道呢？也许就是今天了，每一天都是一个新的开始。幸运当然是最好，不过我情愿做得丝毫不差，这样，当机运来临时，才会有备无患。

【点评】该同学在分享阅读体验的同时，能够设计几个小问题与同伴互动，俨然一个小老师的形式，而且问题设计得紧扣文本，有板有眼，正所谓“独学而无友，孤陋则寡闻”。教学中教师如果能放手，给学生多点空间和自由，可能有意外的惊喜。

☞ 案例 12

小组互动式分析。小组就某一问题进行讨论然后汇报成果，是综合分析课上的重要教学组织形式。在小组汇报时，其他组的同学认真倾听，并可以在此过程中质疑、评价、补充。这样，学生不仅从其他组的汇报中学到了新知识，也学会了勇于发表自己的观点、见解，在小组合作交流中取他人之长来弥补自己的不足。这样既提高了学生的自主学习的能力，也在互动交流中培养了学生的协作精神，在提高学习效率的同时，也有效地促进了学生的全面发展。

Plot pp. 21-25

Beginning of the battle

Group members:

Anki

Dust

Yoko

Eunie

【点评】这是小组四位成员就小说《老人与海》第12至25页的情节做的展示，小组成员通过共同合作和讨论完成了学习任务，在课堂上该小组四位成员上台轮流发言，其他组的同学会根据他们的发言做出评价或者补充(其他组的同学认为这个展示作业图文并茂、简洁明了、形象生动)，这种互动方式活跃了气氛，锻炼了学生的表达能力和应变能力，有利于互相学习和取长补短。

4. 欣赏表演课(Enjoying and Acting)

教学策略：阅读完部分章节或整本书后，根据具体情况让学生观看该书的电影版、电视版或者话剧的片段，然后让同学选取部分章节尝试表演。同学们分工明确，有的改写剧本，有的做导演，有的负责旁白，有的负责剧务，经过分组排练后，再集中表演选取的章节或精彩片段(案例13)；同学间甚至还可以通过手机或相机互拍、共享。但实践中还是会遇到一些困难。首先表演这种艺术形式很难把握，而且由于时间、场地和学生的阅历限制，学生的表演还是流于形式。如何充分利用这种形式促进文学名著的阅读教学，我们可能要更多地向国外学习。国外有许多戏剧表演俱乐部，有专业老师或导演指导，有充足的准备时间。不过随着条件的成熟，以后老师和学生还可以更多地去尝试。

教学效果：英美电影、电视等往往能激发学生学习英语的兴趣。地道、纯正的口语更是学生学习模仿的资料。学生模仿其中的精彩片段进行表演，也是生生互动的模式之一。这个年龄段的青少年大多喜欢表现自己，热衷于表演。表演是一种有效的输出形式，不仅为学生提供了展示交流的舞台，而且让学生体验角色，加深对作品的理解和感悟。

☞ 案例13

Scene 1

Mr. Darcy looked so thoughtful while he was rambling within the park with Mr. Bingley.

B：(glanced at Mr. Darcy, warmheartedly) Why you looked so thoughtful?

D：(looked to the ground) Doesn't matter.

(A silence kept between these two gentlemen.)

D：(seemed to make a gigantic decision) Uh… Actually, there's something I need to tell you.

B：What's the deal?

D：(stood still) Do you ensure you love her?

B：Absolutely do.

D：Why do you think that she deserve it?

…

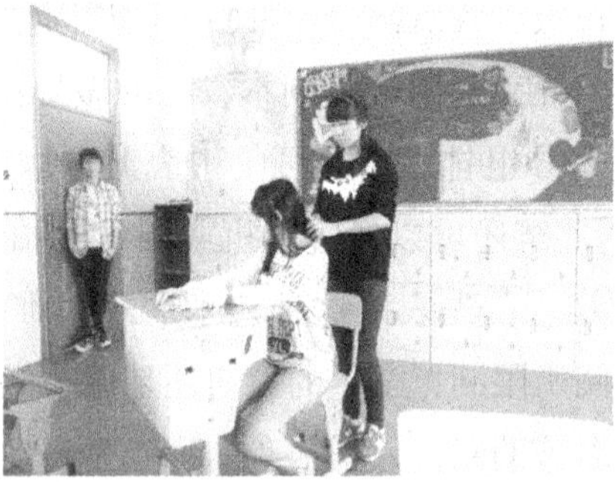

【点评】该案例呈现的是经过改编的《傲慢与偏见》第三章剧本和一张表演剧照。学生充分发挥自己的主动性和创造性，在尊重原著的基础上，适当改编了剧本，还根据原著中的人物情感和情绪的变化，添加了人物动作和旁白。学生的聪明和创意总是出乎我们的意料。

5. 效果监测和评价模式探索

文学名著走进课堂的教学效果如何是决定这一教学模式是否成功的关键因素。笔者在近两年的教学实践探索中建立起一套文学阅读的效果监测和评价模式，并通过调查发现，影响学生文学名著阅读的主要障碍是词汇、背景知识的缺乏。为了扫清这些障碍，提高阅读的效果，在阅读前学生须分组做好每章的生词清单(案例 14)(wordlist，生词清单有统一的格式)，教师在阅读前发给全班学生参考以避免学生重复查阅单词的繁琐任务。在阅读前后教师还会发给学生一些补充的背景知识或者小说阅读指导类的资料以提高阅读效果(案例15)。读后教师会参考高考词汇表从所读章节中精选一些重要单词和短语发给学生背诵和记忆，这些单词和短语也是文学阅读考试中词汇部分的考核范围(案例16)。另外，教师还会发给学生配合所读章节的分析资料以加深学生的理解(案例17)。

对文学名著阅读的评价会影响学生阅读的兴趣和动力，科学、合理的评价能促进有效和高效的文学阅读。通过近两年的实践，评价方面参照《普通高中英语课程标准(实验)》的要求“注重形成性评价和终结性评价相结合，并以形成性评价为主”的模式。形成性评价对学生学习的过程进行干预，其目的是促进学习。因此，它也被称为“为了学习的评价”(assessment for learning)。文学阅读评价的最终目的是促进阅读而不是挫伤同学们阅读的积极性。文学阅读实践中积累的形成评价过程，主要有：①阅读卡模式(案例9)：每章都有阅读卡（Reading comprehension check）来检测学生对名著内容的理解；②阅读日记模式：让学生撰写阅读日记(Reading journal)，让学生来分享阅读的体验(案例18)；③书评模式：通过撰写书评等提高学生的学术写作能力(案例19)；④文学阅读比赛(案例20)、文学阅读海报设计大赛(案例21)、演讲比赛等模式(案例22)；⑤教学反思模式：教师通过撰写阅读日记和教学反思的形式和同学们交流阅读中的感受，和学生分享阅读的体验，同时加强了阅读的效果(案例23)。终结性评价中，高一、高二的校级期中和期末考试中都有文学阅读部分作为考核的内容，这部分内容是参与实验的同学必考的，占考试比重的20%~30%，题型主要有选择题、阅读题、写作题、词汇题等(案例24)。

☞ 案例14

Chapter 8

incessantly [ɪnˈsesntlɪ]　　*adv.* 不停地，不间断地

grotesque [grəʊˈtesk]	*adj*. 奇形怪状的；奇怪的；可笑的
savage [ˈsævɪdʒ]	*adj*. 野蛮的；残酷的；狂怒的；荒凉的
dejection [dɪˈdʒekʃ(ə)n]	*n*. 沮丧
wanly [ˈwɒnli]	*adv*. 苍白地；衰弱地
pavilion [pəˈvɪljən]	*n*. 大帐篷
tumble [ˈtʌmb(ə)l]	*vi*. 摔倒
inexplicable [ˌɪnɪkˈsplɪkəbl]	*adj*. 无法说明的；莫名其妙的
humidor [ˈhjuːmɪdɔː]	*n*. 雪茄盒
stale [steɪl]	*adj*. 陈腐的；不新鲜的
clutch [klʌtʃ]	*vi*. 攫住；企图抓住
malice [ˈmælɪs]	*n*. 恶意
extravaganza [ɪkˌstrævəˈgænzə]	*n*. 狂想曲
capacity [kəˈpæsəti]	*n*. 地位；身份
indiscernible [ˌɪndɪˈsɜːnəb(ə)l]	*adj*. 难识别的；看不见的
barbed wire [ˈbɑːbdˈwʌɪə]	有刺铁丝网
gay [geɪ]	*adj*. 快乐的；放荡的；艳丽的

【点评】单词表节选自一位同学为小说《了不起的盖茨比》第八章整理的生词清单。生词清单包括单词、音标，以及和小说中相符的中文意思等内容，能帮助其他同学节省时间，顺利阅读。

☞ 案例 15

Biography of F. Scott Fitzgerald (1896-1940)

Francis Scott Key Fitzgerald was a Jazz Age novelist and short story writer who is considered to be among the greatest twentieth-century American writers. Born on September 24, 1896, he was the only son of an aristocratic father and a provincial, working-class mother. He was the product of two divergent traditions: while his father's family included the author of *The Star-Spangled Banner* (after whom Fitzgerald was named), his mother's family was, in Fitzgerald's own words, "straight 1850 potato-famine Irish". As a result of this contrast, he was exceedingly ambivalent toward the notion of the American dream: for him, it was at once vulgar and dazzlingly promising.

Like the central character of *The Great Gatsby*, Fitzgerald had an intensely romantic imagination; he once called it "a heightened sensitivity to the promises of life". The events of Fitzgerald's own life can be seen as a struggle to realize those promises.

He attended both St. Paul Academy (1908-1910) and Newman School (1911-1913), where his intensity and outsized enthusiasm made him unpopular with the other students. Later, at Princeton University, he came close to the brilliant success of which he dreamed. He became part of the influential Triangle Club, a dramatic organization whose members were taken from the cream of society. He also became a prominent figure in the literary life of the university and made lifelong friendships with Edmund Wilson and John Peale Bishop. Despite these social coups, Fitzgerald struggled academically, and he eventually flunked out of Princeton. In November 1917, he joined the army.

【点评】这份资料是关于小说《了不起的盖茨比》作者菲茨杰拉德的生平介绍的节选，介绍了作者的个人生活、时代背景、教育背景、主要作品，等等。通过阅读背景资料，学生可以更好地理解小说的情节、人物性格和主题。

☞ 案例 16

Charlotte's Web **(Chapters 1-5)**

1. 生死攸关的一件事　　a matter of life and death
2. 扫尽天下不平事　　rid world of injustice
3. 走近；靠近　　approach

4. 原谅我做了这傻事	forgive me for this foolishness
5. 棒极了	absolutely perfect
6. 把……分发给	distribute sth. to
7. 胃口很好	have a good appetite
8. 对……完全负责	have entire charge of
9. 用深情的眼睛	with adoring eyes
10. 抱怨	complain
11. 朝门里偷看	peer through the door
12. 放心	relieve one's mind
13. 待在烂泥里自得其乐	amuse oneself in the mud
14. 抚养一头猪	raise a pig
15. 遗漏	overlook
16. 冒着……风险	at the risk of
17. 钻出了围栏	squeeze through the fence
18. 发表一场激动人心的演讲	make a stirring speech
19. 充当指挥开始发号施令	take command and begin to give orders
20. 听从指示	follow the instructions

【点评】这是根据小说《夏洛的网》第一章到第五章整理的重点单词和短语，它们大多是高考词汇表中出现的或者语言运用过程中的一些高频词汇或短语。文学名著的阅读过程中，教师可以章为单位整理出重点单词或短语让学生课外去记忆，避免让文学阅读流于形式。只有奠定了扎实的基本功，学生综合语言能力的提升才有保障。

☞ 案例 17

The Fourth Tuesday: We Talk about Death

Plot

Morrie tells Mitch that everyone is aware that they will eventually die, though no one actually believes it. Mitch notes that Morrie is in a business-like mood on this Tuesday, as he scribbles notes in his now undecipherable handwriting. In Detroit, the newspaper strikes continue, and Mitch remains out of work. Once again, he notes the disgustingly violent news stories he has heard and read about, namely the O. J. Simpson murder trial. In Morrie's office, however, news events are inconsequential, and they focus on more meaningful subjects.

Analysis

The O. J. Simpson murder trial is an issue which appears repeatedly throughout the book. Mitch uses the trial as a tool to portray the popular, media-saturated culture as a source of meaninglessness, as he does when he sees the murderous potential on the faces of the people at the airport, or reads about murder and other crimes in the newspaper. These crimes that taint the popular culture are used, in large part, to contrast the good of Morrie's self-created culture against the evil of the mainstream social culture, whose values are entrenched in meaningless and wasteful endeavors, such as watching television and reading tabloid gossip. Why, then, if Morrie loathes the media and the popular culture, does he agree to do multiple interviews with Ted Koppel for "Nightline"? Because only "Nightline" can provide him with the means to reach millions of people, so that he may share his story and influence their lives with his life lessons. It seems that Morrie must use the popular culture he condemns as a vehicle to spread his philosophy of a self-created culture.

【点评】该案例节选自小说《相约星期二》中第四个星期二有关死亡这个话题的课后学习资料。这份资料由国外的文学老师提供，不仅包括该章的情节(plot)介绍，而且有专家对文本的解读、对文本背后文化知识的介绍、对人物性格的分析，以及对小说主题的进一步挖掘等深度分析(analysis)。

☞ 案例 18

A Sample Reading Journal—Chapter 1, Pages 1-14

George

This first chapter shows protagonist Nick Carraway's background and his traveling to New York to visit his cousin, Daisy Buchanan. He meets Daisy and her husband Tom outside their home. As Nick returns home that first night, he sees a mysterious man from the dock reaching out towards a green light on the other end of the bay.

As for the charaters I choose Daisy because even though I dislike her character, I find her interesting. I think she tries to act silly, but has really come to the point in life where she feels that as a woman, she can only be a trophy wife to Tom. Daisy does not really act or think for herself; she only cares about what she has, even putting that above her baby daughter.

I really like the book so far. I think all the characters, especially Daisy, will have big parts to play. Daisy seems to like Nick very much, but much like she only appears to care about superficial things, I can't decide yet whether she only likes Nick superficially as well. She certainly does not seem to think for herself much, as she always listens to what her controlling husband Tom has to say.

My favorite quote from this chapter is Nick's first description of Gatsby: "He stretched out his arms toward the dark water in a curious way, and I could have sworn he was trembling involuntarily... at a little green light at the end of the dock on the opposite end of the bay" (Fitzgerald 14). I think it is beautifully written and a mysterious line at the same time, and will have a part to play soon, too.

【点评】上文是针对小说《了不起的盖茨比》第一章所写的阅读日记，

阅读日记中包括对该章内容的简介、重点角色的评介，以及对重点引语的赏析。写是读的延伸，是对语言综合运用能力和思维能力的考验。

☞ 案例 19

A Book Review of *Tuesdays with Morrie*

It's such an amazing experience for me to read this novel. The book is about a dying man who taught us how to love, and how to pursue a meaningful life. In my mind, Morrie is just like a wise prophet, he always has unique views about life. He is so different from other professors, not only for how easy-going he is, but also for his spiritual world and mental heart.

After reading this novel, I asked myself a question: "Does the book help me?" Obviously, my answer is "Yes"! What impressed me mostly is the topic about Love. "Love" is a key word covering the whole book. I still remember a typical sentence: "Love is the only rational act." According to Morrie, devoting your love to others is the most important thing in our life. I can't agree it any more. In my opinion, giving out our love to others is the way that we can seek our inner fulfillment, which can really make us happy. Love is just like a diamond which can sparkle even in the dark. It's also like water which can clean our dusty mind. So there is no reason for not giving true love from our deep heart.

In a word, I learn a lot from the novel. In particular, it helps me find the correct way to the meaningful life. Personally, this book is the mirror of our life.

A Book Report of *Tuesdays with Morrie*

The book *Tuesdays with Morrie*, which affects most of readers, is fulfilled with sense and philosophy. It is a thesis, a magnificent one, which was completely finished by Morrie and Mitch. They produced the creative value of their lives. Morrie, such an old but wise man, enjoyed his ultimate days, providing us with a series of profound classes. It contains the real meaning of love, family, forgiveness, and so on. During his dwindling days, Mitch was totally impressed by his old professor, and he started to create the culture of his own.

I like the book very much. It feels like a powerful rinse of spiritual world. I long for the attitude which Morrie took towards life. It's a detaching way of living, taking no notice of material things and devoting yourself to anyone that really needs your help. Everyone is not as clever as Morrie. All in all, the book can bring us a new perspective to appreciate our lives.

【点评】两位同学都是读了《相约星期二》后写的书评，她们都能够遵循书评的常见格式，介绍该书的内容，陈述喜欢的原因和阅读体会。书评也是学生语言综合运用能力的展现。

☞ 案例 20

Contest for Literature Comprehension (1)

Literature Translation

Class ________ Name ________ Mark ________

You are expected to translate two paragraphs into Chinese from the book *The Old Man and The Sea*. Please write your answers in the following blanks and the full mark is 50 and it will account for a certain percentage of your final exam. You can turn to a dictionary for help but any Chinese version or discussion isn't permitted.

Passage 1: You can choose one between the following two passages.

(20 marks)

P. 7. When the boy came back... He was barefooted.

P. 11. He no longer dreamed of... he would be rowing.

Passage 2: You can choose one between the following two passages. (30 marks)

P. 39. As the sun set he remembered... as the breeze moved the lamps.

P. 47. He woke with the jerk of his right first coming up... and he could not move.

部分学生译文：

The Old Man and the Sea

P. 7：

等男孩回来的时候，老人已经在椅子上睡着了，太阳也落下了。男孩从床上捡起一条旧的军毯，铺在了椅背上，盖住老人的肩膀。奇怪的是，虽然老人已上了年纪，可是他的肩膀依然健壮，脖子也很壮实。而当老人睡着了，轻轻地耷拉下脑袋，他的皱纹也就不大明显了。他的衬衫已经被补过了好多次，就跟他那张帆似的。上头的补丁被太阳晒得褪了色，一块块的颜色都不一样，有深有浅。老人的头部显得十分苍老，以至于当他闭上双眼时，脸庞上毫无生机可寻。报纸摊开着铺在他的膝盖上，用一条手臂压着，免得被风吹走了。老人光着脚，感受着轻轻吹来的夜风。

P. 39：

当太阳落下的时候，为了给自己增加点儿信心鼓鼓劲儿，老人回想起了曾经一次他在卡萨布兰卡的一家酒馆里，和一个来自西恩富戈斯的黑人比赛手劲儿，那个黑人是码头上最强壮的家伙。他们两个人僵持了一天一夜，他们把手肘搁在桌子上画好的粉笔线上，胳膊伸直，双手紧握，都试图用力量将对方的手按倒在桌面上。那会儿在屋里的煤油灯下，不停地有人进进出出，好多人都在赌这场比赛。他仔细地打量了这个黑人的胳膊和手，还有黑人的脸。在刚开始的八个小时里，人们每过四个小时换一次裁判，好让自己能轮流休息。鲜血从老人和黑人的手指甲缝中渗出，他们紧紧地注视着对方，还有对方的胳膊与手。赌赛的人们走进走出，倚着墙坐在高高的椅子上看比赛。四周的墙壁被涂成了明亮的蓝色，灯光把他们的影子投在了上面。那黑人的影子显得格外高大，并随着夜风吹动油灯而轻轻晃动。

The Old Man and the Sea

P. 7：

当男孩回来的时候，老人已在椅子上睡熟，太阳也落下了。男孩从床上抱来旧军旅毛毯，将它展开盖在椅背上和老人的肩膀上。这是奇怪的肩膀，虽然很老了但依旧强健有力。那颈脖也很强壮，并且当老人耷拉着脑袋睡熟的时候，他的皱褶并没有表现得过于明显。他的衬衫被缝补了很多很多次，像是船上的帆。那补丁都被太阳晒褪了色，呈现出各种深浅不一、色彩不同的样子。老人的头、脸已极苍老了，当他闭上眼睛时，脸上毫无生机。在晚风的吹拂下，老人将报纸摊在膝盖上，同时用胳膊压着，风是吹不走的。他赤着脚呢。

P. 39：

夕阳西下时，他为了给自己更多信心，回忆起当年他在卡萨布兰卡酒馆的经历，他与一个来自西恩富戈斯的码头工人，也是当时那儿身体最壮的黑人大汉扳手腕。他们前臂竖直，手与手紧紧地攥着，胳膊肘有力地抵着桌上的那道用粉笔画出的线，搏斗了整一天一夜。他们两个都竭尽全力想要把对方的手扳倒在桌面上。煤油灯下，许多看客来来往往，下了很大的赌注；可他的眼睛从未离开黑人的手臂、头和脸。比赛进行八小时后，裁判累得要回去睡觉，于是裁判每隔四小时就换一次。他和黑人的指甲都出了血，却还坚定地互相直视着对方的手臂和手毫不懈怠。而打赌的人进进出出，或坐在靠墙的高脚椅上观看。拼接的木板墙漆上了鲜艳的蓝色，灯光将他们的影子照在墙上。每当微风拂动吊灯使它摇晃时，黑人那巨大的影子也在墙上来回摆动。

Contest for Literature Reading（2）

Word Attack Competition

Name ________ Class ________ Mark ________

Part A：Fill in the blank with a proper word based on the first letter and the context of the sentence. (30 marks)

1. A b ________ is a shopkeeper who cuts up and sells meat.
2. Most people visit Las Vegas to g ________ their hard-earned money.
3. He won no less than £ 5000 in the l ________.
4. Santiago couldn't afford a pair of shoes, so he was b ________.
5. Santiago kept the lines straighter than anyone did and kept them with p ________.

…

Part B: Fill in the blank with proper word and its proper form based on the Chinese clues and the context of the sentence. (20 marks)

1. The need for sleep varies ________ (相当地；很) from person to person.
2. Our ________ (最初的) plan was to read *Pride and Prejudice* rather than *Tuesdays with Morrie*.
3. Considering the ________ (障碍) the skiff must have sailed very well. Otherwise, the old man and his skiff couldn't have reached home safely.
4. "A man can be destroyed but not defeated," Santiago said with full of ________ (决心).
5. It is absolutely silly not to hope, which he thinks is a ________ (罪过).

…

奖状模板：

________同学在高一英语文学阅读(翻译、词汇)竞赛中，成绩优异，荣获________等奖，特发此状，以资鼓励！

宁波外国语学校

【点评】该文学阅读竞赛是在高一下学期开展的，是在阅读完《老人与海》和《相约星期二》后进行的，竞赛的内容包括翻译和词汇两部分，内容紧扣所读的两本小说，比赛的形式既提高了学生阅读文学的兴趣，也能检测到学生阅读的效果。虽然教师自己设计的奖状简单，但依然能激发学生参与的热情。

☞ 案例 21

【点评】这是设计海报比赛的两幅作品，分别是基于小说《老人与海》和《夏洛的网》做的海报。海报图文并茂，能形象生动地展现作品主要角色和内容。

☞ 案例 22

The Book That Reclaimed Me

Hello everyone. Today I want to share my experience about a famous book—you may have heard its name because it is so famous—with all of you. A book that reclaimed me.

First of all I want to show my sincere thanks to my former English teacher, who gave me the English version of the book as a present when I graduated. The book is called *The Adventure of Tom Sawyer*. To be honest, it brought back all my childhood sweet memories.

There is a saying that once you are afraid that sunshine, rain, or the mud on the pavement would spoil your new shoes, your childhood is over. Well, my childhood has been long gone. In the story, Tom would gather some of his best pals and go to the deep forest in search of gold, or exchange credit with all kinds of cool stuff such as a grasshopper with his classmates, in order to get good grades, all these cracked me up and held me entirely in its power. What's more, the book is also a good teacher to me. It told me that reality can't always be like what you wish. You have to stand up to it by using your own strength to fit into the atmosphere around you. When I was a kid, I used to be under my parents' careful protection so I can't make dozens of friends and take our own territory just like Tom did. I also tried my best to find a river or a pond, where I could enjoy swimming in the clear and see-through water, but all I can find are rivers whose water is brown or ponds with all kinds of garbage floating on it. I still remember the sorrowful disappointment I felt that I found out I can never lead a colorful life like Tom did.

Years flew by. When I read the book again, what I appreciate is Tom's bravery that he stood against wickedness. And, by the way, the book, thank you for teaching me that a good book begs to be read in different ages, and the reader will benefit totally differently.

My experience with the book will last a lifetime.

Thank you very much.

【点评】这是一位文学演讲比赛参赛选手的演讲稿，虽然不是以我们正在读的文学名著为主题，但文学阅读让这位同学思索自己的童年生活，物质富裕和环境污染给这位同学的童年带来的是悲哀和遗憾。

☞ 案例 23

May 13rd, Fine

Just now very coincidently a university student sat beside me when I was reading the word list made by my student. She was surprised and asked me what it was about. Then I told her it was a word list for a novel. She took it for granted that I was a university teacher before I told her I was a senior school teacher. She was very surprised how senior school students could read and understand such a profound novel. She told me as an English major she has never finished reading an original English novel. In fact she was interested in literature too and she was a senior now and she has even decided to further her study so she will apply for a graduate entrance examination and she will choose literature as her research field. A graduate candidate has never finished reading an original literature classic but we have finished nearly five as a senior high school student. From her expression I can sense how envious she is of what we are doing! It is hard to imagine a senior school should go so far. We have been trying all the time in the past two years. I can't guarantee what I am doing is very successful. At least it is a way worth considering and trying in our English teaching.

I hope my student can form a habit of reading more original books they like with the help of the reading habits we have developed in the last two years. I know they have to face all kinds of school loads and sometimes it is impossible for them to spare some time to do what they like but if they can learn to manage time more sensibly and reasonably, there is still some room for them to develop themselves freely and fully, which depends on their wisdom.

【点评】这是在出差路上发生的一个小故事，这也从侧面表现我们现在正在做的文学阅读是一次大胆的尝试。笔者相信这一尝试是对的，虽然实践的过程充满了各种艰辛。

My Stories with My Teachers

The book *Tuesdays with Morrie* is mainly a story between a teacher and a student. The story has moved so many people since it came out. In our life journey nearly all of us have met teachers. I am sure we also have our stories about our own teachers. But do you have a teacher like Morrie?

Back to my school life, I was not a social person or a top student in the class, and I was a very quiet and ordinary student then. I couldn't say I developed a very good relationship with teachers, let alone I had met a teacher like Morrie. But even so several teachers are still in my mind, who impress me a lot. In my primary school, I studied in my village school and the conditions were very poor. The tables and chairs were all made of stone and the house was in poor condition. Though the condition was poor, I met a very kind and sincere teacher. He was my Chinese and maths teacher—Mr. Zhu. He treated us very well and was very warm-hearted. He had a very wide smile and was always optimistic though we knew his wife was terminally ill and they lived a very poor life. His smile is always in my heart.

In my junior high school I studied in my town. Every day I had to walk about half an hour to school. There I met my maths teacher—Mr. Li. He taught maths very well and was a very strict teacher. I was very careless, and I still remembered one time I made some simple mistakes. Mr. Li was a little angry and asked me to his office and criticized me severely. Though I was criticized, I was very grateful to him. Because of him I did a better job in maths. Several years ago his daughter came to Ningbo, and Mr. Li called me and asked me to take care of his daughter a little. I was very glad that I could help him a little after I had graduated from middle school twenty years later.

In my senior high school I met my Chinese teacher Mr. Hu. He was a bookworm and also a quiet person. We had a lot in common. Actually my Chinese was average but he gave me a lot of care. I remembered one time he asked me to his dorm. We had a very good talk at his dorm and he made lunch for me. I still remembered one dish — bean sprouts. Now every time I have it, it reminds me of my teacher Mr. Hu. Recently I have known he has changed his job after we graduated to be a lawyer.

Do you have some stories with your teachers?

【点评】笔者在文学名著阅读教学中基本每天会坚持用英语写点杂感，这些杂感大多是阅读小说后的感触以及对教学的反思。这既能提高教学水平，也能提高英语表达能力和写作能力。本案例是笔者在教学小说《相约星期二》的过程中写的自己和几个老师的故事。作为一名人民教师，这本小说中莫里教授与米奇的师生情谊对笔者触动很大，随即写了这段文字。

☞ 案例 24

The following part based on the novel *Pride and Prejudice*:

Ⅰ. Choose the right answer according to the novel *Pride and Prejudice*.

1. How does Mr. Darcy offend Elizabeth at the first ball?

   A. He dances with Jane too often.　　B. He insults her father.

   B. He refuses to dance with her　　D. He keeps silent all the time.

2. Jane suffered from a cold and Jane and Elizabeth had to stay at ________ for nearly two weeks.

   A. Pemberley　　B. Longbourn

   C. Netherfield　　D. Rosings

3. Elithebeth's best friend is named ________.

   A. Mrs. Phillips　　B. Charlotte Lucas

   C. Miss Bingley　　D. Mrs. Gardiner

Ⅱ. Choose the words in the box with the right form to fill in the blanks.

suffer	mix	admire	dangerous	victory	discovery	fall

1. Mr. Bennet was so odd a ________ of quick parts, sarcastic humour, reserve, and caprice.
2. To be fond of dancing was a certain step towards ________ in love; and very lively hopes of Mr Bingley's heart were entertained.
3. Had she only dined with him, she might only have ________ whether he had a good appetite.
4. Mrs Bennet, who fancied she had gained a complete ________ over him, continued her triumph.
5. He began to feel the ________ of paying Elizabeth too much attention.

Ⅲ. What is your understanding of the following sentence? (within 20 words)

1. Happiness in marriage in entirely a matter of chance.

...

Directions: The full mark of this part is 40 and those who choose to read *The Great Gatsby* this term must finish this part, otherwise you will lose the mark of this part.

I. Choose the best answer based on the Chapters 1-5 of *The Great Gatsby*. (共 20 小题; 每小题 1 分, 共 20 分)

1. At the beginning of the novel, Nick recounts a conversation where his father tells him to remember that "all of the people in this world haven't had the ________ you've had"...

   A. advantages B. disadvantages C. friends D. luck

2. How does the narrator describe Gatsby?

   A. Gatsby was brilliant, although somewhat smug and self-centered.

   B. Gatsby had an extraordinary gift for hope, and a romantic readiness.

   C. Gatsby was a big, hulking brute of a man.

   D. Gatsby was self-assured and showed boundless enthusiasm about most topics.

3. Describe Tom. What is our impression of him in Chapter 1?

   A. He is short and fat and jolly.

   B. He has an athletic build and an arrogant attitude. He is an old-money snob.

   C. He is tall and slender. He is a grumpy middle-aged man.

   D. He has a medium build and is balding. He is easy-going and pleasant.

...

20. What did Gatsby do to impress Daisy?

   A. He gave her a pearl necklace worth $500,000.

B. He showed her his house and elegant clothes.

C. He took her for a ride in his hydroplane.

D. He showed her the love letters he had written her, but never sent.

Ⅱ. Reading.（共 4 小题；每小题 1. 5 分，共 6 分）

F. Scott Fitzgerald, born on September 24, 1896, an American novelist, was once a student of St. Paul Academy, the Newman School and attended Princeton. University for a short while. In 1917 he joined the army and was posted in Alabama, where he met his future wife Zelda Sayre. Then he had to make some money to impress her.

His life with her was full of great happiness, as he wrote in his diary: "My own happiness in the past often approached such joy that I could share it even with the person dearest to me but had to walk it away in quiet streets and take down parts of it in my diary."

This Side of Paradise, his first novel, was published in 1920. Encouraged by its success, Fitzgerald began to devote more time to his writing. Then he continued with the novel the *Beautiful and Damned* (1922), a collection of short stories *Thales of the Jazz Age* (1922), and a play *The Vegetable* (1923). But his greatest success was *The Great Gatsby*, published in 1925, which quick brought him praise from the literary world. Yet it failed to give him the needed financial security. Then, in 1926, he published another collection of short stories *All the Sad Young Men.*

However, Fitzgerald's problems with his wife Zelda affected his writing. During the 1920s he tried to reorder his life, but failed. By 1930, his wife had her first breakdown and went to a Swiss clinic. During this period he completed novels Tender Is the Night in 1934 and The Love of the Last Tycoon in 1940. while his wife was in hospital in the United States, he got totally addicted to alcohol. *Sheila Graham*, his dear friend, helped him fight his alcoholism.

1. How many novels written by Fitzgerald are mentioned in the passage?

A. 5. B. 6. C. 7. D. 8.

2. Which of the following is the correct order to describe Fitzgerald's life according to the passage?

a. He became addicted to drinking.

b. He studied at St. Paul Academy.

c. He published his first novel *This Side of Paradise.*

d. *The Great Gatsby* won high praise.

e. He failed to reorder his life.

f. He joined the army and met Zelda.

A. f-c-e-a-b-d B. b-e-a-f-c-d C. f-d-e-c-b-a D. b-f-c-d-e-a

3. We can infer from the passage that Fitzgerald ________.

A. had made some money when he met Zelda in Alabama.

B. was well educated and well off before he served in the army

C. would have completed more works if his wife hadn't broken down

D. helped his friend get rid of drinking while his wife was in hospital

4. The passage is probably followed by a concluding paragraph about ________.

A. Zelda's personal life

B. Zelda's illness and treatment

C. Fitzgerald's friendship with Graham

D. Fitzgerald's contributions to the literary world

Ⅲ. Quotation Identification: Identify the character who says the quotation. Some characters will be repeated, but *ALL WILL BE USED AT LEAST ONCE.* (共 8 小题；每小题 0.5 分，共 4 分)

Daisy	Gatsby	Nick	Jordan	Tom	Myrtle	Wolfsheim

1. "That? That's Mr. Dan Cody, old sport."

2. “Daisy! Daisy! Daisy! I’ll say it whenever I want to! Daisy! Dai—”
3. “It makes me sad because I’ve never seen such—such beautiful shirts before.”
4. “Civilization’s going to pieces.”
5. “It’s a libel. I am too poor.”
6. “... This is a terrible mistake, a terrible, terrible mistake.”
7. “Hot and small—yes, but full of memories.”
8. “Tom’s got some women in New York.”

Ⅳ. Fill in the blanks using the right form of the words in the box. (共10小题；每小题1分，共10分)

hasty	sight	occasion	shrink	rise	crawl
stir	fantastic	dim	grotesque		

About half way between West Egg and New York the motor road __1__ joins the railroad and runs beside it for a quarter of a mile, so as to __2__ away from a certain desolate area of land. This is a valley of ashes—a __3__ farm where ashes grow like wheat into ridges and hills and __4__ gardens; where ashes take the forms of houses and chimneys and __5__ smoke and, finally, with a transcendent effort, of men who move __6__ and already crumbling through the powdery air. __7__ a line of gray cars __8__ along an invisible track, gives out a ghastly creak, and comes to rest, and immediately the ash-gray men swarm up with leaden spades and __9__ up an impenetrable cloud, which screens their obscure operations from your __10__.

【点评】该案例是小说《傲慢与偏见》《了不起的盖茨比》学期期中、期末考试的部分考核试题，通常占试卷分值的20%~30%，题型有主、客观试题，试题题型新颖，比如对《了不起的盖茨比》中人物对话的辨认、细节的考核、经典语句的深度解析等，从不同角度全方位地检测了学生的阅读效果。

第五节　创新之处和后续研究设想

一、创新之处

本课题把文学作品作为拓展课教学内容，而且教学选用的文学作品大多是简写本。该课题旨在让高中学生直接阅读文学原著，并且是从高一开始，有计划、系统地进行。本课题是在浙江省 2019 年秋季深化课程改革的背景下提出的，本书尝试论证文学作品思想、人文等诸方面的课程价值。本课题创新之处在于提出名著在高中英语教学中的应用是英语教学走向英语教育的重要途径。另外，本课题尝试中外师资合作研究的形式。课题研究过程中，宁波外国语学校国际部学术校长 Mr. Richard 多次提出课程建议并提供了很多宝贵的外文资料，笔者和宁波外国语学校国际部其他文学教师相互听课、交流，和美国高中文学教师 Mr. Glen 就文学阅读教学话题一直保持邮件联系。Mr. Glen 提供了大量的文学教学资料，保证了该研究成果的前沿性和科学性。

二、存在问题

该课题的研究面临压力。文学名著在英语教学中的应用还是一个新领域，虽然一线教师深知阅读在英语教学中的重要性，但传统的阅读教学仍然以应试为主，文学名著的阅读不如传统的阅读教学一样在考试中能起到立竿见影的作用，所以很多时候任课教师并不愿意冒险或接受新的挑战。整个课题的实践还面临着部分家长和学生的质疑，这可能会影响到研究的深度和广度。

其次，参与本课题的学生处于高二年级，他们面临着学业水平测试和英语高考听力等应试的负担，不得不分散精力去准备这些考试，这就势必影响名著阅读的时间以及同学们的专注度。面对日常教学任务和应试压力的干扰，实验教师从夹缝中挤出时间来做好教学改革尝试，也是需要智慧的。事实上，英文名著走进课堂教学的实践和这些学业考试并不矛盾。从 2014 年 1 月浙江省学业水平考试成绩来看，参与本课题的学生的英语成绩显著提高，其学业水平 A 等率(91%)也大大高于兄弟平行学校(80%左右)；平时英语测试中，其听力平均分也在 27 分(满分 30 分)。

最后，课题研究过程中收集了大量数据，这些数据包括学生的作业、课件、原创的备课资料、考试试卷、调查问卷、邮件、演讲稿、海报、访谈、课后反思日记，等等，如何充分、科学地整理和利用这些资料来展现课程成果还需要进一步积累经验。

三、后续研究设想

本研究主要聚焦文学名著在高中英语教学中的可行性分析，在今后的研究中会借鉴文学阅读的方法，在教学中继续探索文学阅读的有效方式。同时在未来的研究中还要继续实践文学名著走进高中英语课堂教学，进一步完善相关课型，完善相应的考核和评价机制。

◎ 参考文献

1. Brumfit C. J., Carter, R. A.. Literature and Language Teaching [M]. Shanghai: Shanghai Foreign Language Education Press, 2001.
2. Ess, C.. Critical Thinking: A Concise Guide [M]. London: Routledge, 2002.
3. Mackay S. L.. Literature as Content for ESL/EFL[A]. In M. Celce-Muria(ed.) Teaching English as a Second or Foreign Language(the 3rd) [C]. Boston: Heinle & Heinle/Thomson Learning, 2001.
4. Marckwardt, A. H.. The Place of Literature in Teaching English as a Second or Foreign Language [M] Honolulu: University of Hawaii Press, 1978.
5. Tomlison, B.. English Language Learning Materials: A Critical Review [M]. London: Continuum, 2008.
6. 曹敏. 高中生英语写作的问题与对策——一项基于语料库的研究[J].

课程·教材·教法，2010(10).
7. 傅云山. 高中英语文学欣赏课教学实践研究［J］. 英语教师，2012(11).
8. 盖梦丽. 基于语言教学的文学教学[J]. 北京第二外国语学院学报(外语版)，2007(10).
9. 中华人民共和国教育部. 普通高中英语课程标准(实验)[M]. 北京：人民教育出版社，2003.
10. 贾东佳. 英美文学与英语阅读教学［J］. 文学教育，2012.(10).
11. 黄远振. 中学英语文学阅读可行性和有效性研究——优秀学习者个案及其启示[J]. 课程·教材·教法，2009.(10).
12. 柯安利. 中小学英语也要重视文学阅读［J］. 光明日报，2007-07-18.
13. 李振来. 生本理念：让英语文学名著走进高中课堂——开设高中英语名著读写指导课的探索［J］. 现代教育论坛，2011(3).
14. 刘蕴秋，邹为诚. 美国新英语课程标准评析［J］. 全球教育展望，2010(5).
15. 仇云龙，张绍杰. 晚清外语人才培养特色及其当下启示外语教学与研究[J]. 外国语文双月刊，2011(2).
16. 唐洁璠. 论文学阅读指导的评价标准［J］. 语文学刊，2008(7).
17. 张春开. 浅谈英美文学在高中英语教学中的渗透［J］. 英语教师，2012(4).

附　件

【附件一】 课题研究大事记

1. 2012 年 10 月，在宁波外国语学校全体高一学生中开始英文原著《夏洛的网》阅读教学工作。
2. 2012 年 11 月，在宁波外国语学校外语组开设《夏洛的网》教学公开课。
3. 2013 年 2 月，在宁波外国语学校全体高一学生中开始英文原著《相约星期二》的阅读教学工作。
4. 2013 年 3—4 月，和宁波外国语学校国际部学术校长 Mr. Richard 相互交流听课。
5. 2013 年 5 月 3 日，该课题在宁波市四明中学立项，参加立项的专家有张立新、纪勇、薛矿军等。
6. 2013 年 5 月 15 日，北京市骨干教师来校观摩，笔者代表学校开设观摩课，会后交流中老师们都对文学名著走近英语课堂教学产生了很大的兴趣。组内同事不定时多次走进课堂听课。
7. 2013 年 5 月，开始英文原著《老人与海》的阅读教学。
8. 2013 年 6 月 4 日，邀请国际部老师 Richard 为学生做文学阅读的辅导讲座，讲座持续一节课时间，学生就国际部学生的文学作品阅读提出了感兴趣的问题。
9. 2013 年 6 月，高一全体学生开展文学阅读比赛，比赛的内容分为两部分，一部分是小说《老人与海》节选部分的翻译，一部分是词汇检测，两部分总分加起来，最后取一等奖 5 名，二等奖 10 名，三等奖 15 名。
10. 2013 年 6 月，高一、高二同学开展以名著阅读为主题的演讲比赛，笔者任教班级学生胡易韬、刘璇获得高中段二等奖。
11. 2013 年 9 月，在部分学生中开始《傲慢与偏见》(第一部共 21 章)的阅读教学工作。

12. 2013 年 9—11 月，宁波大学英语专业忻盈等实习生在笔者任教的班级参与教学实习，也参与了部分文学阅读教学的工作。

13. 2013 年 12 月 27 日，该课题作为笔者的博士论文选题在华东师范大学开题，参与开题的有马和民、马庆发、吴遵民、张际平、鞠玉翠五位教授，他们肯定了该选题对英语教学的意义，认为文学教学在英语教学中是不可缺少的，肯定了该选题的实践价值，并且鼓励笔者扎根课堂，做出自己的特色。

14. 2013 年 12 月—2014 年 1 月，钱佑尔、舒昱昱、李欣洁、邵华圆圆等同学在 21 世纪英文杯英语演讲比赛中获宁波市一等奖和二等奖，笔者也获得优秀教师指导奖。

15. 2014 年 1 月 14 日下午，宁波市教科所副所长张立新博士对该课题进行中期检查。

16. 2014 年 3 月，开始英文原著《了不起的盖茨比》的阅读教学工作。（截至 2014 年 3 月 14 日已经完成前两章的教学任务。）

17. 2014 年 3 月 19 日下午，本课题在宁波教科所接受相关专家的结题检查，吴晶京老师就课题结题中存在的困难及结题报告的撰写等问题提出了指导意见。

18. 2014 年 3 月 27 日，胡易韬、骆雨菡、俞萌等同学编排的英文剧《傲慢与偏见》片段在学校英语节上表演，获得好评。

19. 2014 年 4 月 10 日，笔者在宁波效实中学浙派高中英语名师班进行英文名著教学展示课，参与听课的老师有五十余人，展示课后与有关专家和听课老师交流，效果良好。

20. 2014 年 4 月 23 日上午，宁波教科所张立新副所长就该课题结题工作进行检查指导，张所长对结题报告的格式和内容、结构都提出了修改意见。

21. 2014 年 5 月 10 日，张立新副所长对该课题的修改稿进一步提出意见，针对张所长的意见，笔者对结题报告进行进一步完善。

22. 2014 年 7 月，该选题顺利结题，并获得宁波市教学成果奖三等奖。

【附件二】 教学案例选

教学案例 1

Day 1: Biography of F. Scott Fitzgerald and Introduction to *The Roaring* 1920*s*

Teacher: He Ze

Date: March 3rd, 2014

Learning Objectives:

After this lesson the students will be able to:

1. Identify several key facts/events from the biography of author F. Scott Fitzgerald's life via a PowerPoint presentation;
2. Describe some of the main elements that characterized the "Roaring 1920s" era in U. S. history, including music, culture, and societal values;
3. Find more information from the internet about the author and the related background knowledge about "The Roaring 1920s".

Teaching Procedures:

1. Introductory Activity/Hook (5-7 minutes)

I will begin this first day of the week (as well as the new unit *The Great Gatsby*) by performing the initial classroom duties, including welcoming my students and taking attendance. During this time, I will direct the students to a given picture on the board (from the computer projector) for their daily introductory activity. To set them in the mindset of the "Roaring 1920s", the photo will be of a "flapper" from the era, as well as the time's jazz music playing. Students will be asked to jot down in their daily journals what they think the "flappers" represented, how the music makes them feel, what they may be studying next, etc. Lastly, I will close this "hook" by asking a few students to share their responses before going over the daily agenda and learning objectives on the board and starting the lesson.

2. Presentation (20-25 minutes)

(1) PowerPoint Presentation about *F. Scott Fitzgerald and the Roaring* 1920*s*. Much of the lesson will not be an immediate immersion into *The Great Gatsby* itself, but to provide a framework beforehand. As such, students will be asked to interact with the teacher with the following questions. Via these questions we will examine author F. Scott Fitzgerald's life and the culture, society, and values of the 1920s decade in the United States. Some key questions to keep in mind:

① What was Fitzgerald's young life like?

② How might his youth have affected his later writing?

③ Who was Zelda Sayre? How did the author's wife affect his life?

④ What was the 1920s decade like?

⑤ Why was the time called the "Roaring 1920s"?

⑥ Describe elements of the Jazz Age and relation to the "Lost Generation".

⑦ What is Modernism?

(2) Class Discussion (5-7 minutes). After the presentation is finished, the teacher will ask students what they thought of the Fitzgerald's life, as well as any other questions, comments, and insights they may have of the "Roaring 1920s". Teachers might also encourage students to make connections of the author and present from the past to contemporary authors and experiences today.

3. Closure

(1) I would close this first day by reminding students to bring their own copies of the novel tomorrow for class, where we will begin our reading together. I will also ask students to have their daily writing journals handy every day of our unit for responses/questions/ comments to the reading.

(2) Assessments: The assessment is a formative evaluation based on students'

participation and correct responses given in the PowerPoint presentation. Throughout our class lecture and discussion, the teacher should check for students' comprehension by noting whether they are taking extra notes, raising their hands, and offering valuable insight into the experience.

4. Homework

(1) Read Chapter 1 with the help of the word list and comprehension check.

(2) The students are instructed to bring their copies of *The Great Gatsby* to class tomorrow, have their writing journals finished and keep them on hand, and be ready to share.

教学案例 2

Day 2: Introduction to *The Great Gatsby* and Daily Expectations

Teacher: He Ze

Date: March 5th, 2014

Learning Objectives:

After this lesson the students will be able to:

1. Read Chapter 1 of the novel (*The Great Gatsby*) out loud via a popcorn reading strategy;
2. Understand the main plot of chapter1;
3. Express their opinions and record evidence from a novel for homework through writing via a daily journal and setting map assignment.

Teaching Procedures:

1. Introductory Activity/Hook(4-5 minutes)

After initial classroom duties, today's lesson will begin with students joining with a partner seated next to them to think and share their thoughts together from a prompt on the board. The prompt would be: "Have you read *The Great Gatsby* before? If so, what do you remember from it? Likes?

Dislikes? If not, what can you infer about it from the cover, the blurb, or yesterday's presentation? Discuss." This will provide students with an opportunity to verbally communicate with one another and get in the mindset of starting to read *The Great Gatsby*. The teacher might also call on some students after the brief paired conversation for some groups to share their experiences with the novel. Lastly, I will direct students to the daily objectives and learning objectives on the board to begin the lesson.

2. Practice and Reading Procedures (20-25 minutes)

(1) Popcorn Reading of *The Great Gatsby*, Chapter 1: The majority of today's class will revolve around the popcorn reading strategy. Students are asked to take out their copies of the novel and open to Chapter 1. The teacher will begin by reading the first page or so, then say "popcorn" and call on a student, who will then read a paragraph and pass on to the next student (and so on). It is intended that all students will be able to read out loud at least once as everyone follows along.

(2) Hand the comprehension check questions out and ask students to do finish it and then check in groups.

3. Closure

Ask if students had any comments/ questions on today's reading. I would then ask some students to share the reading journals and ask some other classmates to make comments.

4. Homework

Preview Chapter 1 with the help of the word list and do the exercise of the reading check of Chapter 2.

教学案例3：2014年4月10日浙派名师高中英语名师班展示课

Date: 10 April, 2014

Teacher: He Ze

Content: *Tuesdays with Morrie* PP. 80-85

Learning Objectives:

After this lesson the students will be able to:

1. Read and understand the excerpt of the novel *Tuesdays with Morrie* by reading loud via a popcorn reading strategy and discussing some questions.
2. Reflect on their own opinion on the central topic death via a class discussion that promotes critical thinking and the use of context clues.
3. Figure out some background knowledge or remove some cultural barriers by referring to some cultural notes.

Teaching Procedures:

1. Introduce the book *Tuesdays with Morrie* and related background knowledge(The disease ALS, for exemple).
2. Read and understand the excerpts better by discussing the questions on the preview reading comprehension check card.
3. Popcorn reading of the excerpt of *Tuesdays with Morrie.* The teacher will begin by reading the first paragraph or so, then say "popcorn to..." and the student who is called will then read a paragraph and pass on to the next student (and so on). It is intended that all students will be able to read out loud at least once as everyone follows along. This reading strategy is effective because it requires every student to pay attention in case they are called next, and highlights the importance of reading by devoting actual class time to the novel itself.
4. Sharing and reflection. Ask the students to write short comments where they are touched and then exchange their comments. Also reflect on their own opinions on the following questions:
   (1) One common thought is that it would be best to live a long, healthy life and then die suddenly in one's sleep. After reading this chapter, what do you think about it?
   (2) Morrie was seventy-eight years old when he suffered from ALS. How might he have reacted if he had had the disease at a Mitch's age even

younger? Would Morrie have come to the same conclusion? The same peace and acceptance? Reflect on your opinion an death after you have read this chapter. (if possible watch two clips of videos)

5. Homework:

(1) Read this chapter again in groups after class using the popcorn reading skills.

(2) Read the following quotes about death and choose two and make comments.

All our knowledge merely helps us to die a more painful death than animals that know nothing.

—Maurice Maeterlinck

The fear of death follows from the fear of life. A man who lives fully is prepared to die at any time.

—Mark Twain

Men fear death, as children fear to go in the dark; and as that natural fear in children is increased with tales, so is the other.

—Francis Bacon, *Essays*

If you spend all your time worrying about dying, living isn't going to be much fun.

—From the sitcom *Roseanne*

Some people are so afraid to die that they never begin to live.

—Henry Van Dyke

He who doesn't fear death dies only once.

—Giovanni Falcone

No one can confidently say that he will still be living tomorrow.

—Euripides

While I thought that I was learning how to live, I have been learning how to die.

—Leonardo da Vinci

Death is a distant rumor to the young.

—Andrew A. Rooney

Death may be the greatest of all human blessings.

—Socrates

Death never takes the wise man by surprise; he is always ready to go.

—Jean de La Fontaine

【附件三】 评价案例选

☞ 案例 1

宁波外国语学校 2012 学年第二学期期末考试试题

（小说《相约星期二》部分试题）

第二题：单项选择（共 20 小题；21～30 每小题 0.5 分；31～40 每小题 1 分，满分 15 分）。从 A，B，C，D 四个选项中，选出可以填入空白处的最佳选项，并在答题卡上将该项涂黑。

31. When Mitch graduates from college, what occupation does he want to pursue?

 A. A writer. B. A doctor. C. A musician. D. An artist.

32. The pink hibiscus is a symbol of ________.

 A. the dying relationship between Mitch and Morrie.

 B. Morrie's decaying body.

 C. Mitch's dwindling relationship with his brother Daniel.

 D. Morrie's career at Brandeis University.

33. Morrie's father can be best described as ________.

 A. a mentor in the education business.

 B. a nurturing and supporting parent.

 C. a person who dies when Morrie is a child.

 D. a poor person who works in a factory.

34. In which of the following ways does Morrie celebrate his death?

 A. Morrie celebrates his death by having a living funeral.

 B. Morrie celebrates his death by visiting his burial site in the weeks before his death.

 C. Morrie celebrates his death by having Ted Koppel interview him for Nightline.

 D. Morrie celebrates his death by teaching a last class about death and dying at Brandeis University.

35. According to the book, "When you're in bed, ________."

A. you're on your last leg　　B. you're dead

C. you're on your last breath　　D. there is little time left

36. Which of the following events allows Mitch to visit Morrie regularly?

A. When Morrie undergoes treatment for ALS, he lives in the same town as Mitch.

B. Mitch's newspaper goes on strike; therefore, Mitch cannot go to work.

C. Mitch is independently wealthy as a result of writing books and is able to take time off from work.

D. Mitch moves in with Morrie in order to take care of him.

37. When Morrie is first interviewed by Ted Koppel, how does Morrie feel about Ted?

A. Morrie feels that Ted is too important of a man to do the interview.

B. Morrie is angered by Ted's reliance on the media to tell his story and as a result, Morrie refuses to do the interview.

C. Morrie is star-struck by Ted Koppel and is unable to contribute much to theinterview.

D. Morrie feels that Ted Koppel is a narcissist.

38. What event is most responsible for Morrie's need for physical and emotional love?

A. The death of his father.　　B. The death of his mother.

C. The death of his son.　　D. The death of his wife.

39. Which of the following is not a subject that Mitch and Morrie discuss?

A. Regrets.　　B. Emotions.

C. Friendship.　　D. Love.

40. Mitch repeatedly tells Mitch that he must create his own ________.

A. religion　　B. life

C. relationship　　D. culture

第Ⅱ卷非选择题部分(共 45 分)

注意事项：用黑色签字笔或钢笔将答案写在答题纸上，不能答在试卷上。

第一节：单词拼写。根据首字母提示和句意在空白处填写正确的单词。(共 **10** 小题；每小题 **1** 分，满分 **10** 分)

81. It is not polite to i ________ while others are speaking.
82. Our school is s ________ by small hills, which makes our school more beautiful.
83. According to Morrie, love is the only r ________ act.
84. You can't s ________ material things for love or for gentleness or for tenderness.
85. The slightest foods were still beyond Morrie's limited strength to chew and s ________.
86. The flight was c ________ because of foggy weather.
87. The professor d ________ himself to doing scientific research into agriculture.
88. The young children are totally d ________ on their parents for food and shelter.
89. Much to our r ________ no one was badly injured and the car was not damaged either in the accident.
90. We a ________ great importance to the headmaster and teachers' visit this Monday.

第三节：书面表达。(满分 **25** 分)

Write a book report of the novel *Tuesdays with Morrie* with a word limit of 100-120, and your book report should include two parts (point 1 is a must, and as for points 2 and 3, you can choose one):

1. The brief introduction of the book;

2. Your evaluation of the book;

3. What you have learn from the book.

用英文写一篇《相约星期二》的读书报告，你的读书报告应该包括两个部分。第一部分包括下面提示中的第一点，第二部分可以从提示中第二点或第三点中任意选择其一。词数100~120词。

1. 该书的简要介绍；2. 您对该书的评价；3. 您从该书中学到的道理。

☞ 案例2

宁波外国语学校2013学年第一学期期末考试
(小说《傲慢与偏见》部分试题)

Ⅰ. Choose the right answer according to the novel *Pride and Prejudice*.

1. How does Mr. Darcy offend Elizabeth at the first ball?

   A. He dances with Jane too often.

   B. He insults her father.

   C. He refuses to dance with her

   D. He keeps silent all the time.

2. Because Jane suffered from a cold and Jane and Elizabeth had to stay at ________ for nearly two weeks.

   A. Pemberley　　B. Longbourn

   C. Netherfield　　D. Rosings

3. Elithebeth's best friend is named ________.

   A. Mrs. Phillips　　B. Charlotte Lucas

   C. Miss Bingley　　D. Mrs. Gardiner

Ⅱ. Choose the words in the box with the right form to fill in the blanks.

suffer	mix	admire	dangerous	victory	discovery	fall

1. Mr. Bennet was so odd a ________ of quick parts, sarcastic humour, reserve, and caprice.

2. To be fond of dancing was a certain step towards ________ in love; and very lively hopes of Mr. Bingley's heart were entertained.

3. Had she only dined with him, she might only have ________ whether he had a good appetite.

4. Mrs. Bennet, who fancied she had gained a complete ________ over him, continued her triumph.

5. He began to feel the ________ of paying Elizabeth too much attention.

Ⅲ. What is your understanding of the following sentences? (within 20 words)

1. Happiness in marriage is entirely a matter of chance.

…

☞ 案例 3

宁波外国语学校 2013 学年第二学期期中考试
(小说《了不起的盖茨比》部分试题)

Directions: The full mark of this part is 40 and those who choose to read *The Great Gatsby* this term must finish this part, otherwise you will lose the mark of this part.

Ⅰ. Choose the best answer based on the Chapters 1-5 of *The Great Gatsby*. (共 20 小题; 每小题 1 分, 共 20 分)

1. At the beginning of the novel, Nick recounts a conversation where his father tells him to remember that "all of the people in this world haven't had the ________ you've had".

   A. advantages　　B. disadvantages　　C. friends　　D. luck

2. How does the narrator describe Gatsby?

   A. Gatsby was brilliant, although somewhat smug and self-centered.

   B. Gatsby had an extraordinary gift for hope, and a romantic readiness.

   C. Gatsby was a big, hulking brute of a man.

   D. Gatsby was self-assured and showed boundless enthusiasm about most topics.

3. How did the author describe Tom? What is our impression of him in Chapter 1?

   A. He is short and fat and jolly.

   B. He has an athletic build and an arrogant attitude. He is an old-money snob.

   C. He is tall and slender. He is a grumpy middle-aged man.

   D. He has a medium build and is balding. He is easy-going and pleasant.

4. When asked about her daughter, what does Daisy say?

   A. "She acts just like her father!"

   B. "Isn't she a little darling?"

C. "I suppose she talks—and eats, and everything."

D. "I wish I had never had her."

5. What are the "eyes of Dr. T. J. Eckleburg"?

A. Seeing eye dogs that the doctor trains for the Association for the blind.

B. A group of security guards who monitor the doctor's home and offices.

C. A new kind of contact lens that the doctor has just developed.

D. An illustration on a billboard.

6. What did Mrs. Wilson buy while she was out with Tom and Nick?

A. Sandwiches for lunch.　　B. A dog.

C. A new dress.　　D. Cuff links for Tom.

7. Where did they go? What was at 158th Street?

A. Tom's favorite restaurant.

B. Nick's office.

C. The dealer where Tom bought his last car.

D. The apartment where Tom met his mistress.

8. Identify Catherine and Mr. & Mrs. McKee.

A. Catherine is Nick's secretary. Mrs. McKee is her sister, and Mr. McKee is her brother-in-law.

B. Catherine is Myrtle's sister. The McKees live downstairs at the apartment complex.

C. Catherine is Tom's cousin. The McKees are the apartment managers.

D. Catherine is Mrs. McKee's best friend. The McKees are old neighbors of Myrtle's.

9. What reason did Myrtle give for marrying George Wilson?

A. She had to do something to get away from her abusive parents.

B. She did it to spite George's former girlfriend.

C. She thought he was a gentleman; later she found out differently.

D. She didn't think she would ever find a husband, and she was grateful to him for asking her.

10. Which one of these does not represent Gatsby's wealth?
    A. Made in the post-war period.
    B. Spending on flashy, extravagant things.
    C. Old, family money.
    D. Wild parties.
11. What kind of people come to Gatsby's parties?
    A. The newly rich, famous, and their friends.
    B. Only the residents of West Egg.
    C. Scholars and intellectuals from area universities.
    D. Mostly Gatsby's business associates.
12. How does Nick meet Gatsby?
    A. Gatsby greets all of his guests in a receiving line.
    B. They met when Nick wandered into the library where Gatsby was reading.
    C. Jordan Baker introduced them.
    D. Nick asks a man he is talking to where Gatsby is and discovers that he is talking to Gatsby.
13. Describe Nick's relationship with Jordan.
    A. They can't stand each other.
    B. They are beginning to get friendly.
    C. They fell in love at first sight.
    D. They are just golfing partners.
14. What does Gatsby tell Nick about himself?
    A. He had never finished high school, he was a boatswains mate during the war, and he had been married twice.
    B. He had a degree in Finance from the University of Pennsylvania, he had been draft exempt because of his vision, and he made all of his money in the theater.
    C. He dropped out of college to go into the army, he intended to be a

career military man, but inherited his money from his wife when she died unexpectedly.

D. He was educated at Oxford, inherited his money from his family, and got some medals in the war.

15. What "matter" did Gatsby have Jordan Baker discuss with Nick?

A. Gatsby had a business deal he wanted to include Nick in on it.

B. Gatsby wanted Nick to arrange a luncheon meeting between himself and Daisy.

C. Gatsby had a cousin who was coming to stay for a month, and he wanted Nick to escort her around the city, if Jordan approved.

D. Gatsby wanted to invite Nick and Jordan to go on a golfing vacation to Europe.

16. Who is Mr. Wolfshiem?

A. He is the owner of Gatsby's favorite restaurant in New York. He secretly arranged to have a member of the mob murdered outside the restaurant.

B. He is Jordan Baker's coach and manager. He thinks Jordan is spending too much time with Nick and not enough on her golf.

C. He is a racketeer and a business associate of Gatsby's. He fixed the 1919 World Series.

D. He is the president of the company where Nick is working. He wants to bring Gatsby in on a new real estate deal.

17. What does Mr. Wolfshiem tell Nick about Gatsby?

A. Gatsby was dangerous and should never be trusted.

B. Gatsby was on the verge of bankruptcy because of some bad investments.

C. Gatsby was thinking of getting into politics.

D. Gatsby was the kind of man to take home to meet your mother and sister.

18. Describe the meeting between Gatsby and Daisy.

A. Daisy did not recognize him. He was embarrassed and tried to leave, but Nick stopped him.

B. It was initially very awkward. Gatsby was nervous. They became more at ease as they talked.

C. Daisy was upset with Nick for not warning her. She did not want to see Gatsby and left as soon as her chauffeur returned.

D. It was love at first sight for both of them. They wandered off into the living room and left Nick alone in the kitchen.

19. How long did it take Gatsby to make the money to buy the mansion?

A. Three years.　　　　　　B. Eleven months.

C. Two hours.　　　　　　D. Fifteen days.

20. What did Gatsby do to impress Daisy?

A. He gave her a pearl necklace worth $500,000.

B. He showed her his house and elegant clothes.

C. He took her for a ride in his hydroplane.

D. He showed her the love letters he had written her, but never sent.

Ⅱ. Reading. (共 4 小题; 每小题 1.5 分, 共 6 分)

F. Scott Fitzgerald, born on September 24, 1896, an American novelist, was once a student of St. Paul Academy, the Newman School and attended Princeton. University for a short while. In 1917 he joined the army and was posted in Alabama, where he met his future wife Zelda Sayre. Then he had to make some money to impress her.

His life with her was full of great happiness, as he wrote in his diary: "My own happiness in the past often approached such joy that I could share it even with the person dearest to me but had to walk it away in quiet streets and take down parts of it in my diary."

This Side of Paradise, his first novel, was published in 1920.

Encouraged by its success, Fitzgerald began to devote more time to his writing. Then he continued with the novel *The Beautiful and Damned* (1922), a collection of short stories *Thales of the Jazz Age* (1922), and a play *The Vegetable* (1923). But his greatest success was The Great Gatsby, published in 1925, which quick brought him praise from the literary world. Yet it failed to give him the needed financial security. Then, in 1926, he published another collection of short stories *All the Sad Young Men*.

However, Fitzgerald's problems with his wife Zelda affected his writing. During the 1920s he tried to reorder his life, but failed. By 1930, his wife had her first breakdown and went to a Swiss clinic. During this period he completed novels *Tender Is the Nigh*t in 1934 and *The Love of the Last Tycoon* in 1940. while his wife was in hospital in the United States, he got totally addicted to alcohol. Sheila Graham, his dear friend, helped him fight his alcoholism.

1. How many novels written by Fitzgerald are mentioned in the passage?

   A. 5. B. 6. C. 7. D. 8.

2. Which of the following is the correct order to describe Fitzgerald's life according to the passage?

   a. He became addicted to drinking.

   b. He studied at St. Paul Academy.

   c. He published his first novel *This Side of Paradise*.

   d. *The Great Gatsby* won high praise.

   e. He failed to reorder his life.

   f. He joined the army and met Zelda.

   A. f-c-e-a-b-d B. b-e-a-f-c-d

   C. f-d-e-c-b-a D. b-f-c-d-e-a

3. We can infer from the passage that Fitzgerald ________.

   A. had made some money when he met Zelda in Alabama

   B. was well educated and well off before he served in the army

C. would have completed more works if his wife hadn't broken down

D. helped his friend get rid of drinking while his wife was in hospital

4. The passage is probably followed by a concluding paragraph about ________.

A. Zelda's personal life

B. Zelda's illness and treatment

C. Fitzgerald's friendship with Graham

D. Fitzgerald's contributions to the literary world

Ⅲ. Quotation Identification: Identify the character who says the quotation. Some characters will be repeated, but ALL WILL BE USED AT LEAST ONCE.（共 8 小题；每小题 0.5 分，共 4 分）

Daisy	Gatsby	Nick	Jordan	Tom	Myrtle	Wolfsheim

1. "That? That's Mr Dan Cody, old sport."
2. "Daisy! Daisy! Daisy! I'll say it whenever I want to! Daisy! Dai—"
3. "It makes me sad because I've never seen such- such beautiful shirts before."
4. "Civilization's going to pieces."
5. "It's a libel. I am too poor."
6. "... This is a terrible mistake, a terrible, terrible mistake."
7. "Hot and small—yes, but full of memories."
8. "Tom's got some women in New York."

Ⅳ. Fill in the blank using the right form of the words in the box.（共 10 小题；每小题 1 分，共 10 分）

hasty	sight	occasion	shrink	rise	crawl
stir	fantastic	dim	grotesque		

About half way between West Egg and New York the motor road __1__ joins the railroad and runs beside it for a quarter of a mile, so as to __2__ away from a certain desolate area of land. This is a valley of ashes—a __3__ farm where ashes grow like wheat into ridges and hills and __4__ gardens; where ashes take the forms of houses and chimneys and __5__ smoke and, finally, with a transcendent effort, of men who move __6__ and already crumbling through the powdery air. __7__ a line of gray cars __8__ along an invisible track, gives out a ghastly creak, and comes to rest, and immediately the ash-gray men swarm up with leaden spades and __9__ up an impenetrable cloud, which screens their obscure operations from your __10__.

【附件四】 教学反思案例选

☞ 案例 1

March 3 Fine

Today it is the first lesson for me to teach the novel *The Great Gatsby*, which is really a touching novel. I have read its Chinese version and English version at least once respectively. I have also watched its movies starred by Leonardo Dicaprio. Today when a student talked about why she liked this novel, she told us some interesting facts. First, this novel ranked 2 among one hundred best novels in English. Still, the Japanese writer Murakami Haruki recommend this novel all the time. In his novel *The Norwegian Wood* the two main characters become close friends because both of them read the novel three times, which has become a bond between them and it turns out that the bond is very strong. I was so surprised that the student has known so much about the novel. I think this is a good beginning.

From my point of view this novel is a mix of many themes: love, hatred, money, fame, etc. The writer is good at using skills and explores the themes very deeply. It serves as a warning and reminder of what kind of life we should choose. Especially nowadays faced with a materialistic era many of us are also driven to seek fame and wealth very blindly. In this noisy and hollow world how we keep an independent attitude and mindset is always what we should strive for.

As for the teaching of this novel, I think I will still respect the students' ideas. During my lessons I will try to leave more space to the students and ask them to express more. After all I only have one brain, which is comparatively much older. But my students all have a young and active brain. So many young and active brains together definitely produce many creative opinions. It is also a good chance for me to learn from my students. In a way

I am trying to be a unique teacher. In this society being unique always causes danger and envy, and I should be careful with my behavior and don't go extreme. In many respects there is still much room for me to improve. I need to work harder and try to improve myself. I need to be more modest and calm to dream bigger. There are so many uncomfortable moments which I need to face. It is no use complaining about what has happened. The only way to solve the problem is to be braver and work harder.

☞ 案例 2

March 5 Fine

Today I taught the first chapter of the novel. First I analyzed the pages 1-3. I talked about the following points: the main plot of this part and some explanations of some difficult sentences. The main plot of this part is Nick's background. Many students think it is very difficult to understand the role of Nick. Nick is an observer in my eyes. He is often a clear-minded person and makes some judgements on what is happening around him. This part also serves as an introduction of the environment of the novel. The main plot of the story happened in the island and the island was divided into two parts: the west egg and the east egg. Two parts represented two social classes. The west egg lives some new rich while the east egg lives some old rich. The two social classes in fact looked down on each other. Especially the old rich scorned the new rich. Chapter 1 also has a lot of description of environments and surroundings, which are also worth telling the students to pay more attention to.

Today two students seemed to be bored and they did something else. I should try to keep alert and warn them more. If they missed the first part they wouldn't like to read the later part. This term it is the last time for me to teach them novels and in Senior 3 it is impossible for them to read novels because in English lessons they will have to devote themselves to preparing the Gaokao. It is urgent to value this opportunity and make the most of the time.

Teaching literature needs reflection and devotion. Around us there are so many distractions we should try to get rid of. How we integrate our teaching into our life and looking on our teaching as part of our life are a way of making me more mature. Self-improvement and promotion is a long process and we should try to value every chance and minute to make our life better. As an individual, I have met various kinds of hurdles and obstacles. There is no need complaining or regretting. We should get used to all the sides life presents us. No matter what side life presents we should accept all the possibilities. If we have realized the fact that life is suffering we may be willing to accept the uncomfortable side of life. As a teacher with twenty years' experience, I should have more insight and judgement and I should be more courageous. Never give up and always try. I think sometimes I am a little down. If l love teaching and reflect on what I am doing more, it will be easier for me to improve. Courage is the prerequisite of living a normal life. Fear is always an obstacle which makes me lack of motivation.

The weather seems to be better today. It has rained for over one week, which makes us a little numb and get used to the cold. For March it is relatively cold and we have no choice but to bear it. In our daily life we should learn to breed tolerance, sympathy and compassion. Only if we have enough flexibility and energy can we have the ability to kindness to others. I have gone through many negative emotions and how I tide over them is always what I am striving for. I need to keep silent and get prepared facing difficulty and uncomfortable situations. No matter what we do we should consider the others' feelings. It is always time for me to keep learning and improving.

☞ 案例 3

April 7 Fine

This Thursday I will give a demonstration lesson to some teachers. I have decided to teach one excerpt of *Tuesdays with Morrie*. The excerpt is about death, which is very serious and gloomy. I know it is a little difficult to grasp. There are several points I need to remind myself this time. First I should center my class on the students. Most of the class time should be spent on the students. It is very easy for me to get nervous facing so many teachers. Nervousness will have a negative effect on my performance. I need to be confident of my teaching. I have taught literature for over two years and also I have decided to do more research into it. This is a very good stage in which I can demonstrate what I have done and it is also a good opportunity where I can learn from others and welcome some advice. I should treasure this chance to learn from my peers and improve myself. For so many years I have struggled all the time and kept studying English in different ways. I have to admit I have improved a lot but how I show up my skills in a confident way is also what I need to consider. The second point I need to remember is to keep focused. Don't detour so much or let the students wander off the main point. I should try my best to concentrate on one central topic. The students should focus on the topic the whole lesson. The students should spend more time on the materials and express themselves on the topic. No matter how much time I have spent on the materials, if the students are bored with it or can't adapt themselves in the environment I have created, it is also a waste of time. I need to consider the teaching way the students like. How I involve the students in my teaching is also a very serious topic I have to consider. I should spend more time emancipating the students and liberating the students. Also I have to remember how I manage time and give a lesson very efficiently. If I can't do it very effectively and efficiently, it is a pity and all my preparations will be in vain.

This time it is a very important opportunity where I can show my teaching skills and my personality. In a way teaching is also an expression of my character and personality. If I am a mean person, the lesson may be very boring and dull. If I am an open-minded person, the lesson may be very flexible and inclusive. If I am a nervous person, the lesson will be in a mess. So I should choose a proper way to teach my lessons. I think I need to respect my work and do my job very smoothly. I have devoted myself to the literature teaching for nearly two years and also it will be my pursuit. I should try to respect my dream and try to achieve my dream. One thing I have to pay special attention to is how I get rid of my fear. The fear may be from different aspects: the fear of losing my face, the fear of being misunderstood, the fear of not being loved... I have to admit that I need more time and energy to keep focused and try to detach myself to all the distractions. I should have a lot of experience and I should be strong enough to tide over all the difficulties. If I am still in a nervous state and in a panic, it is really a pity. I should be capable enough to show my skills and exert myself to finish the job more successfully.

☞ 案例 4

April 11 Fine

Now is the middle of April and time flies. Nearly two months has passed since the beginning of this term. These days I am very busy with an open lesson. This time I got the notice very late and I only had several days to prepare the lessons. To be honest, sometimes I hate me because I don't have a very good ability to demostrate my teaching. Though I don't have much time to prepare, I have ever taught it. I should have had a very clear picture of what the teaching should be like. But yesterday I made a show of myself. An able man should have the ability to show his ability very successfully and fully. Every time I regretted my performance. I need to be more exact and meanwhile I need to improve myself. I have an advantage to show my side of being open-minded, but I need more time and opportunity to think about how scientific I can be. As a PhD candidate I should have my advantage over others. I have read a lot in the past few years, and how I make the best of my ability is really what I should think it over. I have to admit there is much room for me to improve. I need to digest what I have learnt and what I have known, and how I make the best use of what I have and what I own. Yesterday I also get some feedback from some other teachers. Each time other teachers didn't want to talk much about my lessons and how I organized my lessons is really what I should strive. Now I need more time to digest and think about what I have learnt from the mistakes.

Yesterday at first there was something wrong with the electrical appliances so I waited for a while and I didn't know what I should do. At that time I was a little nervous and I don't know what I should do. Also I was a little afraid to open my mouth because I wasn't confident of my English. I don't know how I adapt myself to the new environment. Sometimes I was at a loss about what was happening to me. I really don't know how I conduct myself in the new environment. I need more courage to face all the possibilities. The topic I chose yesterday is also very strange and maybe the other teachers are strange about my choice. I should give my students more scaffolds and give them more supports. Otherwise there is little chance for me to bridge the distance between me and the students. I need a sense of responsibility and dignity. If I have a chance to give a lesson I should prepare myself more carefully and accurately. I don't know what I should do in order to prepare myself more carefully and I need more time to make me more accurate. To be honest, I am at a loss about my situation sometimes and I need to be more careful. Later the lesson was progressing smoothly and my students were very active and put up their hands a lot. The lesson was becoming more and more smooth but the time was limited. At last the ending of the lesson was very soon and I didn't have much time to prepare for it, which is really a pity.

☞ 案例 5

April 29 Fine

Today is such a fine and warm day that we haven't seen for a long time. May Day is coming, signifying the ending of spring and approaching of summer. It is also a busy, lively and awakening season when farmers are busy planting crops. During this season we tend to be active but sometimes a little sleepy. I like this season because it is mild and comfortable.

Today we read Chapter Six of the book, which is not very long and the main contents include the true life story of Gatsby and the direct confrontation among the three main characters: Gatsby, Daisy and Tom. The confrontation hints love and hatred. Pages 60-62 introduce the life story of Gatsby. This part depicts a typical narcissistic character: when he was young he was extravagantly ambitiously but his family background and education couldn't make him achieve his dream. So he changed his name at the age of 17 and he thought he was son of the God. When he studied in a college he wasn't content with the education there so he only attended college for two weeks. Also he had to work as a janitor there to pay his tuition but he despised the job he did. He was trying to find a ladder he could climb over to the upper class and at last he met Dan Cody, a millionaire who made his fortune overnight during the gold rush. Gatsby was clever and sensitive enough to approach him. At last he found a chance to remind him in advance of a potential danger, which made Dan Cody have a good impression on him. In a way Dan Cody was a savior and supporter of Gatsby and as the story progressed, Dan Cody died and Gatsby inherited a large sum of money from Gatsby. Though the money was deprived of by somebody else but it served as a warning that Gatsby would try all his best to make his fortune by himself. He later made his fortune by bootlegging, which was a quick fix to become rich at that time. We could easily spot that Gatsby was a sensitive and clever man. He was extravagantly ambitiously and he also knew how to achieve his dreams so he was also a self-conscious man. He knew the society very much and knew women very early. He realized getting addicted to women would spoil his dream so he chose to get away from women. In this respect he was very determined and lived an abstinent life. I think this point also proved that he was great. But on the other hand he was so attached to Daisy, which led him to die at last. His attachment to Daisy was a tragedy for him.

These days we are talking about the novel. Now we are at a stage when we reach the climax of the novel. I am trying to ask more students to express their opinions from different aspects. I have to admit I have also learnt a lot from their talking. Though the lesson is kind of boring sometimes, we have learnt a lot. I think I need to teach the students the way of learning form others and learning from their own reflections. So far we have finished the most part of the whole book and we will finish the whole book two weeks later. We have read this book very carefully and fully and it is really an exciting teaching experience. I need more reflection to conclude my exciting experience.

【附件五】 调查案例选

☞ 案例 1

告家长书

尊敬的高一年级家长们：

你们好！

孩子们三年高中生活转眼过去了，这三年的高中生活是孩子成长的黄金时期，也将是孩子们未来人生的基石，这段时光的精神吸收决定着他们未来成长的方向和境界。

宁波外国语学校是一所具有浓厚外语特色和国际氛围的现代化窗口学校。近年来，我校初中的外语教学在继承良好传统的基础上，通过加强与国内外知名高校的合作，引进英国原版教材《典范英语》，在宁波乃至全省都声名远扬，成绩斐然。但高中教学在高考应考的压力下，围绕教材，讲解语言点，较多地通过练习来准备应考，教学方法相对单一。为了改变这一状况，从这一届开始，我们计划除完成高中课标要求的教学任务外，教学中将把经典英语原著的阅读作为教学的重要内容。这样做不仅延续了初中英语教学的良好传统，有利于提高孩子的语言综合运用能力，而且还可以让高中生在成长的黄金时期浸润在经典、地道的语言中，从而达到英语教学对孩子精神成长的引领作用。

高中生英语学习能力不断提高，其抽象思维能力和批判思维能力迅速发展，有能力阅读英语原著。本学期期中考试后，我们已经阅读了美国作家怀特的经典作品《夏洛的网》。我们把小说打印出来发给学生，但这丝毫没有减轻学生的阅读兴趣，这部经典的动物小说深深地吸引着你们的孩子。他们在阅读中或欢笑、或思考，他们的语言能力就是在这样美妙的阅读过程中不断提高的，他们的精神也在愉悦和感动中得到提升。

基于以上思考和初步尝试，我们决定把阅读原著作为寒假作业的一个重要部分。高一外语组经商量决定让孩子们在寒假阅读美国著名作家米奇·阿尔博姆的作品《相约星期二》(*Tuesdays with Morrie*)，该书名列全美各大图书畅销排行榜已有四年之久，已被译成包括中文在内的31种文字，成为近年来图书出版业的奇迹。下面就这个作业和家长们交流几点建议，希望家长们予以指正：

1. 建议孩子每天读一到两章，希望你们定期检查孩子的阅读进展，欢迎家长和孩子一起阅读这部名著，阅读后共同分享阅读体验。

2. 在阅读过程中如果发现孩子因为生词较多而无法往下阅读，建议家长鼓励孩子翻阅词典，或协助孩子买到中文译本(建议参考上海译文出版社的版本)，遇到有困难的章节时，可以参考中文译本对照阅读，但千万不要只读中文译本。

3. 希望家长能够督促孩子做好阅读笔记和摘录，鼓励孩子们从每章中选择一到两个精彩段落，在空白处写简单的个性化的评注，也可就每章的内容写小结或评论。开学后我们会进行相应的教学测试。

4. 建议有余力的学生在读完《相约星期二》后，试读小说《傲慢与偏见》。开学后我们在共读分析完《相约星期二》后，再根据同学们的实际情况，选择一到两本名著作为教学的补充内容。

5. 我们先前读过原版《夏洛的网》，是打印下来发给孩子们阅读的。寒假期间可以选取某些章节进行回顾，经典文学作品的阅读要注重回味。

希望家长能够对我们高一英语教学的新尝试提出切实建议，我们热烈欢迎家长们在下学期走进我们的课堂，来看看孩子的表现，更希望得到你们对教学的指导和建议。

祝高一全体家长新年快乐，万事顺意！祝你们的孩子在新年里学习进步、健康成长！

高一英语备课组

2013年1月

☞ 案例 2

调查问卷 1

同学们！请配合下面关于期中考试后英语教学的小调查，谢谢！

1. 我们已经读完两本文学名著《夏洛的网》和《相约星期二》，你觉得对你的英语学习有帮助吗？

   A. 很有帮助　　B. 有帮助　　C. 没什么帮助

2. 如果期中考试后我们选择继续读一本文学名著，你的态度是：

   A. 同意　　B. 不同意

3. 如下为备选的两本文学名著。你对哪本感兴趣？请填写你自己感兴趣的文学名著。

   A.《老人与海》　B.《汤姆索耶历险记》　C. ________

4. 如果你同意我们继续进行文学名著的教学，你有什么好的建议吗？

调查结果如下：

各班情况：

高一(2)、高一(3)

共 37 份问卷，有效问卷 37 份。

1. 觉得很有帮助和有帮助 28 人(占 75%)，没什么帮助 9 人。
2. 同意期中继续文学名著教学 33 人(占 81%)，不同意 4 人。

高一(1)、高一(3)

共 34 份问卷，有效问卷 34 份(是在做了一份英语试卷后展开的)。

1. 觉得很有帮助或有帮助 29 人(占 85%)，觉得没什么帮助 5 人。
2. 同意期中继续名著教学 21 人(占 61%)，不同意 13 人。

高一(1)、高一(2)

共 40 份问卷，有效问卷 40 份。

1. 很有帮助或有帮助 38 分(9 占 5%)，没什么帮助 2 人。
2. 同意期中继续文学名著教学 36 人(占 90%)。

高一年级：

高一共发放 111 份问卷，有效问卷 111 份。

同意期中后继续名著教学 90 人(占 81%)；觉得有帮助和很有帮助的 95 人(占 85%)。

集中的建议如下：

1. 名著教学形式可以多样化，如多些表演、辩论、阅读报告、话剧表演、小组合作展示、看电影写影评等。
2. 建议阅读短篇小说，长篇小说有些乏味，每周上一两节文学名著课，名著教学与教材教学结合起来。
3. 文学名著课上少些细节解读，多些鉴赏、诵读的机会。
4. 增加听力练习，增加词汇、语法的讲解，把名著教学和应试尽量结合起来。或 4 天教学名著，1 天教学语法。
5. 增加读名著的时间，少些讲解，多领悟，但课堂上过多阅读会使同学昏昏欲睡，建议老师多介绍阅读的方法。
6. 进度是否可以慢点，部分重点章节重点讲。
7. 布置每周阅读量，每周抽出一节课的时间分享读书体会。
8. 可以采取让学生教学的形式，让每个小组读一个章节，然后进行 PPT 展示。
9. 增加对所读的书的检测，多设置一些过关类的测试督促阅读，同时可以要求背一些精彩的段落，定期抽查。
10. 不一定读完整本书，可挑选某些精华部分来阅读。

☞ 案例 3

调查问卷 2

Please Answer the Following Questions

Name ________

1. In what ways do you think the literature teaching does good to you?

2. In what ways do you like our current literature teaching?

3. Could you give some advice on our literature teaching?

部分学生答卷如下：

Please Answer the Following Questions

Name Yolanda

1. In what ways do you think the literature teaching does good to you?

It colors our study time, offers us something different from the texts, so that it releases us from study burdens and makes us study English in a more nature and easier way. Despite some difficulties in understanding new words and complex sentence structures at beginning, we appreciate original English language and western culture. It is more meaningful than learning texts in the books, even more meaningful than reading classic literatures' Chinese version.

2. In what ways do you like our current literature teaching?

1 Letting students share their own opinions is really good. But the teacher's thoughts are also meaningful for us. Comunication between teachers and students is an important part.

2. Watching movies is also an important part in learning literatures. Sometimes the atomosphere the writer wants to describe can be felt directly in the movie, as well as the complex relationship between characters.

3. Could you give some advice on our literature teaching?

1. I think that guessing the meanings of new words can be a kind of interesting thing. And the student who make the word list is really tired. So the word list can be briefer, or cancel it.

2. A whole book is a little bit too much for us to learn in one semester. It's a pity that we can't learn it completely. Maybe choosing short-sized novels in an album can be better.

Please Answer the Following Questions

Name

1. In what ways do you think the literature teaching does good to you?

By learning some significant literature can efficiently enhance our vocabulary. Also it can ameliorate our reading ~~compreh~~ comprehend. and it's very beneficial for our gaokao to some extent. And during our adolescence, it's dispensable and vital for us to learn something, which can ~~tell us~~ teach us how to behave and how to respect others. ~~I'm very~~ I feel very ~~fortunate~~ lucky to have this chance to shape myself.

2. In what ways do you like our current literature teaching?

Many school just force students to practise grammer by a large amount of exercises. I suppose it's useless for a student, for a teenager who ~~should~~ is just shaping his character now. But our school offers this chance. It's the best way to improve our English capability.

3. Could you give some advice on our literature teaching?

Both plot and vocabulary should be concerned. Using modern methods, such as ppt, as well as movie, ~~can be~~ will be much ~~better~~ more attractive. And ~~talking~~ some famous writer's comments about the novel are very good for us in writing. And I hope we can have more chance to show our understanding in group, ~~in order to~~ which can practise our spoken-English.

Please Answer the Following Questions

Name Serena

1. In what ways do you think the literature teaching does good to you?

The most important and meanfulling thing is that literature teaching can let us have more interests in learning a language. And it can help us gain a lot of good habits and abilitys. It can enlarge our vocabulary and deepen our understanding of most materials. Also from the literature we can learn some culture and. the way in which we can live a better life.

2. In what ways do you like our current literature teaching?

I may like the part that we making comments on sentences and pharagraphs which can let us think more and hear different opinions. Among these comments, some are very unique and valurable. Also I like the part we solve questions together and have a better understang.

3. Could you give some advice on our literature teaching?

Sometimes maybe we can discuss more about the theme of the novel and changes it brought to us since we read it. Also for some chapter, we can have some performances.

【附件六】 作业案例选

Maggie

Reading Comprehension Check 2 (the Great Gatsby)

Chapter 2

1. What is the "valley of ashes"?

A fatanstic farm where ashes grow like wheat into ridges and hills and grotesque gardens. ...

2. What are the "eyes of Dr. T. J. Eckleburg?

It's an advertisement that an oculist set them to fatten his practice in the borough of Queens.

3. Who did Tom take Nick to meet?

His mistress Myrtle Wilson.

4. Identify Myrtle and George Wilson.

George Wilson is a proprietor of a garage. He is a blond, spiritless man, anaemic and faintly handsome. He's really dumb.

Myrtle is George's wife and Tom's mistress. She is in middle thirties, faintly stout, worldly and also coarse.

5. What did Mrs. Wilson buy while she was out with Tom and Nick?

She bought a copy of Town Tattle and a moving-picture magazine and in the station drugstore some cold cream and a small flask of perfume. Also she bought a dog on her way.

6. Where did they go? What was at 158th Street?

They went to 158th Street.

An apartment which is Tom and Myrtle's "home".

7. Identify Catherine and Mr. & Mrs. McKee.

Catherine is a slender, worldly girl of about thirty. She likes gossiping sth not really triumphantly.

Mr McKee is a pale, feminine man from the flat below. He is a photographer.

His wife is shrill, languid, handsome and horrible.

8. What does Mr. McKee tell Nick about Gatsby?

Gatsby is a nephew of Kaiser Wilhelm's

That's where all his money comes from.

9. What reason did Myrtle give for marrying George Wilson?

"I married him because I thought he was a gentleman.

I thought he knew sth about breeding."

10. What did Tom do to Myrtle when she mentioned Daisy's name?

Tom argued with Myrtle about whether Myrtle had any right to mention Daisy's name.

Tom broke her nose with his open hand.

Clement

Reading Comprehension Check 3 (The Great Gatsby)

Chapter 3

1. Describe Gatsby's wealth. List some of the things that represent wealth.

Gatsby will hold a party every week, using his Rolls-Royce for delivering guests. In party, there will be a lot of fruits, pastry pigs, turkeys and so on. It will also invite bands and actors to performance. Gatsby has two motorboats and a hydroplane.

2. What kind of people come to Gatsby's parties?

Every kind of people come, they can come to party by introduced by somebody who knew Gatsby even though they didn't be invited. Sometimes they came for the party with a simplicity of heart that was its own ticket of admission.

3. Why did Nick Carraway go to the party?

Because the ~~dr~~ chauffeur of Gatsby send the invitation to Nick, and Nick wants to meet Gatsby.

4. How does Nick meet Gatsby?

Nick met someone in the party who stroke up a conversation with Nick, and then he said he was Gatsby.

5. What are some of the stories about Gatsby?

① Gatsby had killed a person, he is a soldior when at war.
② He graduated from Oxford

6. Is Gatsby a "phony"(liar) ? What is your comment?

Maybe. In fact he ~~is a~~ told a lie but it dosen't matter in my opinion, he only want to make his background more lustrous.

7. Describe Nick's relationship with Jordan.

There are ambiguous atmosphere between them, they didn't disguset each other and have some same commones, thoughts.

Reading Comprehension Check Chapter 4

Name Serena

1. Who is Klipspringer?

He was a man at Gatsby' mansion so often and thus became known as " the boarder".

2. What does Gatsby tell Nick about himself?

He said he was the son of some wealthy people in the Middle West—all dead now. He was brought up in America but educated at Oxford, because all his ancestors have been educated there for many years. Once he lived like a young rajah in all the capitals of Europe—Paris, Venice Rome—collecting jewels, chiefly rubies, hunting big game, painting a little.

3. What "matter" did Gatsby have Jordan Baker discuss with Nick?

Whether Nick will invite Daisy to his house some afternoon and then let Gatsby come over if possible.

4. Who is Mr. Wolfshiem?

He is a friend of Gatsby and, they share some secrets. Maybe he helps Gatsby earn money and deal with his business.

5. What does Mr. Wolfshiem tell Nick about Gatsby?

Gatsby is a fine fellow, handsome to look at and a perfect gentleman. He is an Oggsford man. And Gatsby, he is very careful about women. He would never so much as look at a friend's wife.

6. What does Jordan tell Nick about Daisy, Gatsby and Tom?

Daisy and Gatsby once fell in love but they were drifted apart by Daisy's mother effectually. Later Daisy met Tom and they got married in June. But their marriage wasn't successful. Daisy changed her mind. Next day after their marriage, they started off to South Seas and have their little girl the next April.

Course Paper: Literature Reading

Name Serena **Class** 51502

Dear classmates: You are required to write a course paper with a word limit of 400-600 for the novel *Pride and Prejudice* you read this term in English or your advice on our current literature teaching. Your paper is advised to include any of the following points: what you have learnt from the novel; your understanding of the theme of the novel; your advice about literature teaching; any other book you recommend and why you recommend it, etc.

Choosing a literature to read is definitely an efficient and rapid approach to improving our English level and attainment. There is no doubt that Pride and Prejudice is a good choice for us, for it can mirror the culture of England in 18 or 19 century.

This book is mainly talking about love and family. The Author also shows different kinds of love concepts. Some chasing for true love, their love are based on deep understang and long period spending together. Money and status are not important in their eyes and love comes first. These people include Darcy, Bingley, Elizabeth and Jane. And others are totally different. Lydia and Wickham are unconventional and unrestrained. Their life is full of freedon and love is more like company. Nowadays, many people share the same value and attitude with Charlotte, Elizabeth's best friend, who just want to have a peaceful and steady life. Some even managed to find a rich man to change their fate. Even though Jane Austin didn't emerge her thoughts and comments, judging from their own endings we can see she prefers true love among all and she intends to guide readers to owe a meaningful and happy marriage.

Except love, family also plays an essential part in this valuable novel. Readers can feel that Mr. Bennet loves his five daughters who are still on the shelf and almost everyone dislikes the hostess of the house at first sight. I should acknowledge that I was one of them. But later I seemed to understand and sympathize the pains of Mrs. Bennet. In a way, she could be agreed to be a standard mother. Because she really wants her daughters to find their happiness and to go up a notch in status and lever of life.

I should say this book is as successful as The Old Man and The sea and it is also as meaningful and readable as Tuesday With Morrie. It's fluent writing styles, vivid and detailed description speak for itself. And it is a book worth reading again and again.

Till now, we have already read many original novels. It is obvious that my interests enlarged and my ability increased proportionately with more and more reading. Also, I take to reading during the process. As for the following book we are going to read, I hope we can choose a short and easy one. A book with too many chapters may gradually become our burden and let us get tired of it. In that case, we may lose enthusiasm and deflect our original intention. And I'd like to talk about some of my advices. Besides sharing some favorite parts, maybe we can also be divided into several groups and act the plots out. Sometimes we can even go out and read the book under the sun. Much relaxation, much effect. By the by, I hope our next period of reading novels could be a great success.

Course Paper: Literature Reading

Name Frank Hu Class S1501

Dear classmates: You are required to write a course paper with a word limit of 400-600 for the novel *Pride and Prejudice* you read this term in English or your advice on our current literature teaching. Your paper is advised to include any of the following points: what you have learnt from the novel; your understanding of the theme of the novel; your advice about literature teaching; any other book you recommend and why you recommend it, etc.

Part I: Understanding of the novel <Pride and Prejudice>

Firstly, I'd like to say that it's a very ~~a~~ good novel, except that the text itself is sometimes hard to understand. The theme, ~~in~~ from my own perspective, is the conflict between true love and happiness, 'cuz the sentence in the novel "happiness in marriage is entirely a matter of chance" surely ~~impression~~ impressed me a lot. The plot, which is perfectly organized, somehow I felt I was "brought into" the novel, in another way of expression, being one of the characters, and was deeply held by the plot, hoping to know what will happen next at once.

~~Anther~~ Another main attraction of the novel is characters, Jane Austen is so a talented writer that she was able to make every character full of characteristics, for instance, Elizabeth — ~~rational~~ wise, Mr Bennet — rational, Bingley — hypocritical, etc. I suppose, there is no so-called "main character", 'cuz all character has a special spark, which can't be seen in anybody else.

In all, I suppose, the No.2 among the top 100 literature, the book itself is a very good mental supply. But, it might be a a little not suitable for our high-school students, since it has too many complex sentences.

Part II: My idea of literature teaching

We are the students of Ningbo Foreign Language School, we are supposed to be the ~~most~~ best at English among the students in Ningbo, so, our English teaching methods must be special. In my opinion, our textbook is ~~kd~~ kind of "out of fashion", we need fresh English everyday, ~~and~~ which is beneficial for a second langage learning. Youdao, for instance, provides fresh English, is very good for us, as well as the news. The most important, literature, which is the ~~essence~~, essence of the language, I suppose, literature learning must:

(i) Choose the right literature, which must:
(a) Have positive theme;
(b) not too much complicated text;
(c) good for students.
(ii) use proper teaching methods, which includes:
(a) feedback;
(b) discussion;
(c) presentation.
1 (iii) Have high ~~sprit~~ spirits in learning them.

And, the book I recommand, is < The Adventure of Tom Sawyer >, which I suppose is the most interesting, and the most suitable for our teenagers.

◎ 本章小结

传统的英语教学大多遵循“教学—考试”的路径，习惯于把语言肢解成语言知识和语言技能灌输给学生，这种教学方式容易造成片面注重语言的工具性而忽略语言的人文性的被动局面，可以说这也正是目前语言教学“费时多、效率低”的罪魁祸首。本书的立意是针对语言教学中的不足，尝试在高中英语教学中引进英文文学原著作为教学内容的方式，旨在凸显语言的工具性的同时，更加注重挖掘语言的人文性。

本章总结了笔者在宁波外国语学校进行教学实验两年来，与学生共同完成的《夏洛的网》、《相约星期二》、《老人与海》、《傲慢与偏见》(部分)、《了不起的盖茨比》等文学名著的阅读任务。笔者根据自己的教学实践，结合大量的案例总结和展示了文学名著在高中英语教学中的基本范式和教学策略。文学名著教学的范式有“任务展示课、读写实践课、综合分析课、欣赏表演课等”；教学策略包括调动学生积极性、读写结合、合作分享、欣赏表演等。

通过两年的教学实验，笔者认为文学名著阅读教学不仅培养学生健全的人格和独立思考的能力，而且还能使过去只注重教学的路子逐步过渡到英语教育的路上来。

第二部分　中小学英语文学阅读方法例举：文学圈阅读模式①

第一节　引　言

随着网络信息化时代的到来，人们的生活节奏加快，中小学生很难有机会静下心来接触、品读和欣赏人类文化的精髓——优秀的文学作品。而且从目前大部分高中阶段采用的教材来看，其设计编写大多围绕着语言结构、功能、话题和任务进行，阅读的主要目标是获取信息。这样的阅读取向直接导致中小学生功利性阅读大行其道，英语文学阅读的经历和体验极度贫乏。“大多数英语教师只看到了语言的交际功能，语言的工具属性，忽视了语言的认知、社会文化和生物属性。如果只把外语当作工具和手段，外语教育之追求掌握手段而忽视对学生的基本素质，尤其是人文素质和思维能力的培养，到头来只会是竹篮打水一场空。为了给学生的全面发展打下一个良好的基础，具备一个全面而深刻的语言教育观是十分必要的”(韩宝成，2010)。

近些年来，国内学者对加强英语文学阅读教学的呼声越来越高，英语教育界也有人尝试文学阅读教学(黄瑞贤，2015)。本课题组从 2012 年 9 月开始就在课堂中尝试利用英文原著和简写本(《典范英语》)作为

① 该部分使 2015 年度浙江省教育规划课题“基于‘文学圈’模式下的高中英语文学原著阅读研究”(项目编号：2015SC079)的研究成果，稍有修改，感谢宁波效实中学何小庆老师、陈晓红老师、郑朝霞老师的参与。

补充材料开展阅读教学，目前已完成两届高一和高二的的教学实验。本课题主要探索如何利用"文学圈"模式阅读简写本《典范英语10》和进行英文原著的教学实践，并讨论实践的效果和文学阅读的课堂教学模式。

第二节　研究的理论依据

《普通高中英语课程标准(试验)》(以下简称《课程标准》)(教育部，2003)对阅读能力的八级要求是："学生能在教师的帮助下欣赏浅显的英语文学作品；除一般教材外，课外阅读量应累计达到30万词以上。"九级目标指出："学生能阅读一般英文原著，抓住主要情节，了解主要人物。"文学阅读是所有阅读的核心，具有发展语言和思维的特殊功能(黄远振等，2014)。

在文学阅读教学模式方面，国外主要有文学圈(Literature Circle)(Daniels：1994)和持续默读(Sustain Silent Reading)(Krashen：2005)等模式，国内主要有READ(黄远振等，2013)等教学模式。(何泽，2016)《课程标准》中提出要逐渐转变传统的学习方式，变被动的学习方式为自主、合作、探究的学习方式。"文学圈"阅读模式正是这一理念的体现。"文学圈"起源于哈伟·戴勒斯(Harvey Daniels)一本名为《文学圈：以学生为中心的教室里的呼声与选择》的著作。他对"文学圈"的含义概述是：文学圈的小组成员在教师引领下自主选择并阅读同样的小说或其他文学作品，在完成独立的阅读之后，小组共同决定要讨论与分享的内容。每一位成员根据自己在小组中特定的角色和职责为即将到来的分享课做准备，按照角色设计作业纸，填写讨论发言的提纲。教师在其中起着引领、辅助、监督等作用。教师的引领作用和学生的自主阅读是本研究的重点内容。

目前新一轮的课改和课标的修订都指向各科的核心素养，高中英语学科的核心素养主要由语言能力、思维品质、文化意识和学习能力四方面组成(王蔷，2015)。文学名著的阅读正是以主题意义探究为目的，以语篇为载体，在理解和表达的语言实践活动中，发展语言能力，在自主阅读和探究活动中发展学习能力，在分析问题和解决问题的过程中发展思维品质，在潜移默化、理解共情中培养文化意识。《典范英语》提出的理念是，英语教育是用英语“学文化，启心智，爱生命”，这样的理念符合新课标提出的学科核心素养，突出了育人功能。在方法上，《典范英语》提出“基于原版文学作品的整进整出”外语教学模式，强调以故事内容为核心，围绕故事内容去听、去读、去理解、去感悟、去思考、去说、去写，在“整体输入、整体感悟、整体输出”的过程中，自然习得英语，从而培养语言综合运用能力、自主学习能力，在合作共享中发展学生的思维能力，在大量原版阅读中传递异域文化，培养文化意识。

第三节　文学阅读的选材和具体操作

本研究在初期主要选用英文原著作为阅读补充教材，笔者在2012年秋季开始在宁波外国语学校支教两年，期间在高一和高二年级完成了《夏洛的网》、《相约星期二》、《老人与海》、《傲慢与偏见》(第一部共二十三章)、《了不起的盖茨比》等英文原著的课堂教学任务(何泽，2016)。从2014学年秋季开始，为了配合浙江新高考实施走班制，经过英语集体组讨论，我们决定英文原著阅读教学主要放在选修课班级，这更有利于学有余力和对原著阅读感兴趣的同学选择，而在必修班级我们选择《典范英语10》作为补充阅读教材。《典范英语》是风靡英国的母语学习教材，这套教材的特点是集故事性、趣味性、知识性、科学性和人文性于一身，对于中国学生学习英语产生了重大的推动作用。《典范英语》共14本，都是名著的简写本，包括《简爱》《呼啸山庄》等经典作品。本研究重点聚焦在英语必修课堂中如何运用“文学圈”模式进行文学名著(《典范英语10》)的阅读教学。

我校教研组决定，高一、高二年级每学期除完成教材教学任务外，应抽出2~3周时间来阅读和教学2~3本《典范英语》，每本书安排的时间是一周左右，在高一、高二两学年(包括寒暑假)里读完《典范英语》

共 14 本文学名著，以每本书 7 万字计，阅读量超过 100 万字。14 本文学名著按话题或题材分类，高一主要读 A/B 类，高二主要阅读 C/D 类，高三上学期读 E 类，分类图表如下：

A 类(Animal & human & nature)：《秘密花园》《白牙》《黑骏马》
B 类(Sci-fiction)：《海底两万里》《失落的世界》《弗兰肯斯坦》
C 类(Travel & adventure)：《格列佛游记》《鲁滨逊漂流记》《金银岛》
D 类(Biography)：《大卫·科普菲尔》《简·爱》《呼啸山庄》
E 类(Detective story and drama)：《福尔摩斯故事集》《麦克白》

《典范英语 10》是原著简写本。小说通常包括环境(setting)、人物(character)、情节(plot)和主题(theme)等要素，根据这些要素和文学圈阅读模式，我们把全班同学分为 5 个组，每个组由 5 名左右同学组成，每个小组按章节或阅读内容以"文学圈"阅读模式选定本组的任务。"文学圈"是由小组成员组成的临时阅读小组，每个小组通常有 Plot Peeler(情节分析师)、Character Captain(人物分析师)、Language Master(语言大师)，还有 Theme Analyst(主题分析师)、Connector(链接员)、Illustrator(绘画小天使)、Word Master(词汇能手)等角色。一般前四个角色是基本角色，由小组成员轮流担任，后三种角色可根据情节内容的需要或者学生的兴趣灵活补充或替换前面的角色。Plot Peeler(情节分析师)呈现故事发展情节及推展进度；Character Captain(人物分析师)则理顺作品中主要人物和人物关系，挖掘主要角色的性格特点，并提供证据支撑自己的观点；Language Master(语言大师)负责把书本中有意义的词句、段落挑选出来，朗读并简单分析挑选这些语句的原因；Theme Analyst(主题分析师)挖掘作品的主题并提供证据支持；Connector(链接员)把故事内容与外部世界联系起来分析、比较，发现作品和生活的关联性；Illustrator(绘画小天使)把作品的情节、人物和场景等用绘图方式呈现出来；Word Master(词汇能手)赏析重点词汇或者解释作品中的重点生词。任务完成呈现形式可以是 PPT、流程图、思维导图等。每个小组有一位 Discussion Leader（讨论主持），由他/她来引导小组内课外任务的完成和课堂展示。

第四节　研究与实践情况

文学作品承载了复杂的人物关系、错综的故事情节、多元的叙事角度等，是一种多棱面的复杂阅读。再加上语言障碍，对绝大多数学生来说，英语文学作品的阅读极具挑战性，所以阅读初期尤其需要教师恰当引领。而“文学圈”阅读模式的最大特点之一是尊重学生的主动阅读，这种模式旨在充分发挥学生的积极性和主动性以改变传统的阅读模式。在研究和实践中必须处理好教师的引领和学生的自主阅读的关系，下面以《典范英语 10》中 *The Secret Garden* 的教学实例来说明这一关系在实践中是如何实现的。

一、教师的引领

教师的引领作用主要体现在“微型课”和“分享课”两个环节（Harvey Daniels，2004）。“微型课”（mini-lessons）指的是教师在学生进入独立阅读之前、之中策划好课外指导，即教师召集各小组学生，指导他们做阅读文本的种种准备，如确立阅读目标（goal-setting）、选择读本（book-selecting）、形成合作小组（group-forming）等；而“分享课”（class-gathering 或 sharing-time）指的是课堂教学环节，即师生共同分享小组阅读的合作成果，肯定或改进阅读计划和某些阅读行为，更重要的是给下一次乃至以后的自主阅读指明方向。教师在这两个环节所做的一切引领（guide & steer）和监督（oversee）的目的很明确：使各文学圈小组的规则、程序以及自主性阅读都能有序、有效地进行。

在“文学圈”阅读模式中，课题组也融入了几种“支架式”教学策略，作为科学引领学生阅读的手段，如“概念支架”和“图表支架”等。“支架式”教学模式是基于建构主义理念的核心教学模式之一，源于苏联心理学家维果斯基的最近发展区理论。支架式教学理论主张教师应该为学生提供暂时的、必要的框架，以帮助学生建立新的理解、新的概念和新的能力。

本章拟以《典范英语10》Book 1 *Secret Garden* 为例，主要从以下三个方面展开：1. 以“文学要素”为“文体支架”；2. 以“思维地图”为“图表支架”；3. “多重对话”不断“追问”，阐述教师在“微型课”“分享课”环节所起的种种引领作用。

1. 以“文学要素”为“文体支架”，铺设思维的底层框架

从文学要素入手进行文学阅读犹如庖丁解牛。这里的“庖丁”指具有丰富阅读经验的教师。教师以文学元素为抓手，以此锲入读本，使小说阅读有了目标，思维模式有了明确的指向性，从而使学生易于驾驭人物众多、头绪繁杂、背景深广的小说类文学作品。这符合《典范英语》倡导的大量地整体输入、整体输出，从中自然吸收语言的“整进整出”阅读方法。

《典范英语10》为小说系列。笔者把人物（characters）、背景（setting）、情节（plot）、主题（theme）、写作视角（perspective）“五大文学要素”作为抓手，锲入文学读本，作为学生阅读过程中贯穿始终的思维基础，帮助学生建立文体结构的概念框架。

学生自读之前，通过第一次“微型课”及教师的导学问题，开始了解五大要素的基本内容；在“分享课”，教师不断强调文学要素推动作品情节发展的重要功能，引导学生感受作者如何通过对典型环境下的人物外貌、动作、语言、心理、神态等的描述，来完成人物形象的塑造与主题的刻画。

导学问题设计如下：

问题 1：What do you know about 5 important literary elements in reading a novel?

问题 2：What's the setting of *The Secret Garden*?（自然环境和社会环境）

问题 3：How many characters are there in the story? Who is the

protagonist? What other characters are involved in the story?（人物形象）

问题 4：Please tell the story briefly by using the flowchart or plot mountain.（情节）

问题 5：What is the theme of the story?（主题）

另外，教师还引领学生从小说 *The Secret Garden* 的写作视角，再度审视人物情感变化与主题表现的密切关系。

问题 6：What is the perspective of the story? How does the perspective contribute to the development of characters and the theme?

作者运用“上帝之眼”（Eye of God，又称“全知”）这一叙述模式，笔墨游走在人与自然万物，乃至超自然的神界，竭尽其描述之能事：从 Mary 外来者的角度看 Colin 一家人的今昔命运变化；通过 Dickon 的视角看大自然的万物生长规律与灵性；知更鸟 Robin 的出现与引领，则是作者运用了超自然的手法，借此喻指主题之一——颇通人性的 Robin 与有着灵性的 Mary 和 Dickon 象征着人与自然和谐共生的动人与精彩。

学生首次“持续默读”全书之后，完成每章节的概要写作，了解故事情节的同时，进一步融会贯通地去理解各文学要素在小说中的提纲挈领式的作用。让这一“文学要素”的概念框架深植学生心间，整体把握读本，使他们触类旁通：读好一本人物传记或科幻故事，他们就能自读同类作品的任何其他读本；读好一本简写本，以后就可以自读原著；现在教师带着读，学生以后可以开始任何文学作品的自主阅读。希望能用这种简单易行、程式化的方式引导学生进行小说类文学阅读，激发他们对文学的兴趣，帮助他们形成良好的阅读小组合作氛围，逐渐培养他们自主性阅读能力，为其终身阅读打下良好基础。

2. 以“思维地图”为“图表支架”，使思维可视化

宏观上，教师帮助学生搭建“文学要素”的文体大支架，铺设思维的底层框架；微观中，则辅之以“思维地图”等可视化工具作为小支架，使抽象的思维具象化。

"思维地图"是 David Hyerle 博士在 1988 年开发的一种可视化工具。它建立在语义学、认知心理学等理论基础之上，帮助学生进行知识的有序整理，有目的、有系统地进行局部乃至细节处理，无形中简化了读本，降低了理解难度；注重学习能力的培养，尤其提高小组合作解决问题的能力；在教学中赋予思维以灵活性和开放性，有助于培养思维的深刻性、全面性和创造性。小说阅读最具挑战性的是错综复杂的人物关系与多维的叙述角度，而思维地图可视化工具可以使各组复杂关系条理化，思维表达简洁又形象。

思维地图包含圆圈图(Circle Map)、气泡图(Bubble Map)、树型图(Tree Map)、流程图(Flowchart)、桥型图(Bridge Map)等八种基本类型，能够促进学习者进行交流和思考。笔者在学生个人阅读、课堂分享环节等教学实践中引入了几种常用图形，具体举例如下：

(1)气泡图(如图 2-1)：主要是使用形容词、名词短语等关键词来描述人物、事情等。人物关系网(Character Web)是在此基础上的衍变，为厘清作为主角的 Mary 与她所接触的其他人物的关系，为后面的讨论做铺垫。

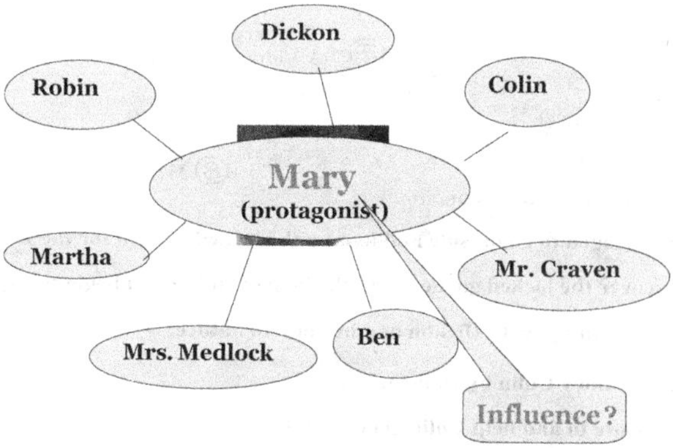

图 2-1 人物关系图(气泡图)

问题 1：Who is(are) the main character(s) in the story?

问题 2：Besides Mary, what other characters are involved in it? Who are they?

(2)双气泡图(如图 2-2)：主要用来对比两个人物或事件的异同点。两个被比较的术语的特点分别放在各自圆圈内，中间重合部分展示二者通过对比的相同点，如比较本书 Mary、Colin 两个主要人物的经历与性格等异同点(similarities & differences)。

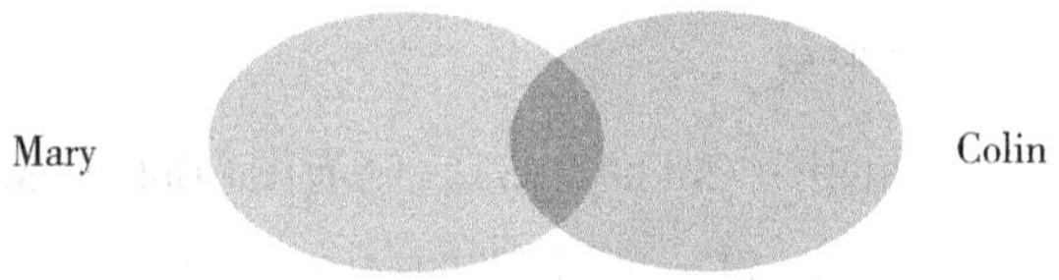

图 2-2　人物分析图(双气泡图)

(3)山形图或流程图：主要用来解释事件发生的顺序，能够分析一个事件发展过程之间的关系。流程图比较常规多用；山形图(如图 2-3 所示)虽不归属于八种类型中，但可以看做桥型图的一种衍变。它更能形象地表现故事发展的起伏跌宕，并突出高潮部分(mountaintop)。

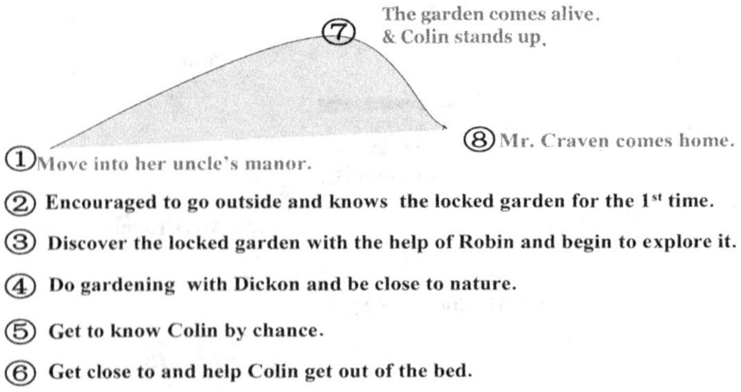

图 2-3　情节图(山形图)

思维地图有助于学生理顺错综复杂的人物关系、情节推动过程中大小事件发生的顺序与内在逻辑等，显示了思维的深广度，也是一种很有效的师生互动的形式。

3. “多重对话”中不断“追问”，培养和激发学生审辩性思维

审辩性思维(或批判性思维)不是我们常说的普通思维，是思维发展到较深层次的体现与最华彩部分。当人们经过缜密的思考，提出问题并找到论据来支持其论点，这个思维过程就是审辩思维。

“文学圈”模式下，师生成了一个学习的共同体，在教师的引领、辅助下，通过小组合作，学生充分发挥自己的主观能动性，完成自主阅读，在课堂分享环节，师生、生生互动，促进无限的生成，激扬思维的敏锐度与深刻性。“独立阅读、多重对话、个体表达”，揭示了每个阅读者在文学欣赏的认知过程中必经的心理体验与发展过程(黄远振，2014)。教师运用导读问题来引领学生浅读深读、反复咀嚼文学读本，通过英语学习另一种思维方式，从而提高语言表达的准确性和地道性。而课堂教学中的“追问”，是在学生基本回答导学问题后，教师或学生有针对性地“二度提问”，即“一次提问”基础上的延伸和拓展，是关于设疑、质疑、释疑的综合性技巧。

在讲授《秘密花园》及其他小说的过程中，教师特别注重培养学生基于事实阐述观点的审辩性思维，如对人物的性格分析、主题的挖掘等。

(1)发掘小说人物成长历程的多元性

图 2-4 是对本书主角之一 Mary 进行的人物性格分析。尽管不同阶段设计的问题角度不一样，但可以基本概括如下：

问题 1：What kind of family background does Mary come from? (supporting details) Does her family influence her? Yes or No, please give the reason.

问题 2：After Mary moved into her uncle's manor, it seems that there is a great change in her. What do you think has changed her?

问题 3：As one of the major characters, there are many other characters around Mary. Who have great influence on her? Who are they? In what way do they influence her?

问题 4：What kind of person do you think Mary is? (Please illustrate your view by finding supporting evidence in the form of looks, speech, actions...)

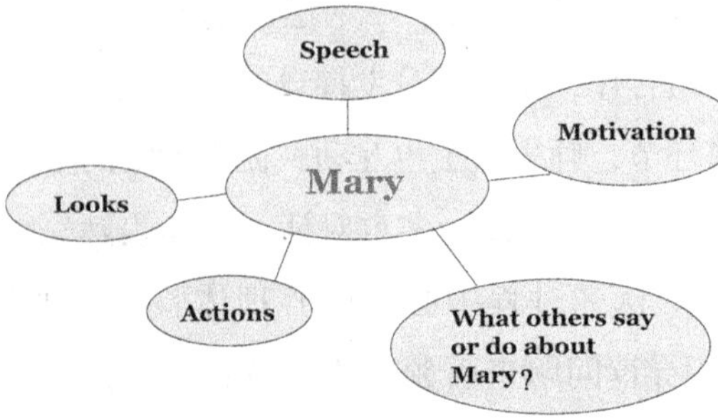

图 2-4　气泡图

(2)探究小说主题渗透的多维性

引领学生思考本书主题，如小说明暗线的交织、作者背景与主题的关系、题目寓意等。

《秘密花园》一书的主题较多维：同伴间的相互鼓舞、家庭成员间的关爱与冷漠、相信自己与他人、行动与毅力等。作者佛朗西斯·霍奇森·伯内特(Frances Hodgson Burnett)在本书的写作中融入自己的经历，如神秘主义的影响等。伴随着内心秘密的成长，相信积极的想法等精神力量可以自愈，这在 Mary 和 Colin 两位主人公身上得到充分体现。这组问题设计综合性强，也极具挑战性，但学生的分享非常精彩，思考颇具深度。

问题 1：What is the theme of the secret garden? What is the underlying theme of the story?

(Please present your idea by giving supporting facts in the book.)

问题 2：Would you try to make connections between the author's background and the underlying theme by finding supporting facts in the book?

问题 3：What does the author try to tell us in the story by the title of *The Secret Garden*?

问题 4：Please find out the descriptions of 5 different scenes of *The Secret Garden* in the book and say why the author describes it so many times from the different angles.

文学活动不仅仅由几个要素简单组合，更是由作品、世界、作者和读者等要素共同构成的一个有机整体。因此，文学欣赏是一个极其复杂的心理活动过程，不仅包括感受与重建、体验与共鸣、理解与领悟，还包括判断和回味，即对文学作品的意义、价值和优缺点作出审美评价，并通过这一过程对作品进行回味、再体会。如果说，前两种策略从宏观与微观的层面平面地解读小说读本，那么“多重对话”则是教师基于前两种策略的综合运用，帮助学生立体地解构作品。

(3)加强简写本与原著的链接

经过多次“持续默读”、影片观摩以及课堂分享，学生对简写本的情节已经非常熟悉。至此，教师趁热打铁，从原著中选取了对 Mary 和 Mr. Craven 的两个描写片段，让学生进一步赏析。经过对照赏析，学生更深刻、丰满地了解了 Mary 和 Mr. Craven 的性格特点。有学生精彩地分享道：“Mr. Craven 的心犹如被尘封十年的秘密花园，而 Mary 则是打开他和儿子 Colin 心锁的小精灵。”简写本与原著描述的内容虽然基本一致，但原著细腻的描写与巧妙的伏笔则是简写本无法比拟的。

在课堂分享过程中，教师及时发现问题，循循善诱，静等花开，鼓励学生用开放、思辨的态度，从文本细节寻找证据来支持自己观点，从而锻炼学生准确、简洁表达观点的能力。随着阅读的深入，思维深广度也在继续推进，学生学会了有理有据地分析问题。

教师也应引导学生链接文学读本、作者与现实世界。链接简写本与原著，离开教师引领，学生很难做到。学生一致认为，若没有老师引导，他们无法体会某些文辞在其中的妙用，以及父母与家庭背景在小孩成长过程中所产生的巨大影响。笔者链接简写本与原著，是有意为学生创设一个“跳一跳，摘到桃”的平台。事实上，效果是显而易见的：有些学生对原著产生了浓厚兴趣，课后纷纷要求老师推荐一些难度相当的原著，准备假期去看。

随着教育改革的深入和新高考的实施，在高中英语教育中引入具有人文性、跨文化意识的英语文学阅读将是一种时代的必然。这对教师来说是一种必须迎接的挑战。教师应该树立正确的教材观，选择并充分利用优良阅读教材，并要求自身成为一个好的阅读者，师生共读一本书，共同体验并关注书中人物命运遭际与情感起伏，成就课堂的精彩，保持学生的阅读兴趣。另外，应成为一个审辩性思维教师。没有批判性思维的老师，如何教出具有批判性思维的学生？教育者应勇敢地面对时代的挑战，转变教育理念、思维模式以及课堂教学方式，以开放、吸纳的心态，鼓励学生去质疑、探究，促进生动活泼、富有生命力的语言、思维的精彩生成。

小说《秘密花园》中那只神奇的知更鸟（Robin），引领着 Mary 和小伙伴们探索尘封了十年的秘密花园，并使万物凋敝的花园又姹紫嫣红，恢复了原有的生机。而这时的知更鸟则退居一角，雀跃、吟唱在枝头，与小伙伴们一起陶醉在春色满园的喜悦中。知更鸟让笔者联想起教师的角色——循循善诱的引领者，静等花开的幕后隐士，欢乐共情的欣赏者。

二、学生的自主阅读

语言学习是一个积极动态的过程，是学习者综合运用各种策略模式对信息积极加工、对学习过程自我监控，从而达到自然运用语言的过程。简言之，自主学习应包括五个方面的内容：确立目标，确定学习内容，运用合适的学习方法，控制适合自己的时间、地点和进度，评价学习结果。在“文学圈”模式下，文学阅读的体验活动不仅促进学生合作学习能力，自主学习能力的培养也贯穿始终，而且最重要的是自主阅读留给学生独立思考的时间和空间，为“文学圈”模式的阅读体验保驾护航，也为学生对文学作品的正确解读和赏析提供保障。

1. 自主阅读在“文学圈”阅读模式中的呈现

如前所述，自主阅读是自主探究学习的重要组成部分，在“文学圈”阅读模式中举足轻重。所以，教师一定要引导学生形成正确的阅读策略，使他们成为真正独立自主的读者。

(1)阅读前的自主选材

倡导“文学圈”的丹尼尔最重视的观念即是“真正的选择权”(real choice)。他在《文学圈：以学生为中心的教室里的呼声与选择》(Daniels，2002)一书中提出了“文学圈”的11个要素，其中包括自主选择材料、自主形成小组、不同组选择不同书籍、自定小组讨论时间、自定小组讨论内容等。其中第一要素强调：阅读作品的选定方式是学生自主选定阅读作品。考虑到高一学生的实际英语水平和学习情况，“文学圈”模式可稍作调整：先由教师引导学生选择阅读材料，然后整个班同读一部作品，再在自建“文学圈”中讨论。

我们发现，自主选材可以更好地激发学生的阅读积极性。心理学家布鲁纳(1960)认为：学习是一个主动的过程，对学生学习内因的最好激发是激起学生对所学材料的兴趣，即来自学习活动本身的内在动机，这是直接推动学生主动学习的心理动机。

(2)导学案引领下的自主阅读

在选定阅读材料之后，教师可以先根据文本制作一份导学案，设计一些引领阅读的相关问题，让学生带着问题自主阅读。导学案的目的并不是束缚阅读者的探究性学习和对作品意义的思考，而是有的放矢地让他们建立起对文学要素的认识。

以 *The Secret Garden* 的自主阅读导学案为例，我们可以尝试让学生从以下几个方面对文学作品作初步理解(见图 2-5)。

Self-Study Plan of *The Secret Garden*

Individual work:

1. Listen and read the book carefully at least twice;

2. Get to know about the literary elements of the story: Setting ((事件发生的)背景); Plot(故事情节); Character(人物); Symbol(象征); Theme(主题)。

3. Story line/scenario:

Read the contents! With the help of the chapter titles, get the main idea of each chapter (each within 20-30 words).

(Altogether there are 11 chapters in the book.)

4. Critical thinking:

- Why is the novel entitled with "The Secret Garden"?
- What is your favorite part? Why?
- Who is your favorite character? Why? (with supporting facts in the book)

图 2-5　*The Secret Garden* 自主阅读导学案

通过导学案引领下的任务型自主阅读，学生对作品的相关文学元素，如背景、情节、人物等有了一定的认识，提供的评判性思考问题为后续的课堂讨论起到抛砖引玉的作用。学生有了独立思考的时间和空间，有的放矢体验阅读，为接下来的小组成员间的有效交流解除壁垒，做好铺垫。

(3)自建"文学圈"后的自主阅读

同理，对"文学圈"的人员组成，应遵循学生的意愿，让学生拥有真正的选择权。同时，由学生自建"文学圈"也是培养其自主能力的一种尝试。我们鼓励学生自主选择、形成"文学圈"，分配任务角色，从不同角度来解读课文，分享、讨论各自对作品的理解。

自建"文学圈"的操作过程如下：首先通过班级讨论，选出 5 位同学作为组长；然后由组长和其他同学双向选择，组成 5 个小组，每个小组由约5人组成。组合过程中，组长和其他同学都会尽量考虑、平衡组内成员的英语水平和其他能力，如绘画技能、文学素养和功底等。然后，在组长的带领下，小组确定每位成员承担的任务、组员自主阅读的作品和小组讨论的时间进程等。

自建“文学圈”的过程不仅能体现学生个体自主性，增强他们的归属感，也能培养他们的责任感。组建“文学圈”后的自主阅读更有针对性，任务更明确，赋予学生特定的使命感，促使他们更认真地自主阅读选定的材料。

(4)合作中的针对性自主阅读

“文学圈”活动与其他读书会形式相比，最大的特色在于“角色扮演”和“积极对话”。学生在阅读体验和分享过程中会有以下收获，如学会如何主动积极地学习、讨论与分享，学习阅读与写作能力的结合，培养反观自我与观察的能力，拓展生活的视野和情感的认同等。

在完成了第一次的自主阅读任务之后，“文学圈”成员的任务分工会更有针对性。我们参照了“文学圈”模式的任务分担表，并结合高一学生表演欲望较强的特点，增加了一个新的角色，即表演组织者(performance organizer)。以 *The Secret Garden* 为例，我们将任务分配如下：

①As the Plot Analyst(情节分析师), it is your job to read *The Secret Garden* carefully and figure out the main plot using some key events or some key words. (Plot mountain or flowchart is encouraged.)

②As the Character Captain(人物分析师), it is your job to share observations you have about the main characters: Mary, Colin, and Dickon, etc. Select at least three adjectives that describe two of the main characters in *The Secret Garden*, and support your description with evidence taken from the novel. (Bubble map is encouraged here.)

③As the Connector(联系人), it is your job to search the information about the author: Frances Hodgson Burnett, find some connections between the author's life experience and *The Secret Garden*, and learn the background information about the novel!

④As the Theme Analyst(主题分析师), it is your job to find connections between the novel your group is reading and the outside world.

* Your understanding of the title *The Secret Garden*;

* Your own life (the similar story you've seen, heard around you).

Think about a minimum(最少) of two connections the novel reminds you of. List the connections and explain how the events are similar.

⑤As the Language Master/Literary Luminary(语言分析师), it is your job to read aloud some sentences or paragraphs worth reading in *The Secret Garden* and help your group members decide the highlight sections of the text.

⑥As the Performance Organizer(表演组织者), it is your responsibility to choose your favorite part, and write a related script including stage instructions, narration, dialogues and so on. And then organize and rehearse the whole performance!

按照角色任务单，“文学圈”成员自主分配任务。每个人带着组内分配的任务，再次进行自主细读，而这次的阅读认真与否、准备充分与否将直接影响学生在接下来合作活动中的表现。在一定程度上，每一个体对文学作品的理解会更好地促进“文学圈”合作阅读。因为自主阅读，自主完成相应的任务使“文学圈”分享过程中的信息补差和思维碰撞成为可能，它将有助于学生对文学作品有更好的把握。

(5)分享自主阅读成果

为了更好地检测学生的自主阅读情况，以及便于学生记录“文学圈”分享过程，我们设计了一份阅读分享反馈单(reading and sharing response)，大致包括 setting, plot analysis, character analysis, author and related information, symbol, theme, language。分享课前，学生人手一张阅读分享反馈单，了解分享的内容进程；在分享过程中，他们将根据反馈单，记录笔记。

在“文学圈”成员交流讨论开始时，我们鼓励学生尽量脱离自主阅读任务单中的笔记，整理好思路，慢慢地向同伴讲述，同伴可以记录，可以根据讲述者的思路画出思维导图(mind map)，也可以向讲述者提出问题，提出质疑，提出自己的见解，在分享讨论中改进每一项内容，加深对这部文学作品的理解。

经过一节课的分享讨论之后，同学们对文学作品的理解和见解逐渐跃然纸上。我们选取了学生绘制的 *The Secret Garden* 人物分析图(见图 2-6、图 2-7)，希望能达到“一斑以窥全豹”的效果。

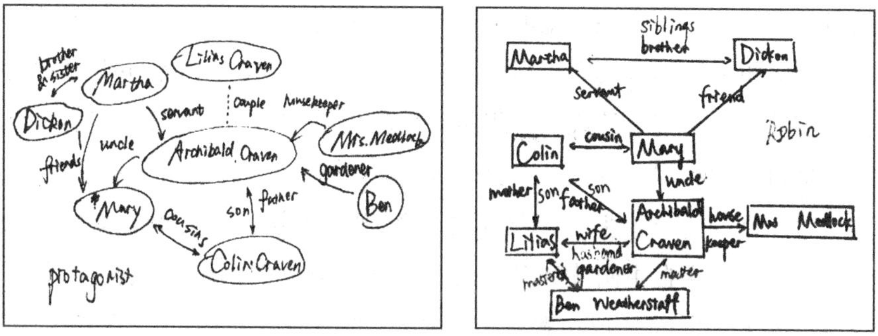

图 2-6

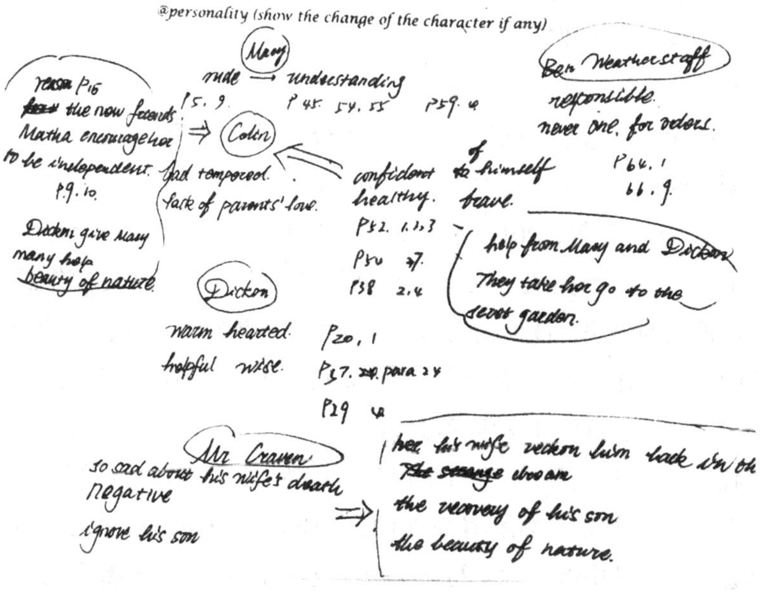

图 2-7

图2-6展示了两组学生为文学作品中出现的人物绘制的关系图(character web)。图形虽大同小异，但这“小异”却正好体现了学生个体思维差异性，也是自主阅读、自主探究的效果体现。图2-7是学生对人物的性格分析，并附上充足的来自作品的细节支持(supporting evidence)。我们在观察“文学圈”成员分享的过程中发现，组内负责人物分析的同学将自己整理出来的人物和彼此的关系陈述给其他组员，组员彼此讨论、补充、改进，形成“文学圈”的集体智慧，即人物关系图。通过这张图，即使错综复杂的关系网也被表现得清清楚楚。然后负责人物性格分析的同学继续和组员分享自己对主要人物的认识，并从作品中找出细节，支撑自己的说法。组员有反驳、有支持、有补充，各种认识在分享讨论中交织、碰撞，最终对人物的认识丰满起来，深刻起来。

对作品的情节、主题、象征意义的讨论和分享也获得了类似的效果。之前的两次自主阅读和独立思考促进了合作学习的成效，反过来，因为每一个“文学圈”成员都怀有“贡献”的精神和“不甘人后”的想法，合作学习的讨论促动每个成员必须认真仔细完成自主阅读和独立思考。所以，“文学圈”模式的阅读，强调了合作学习的作用，也显现了自主学习不可或缺的重要性。

⑥自主阅读中的自主创作

阅读和写作总是息息相关，密不可分。阅读为写作铺路，写作是阅读后创意的表达。而且文学阅读是所有阅读的核心，具有语言和思维的特殊功能(黄远振等，2014)。在自主阅读和“文学圈”成员合作学习的基础上，学生基本完成了对文学作品的品、赏、鉴：读文学作品的语言，读他们的语法，读他们的思想，读出各种韵味。同时，阅读为学生随后的英语写作做了铺垫，形成读写联动。比如教师可以让学生写故事梗概或书评，还可以让学生学习并运用小说语言，写一个片段等。因读得意犹未尽，学生会再一次自主地品味作品，将自己的想法写成文章。

在自读、共读、讨论《秘密花园》(*The Secret Garden*)之后，不少学生有感而发，其中有位学生写下了他对这部作品主题的感想：每个人都应有自己的归属，那就是心中的秘密花园。

Somewhere I belong

It's been a long day,

Without seeing the garden in pain.

Lilias, all the mountains remain,

Where had you been all the way?

（注：Lilias 是小说中 Colin 的母亲，Mary 的姨妈）

也有一位学生对作品的人物进行剖析，通过一首诗写出了对 Mr. Craven(Colin 的父亲)的认识，篇幅不长却不乏细腻。

However

——A Poem for Mr. Craven

Dropping your head, hunching your back,
Acting as a mean and miserable man,
And hiding your kindness inside thorny bushes,
People teased behind your back,
However, you just didn't care.

Locking your garden, burying your keys,
Keeping Colin's existence as a secret,
And pretending to forget everything,
Going abroad to spend a meaningless life,
However, hurt still remained.

Holding your breath, watching your steps,
Slowly opening the large heavy door,

And looking at Colin's peaceful face,
Only then could you avoid facing his eyes,
However, you would always regret.

Until that autumn afternoon, within the fascinating sunlight,
You walked in the garden which came back to live,
Along with Colin who was tall and handsome.
Your pupils reflected Colin's eyes which were given by his mom,
However, still beautiful.

还有一部分学生，在"文学圈"合作学习时，共同协作归纳了作品中对秘密花园景观描写的词汇，然后自觉自主地将其运用于景物描写的片段，其表达生动有趣，生意盎然。

In the corner of the garden, spring is coming silently. The vegetation juts out of the soil quickly with a sound of rustling. Green covers the corner step by step. Birds are chirruping. They perch on the brown tree branches and begin to sing lovely songs. Flowers burst with blossoms, and a pleasant smell floats past. Spring has already taken over the garden!

（注：其中画线部分是学生活学活用小说中描写花园景色的词汇。）

学生作品使我们不禁惊叹文学作品的感染力，欣喜地看到学生在解读文学作品的过程中，慢慢提升的个体自主阅读能力和自主探究能力，以及"文学圈"成员的探讨和分享等一系列活动所带来的影响力。

在践行"文学圈"阅读模式的过程中，我们看到学生逐渐养成了自主阅读的习惯，而且自主阅读促使他们独立思考，较好地完成"文学圈"内所担当的任务；自主阅读还能帮助他们对其他成员的想法作出判断，而不是简单地认同。"文学圈"模式下的自主阅读为学生的语言学习和积累提供了空间。通过反复独立自主阅读文学作品，定期进行“文学圈”内合作交流，在看、听、说等多种形式的语言输入和熏陶下，学生能自然地接触、使用英语，最后促成英语写作。

同时，我们也意识到教师应多关心学生的学习动态，帮助学生及时调整阅读节奏，使他们不因其他学科的压力而敷衍了事或中途放弃；教师也要关注学生组建“文学圈”时，是否会出现组与组之间的能力水平不平衡，适当地予以帮助和指导；“文学圈”成员合作分享时，教师可以作为旁观者，聆听、了解学生的分享情况，等等。总之，在“文学圈”阅读过程中，教师要为学生营造良好的自主阅读氛围，使阅读活动更有成效。

三、几种适合文学阅读的教学课型

课堂教学是进行教学实践的主战场，课堂教学的成败决定教学改革的成功与否。文学阅读作为语言课堂教学的补充和尝试，已经渗透到课堂，如何更加有效地实施文学阅读是值得在课堂教学中反复实践和探索的。笔者经过多年的文学阅读实践，总结出以下几种文学阅读的课型，得到了有关专家的肯定并逐渐在推广。

1. 任务展示课(Task Presentation)

各小组成员根据不同的任务分工，可以PPT、流程图、思维导图等形式展示。每个小组有一位Discussion Leader(讨论主持)，由他/她来引导小组内的课外任务的完成和课堂的展示。组内的任务通常有撰写展示文稿、润色文稿，制作展示课件或海报等微任务，由组长在组内分配，任务分配既考虑组员的特长，又尽力让组员每次完成不同的任务，这样可发挥组员之间互相协作和能力互补等优势。任务展示通常是在周末或假期前分配给各小组，以确保学生有充足的准备时间和方便使用各种媒体查阅资源等，展示的形式灵活多样，可通过课件、板书文字，甚至表演或者播放录制好的微视频等形式展示。下列案例是通过流程图的形式展示故事情节的。

在阅读完小说《老人与海》的第21～25页后，以Clement为组长的小组负责 Plot Peeler(情节分析)。课堂上他们以 the beginning of battle 为主线，通过事件发生动作的先后用流程图形式展示故事情节：found the line shivering—was completely hooked—a big fish bit the bait—slipped the line down—a harder pull—still endured—began to move slowly off toward the north-west—was still towed after the sunset。该小组还制作了课件，配有电影中相关动作的图片。

设计意图：该小组四位组员轮流上台发言，其他组的同学会根据他们的发言做出简短的评价(同学们认为这个组的发言图文并茂，简洁明了，形象生动)。这样的小组间的互动活跃了气氛，锻炼了学生的表达能力和应变能力，有利于学生之间相互学习和取长补短。

教学效果：让学生在课外用文学圈模式分组完成阅读任务，在课内展示任务的实践，能充分发挥学生学习的主动性，在完成任务的过程中，学生学到了摘录要点、链接延伸、评价判断等阅读策略，发扬了团队合作的精神，提高了资料搜集和整合能力，能学会讨论和分享，这有利于发展学生的自主学习和终身学习的能力。

2. 综合分析课（Comprehensive Analysis）

任务展示课主要是学生课外自读、课内分享的环节，它帮助学生理解了作品的情节、人物和主题等主要元素，而作品的深度挖掘和语言综合能力的培养是在综合展示课中进一步完成的。综合分析课的特点是师生共读、共享作品，以讨论分享、出声朗读、角色扮演、影视欣赏等形式进一步解读作品内容、挖掘作品内涵、探究作品寓意、欣赏语言魅力、升华情感体验、培养思维能力等。对于该课型中不同的作品内容，可引导学生采用不同的方式来分析。比如，描写类的内容，可让学生出声朗读、赏析语言的魅力；故事情节突出的内容，可让学生观看影视片段或角色扮演，还可以让学生进一步评价作品人物、分享阅读感受、预测作品的后续内容。在综合实践课中教师要充分发挥其引导作用，对作品挖掘的深度在一定程度上取决于教师对作品主题和内容的熟悉度。教师不仅要引导学生独立阅读，自己还要提前阅读，以理解和把握作品的语言和主旨，这样才能与学生分享、交流(黄远振等，2013)。比如在任务展示课中，学生在进行对《夏洛的网》第四章的语言展示时，该组成员只停留在标示出的好词好句，而笔者在课堂上通过问题“Can you find some sentences describing Wilbur's loneliness and underline the specific words or expressions?”让同学们找出关键词，这样就通过一个主问题把学生列出的零散语言串起来形成语言链；有上下文的语言组块会激发学生语言学习的兴趣，提高思维能力。综合分析课还能就一些问题达成共识，甚至抛砖引玉，激发学生对作品的深入探究，从不同角度去解读作品，课堂上经常会撞出思想的火花，很多观点往往能让人眼睛一亮甚至忍俊不禁。比如有学生在阅读《傲慢与偏见》过程中就说：I don't agree to their lifestyles because they seem to throw parties every day and don't need to go to do any work.

教学效果：综合分析课不仅能够引导同学们赏析和内化作品语言，而且还能进一步激发探究兴趣、诱发思维和促进进一步阅读的兴趣，为下一步输出打下语言和话题基础。还可以结合青少年的特点，挖掘作品中的积极元素来激发学生对文学的热爱、对生活的热爱，在这个过程中要充分尊重学生对文学作品的个性解读，激发他们的探究精神和创新能力。

3. 读写实践课（Reading and Writing）

阅读和写作是紧密相关的。阅读促进写作，写作基于阅读；阅读是一种输入，写作是一种输出，输入是输出的基础。阅读过程中，学生既可以积累有用的语言知识和写作素材，还可以学习文学名著中的写作方法和技巧。反过来，写作也能检查和加深对阅读内容的理解。读后续写把语言输入和输出紧密结合，把语言的模仿和创造使用有机结合，将语言的学习与运用切实结合，是提高外语学习效率的好方法（王初明，2012）。读写实践课的实质就是基于阅读的续写，它的落脚点是写，写的内容根据不同教学时间和不同的阅读内容而变化。读写实践课前期的主要目标是夯实基础，培养写作习惯，写作任务有摘抄好词好句、听写好词佳句、朗读和赏析好词好句、回答问题、翻译句子、句型转换（paraphrase）、加批注，以及写简短评论（评论包括对语言、内容或者人物等的个人看法，每个章节要求在书眉或空白处写3条20~30字小评论），等等。经过一段时间的读写实践后，教师可根据阅读内容设计更高级的写作任务，比如针对名著中人物、情景、情节等的精彩描写，让学生仿写生活中相关的内容，或者读后写作活动，比如写章节梗概（50字左右），续写故事情节，改写故事情节，选取一个角度发表评论，写书评（book review）（100~120字）或者课程小论文（course paper）（150~200字）等。该课型的教学步骤通常是读、议、写、评，这里的“读”不同于课外对作品全面的阅读，而是针对写作需要的语言素材和写作技巧进行的精读。“议”是让小组交流和内化阅读获取的信息，并讨论“写”什么（写作内容）和怎么“写”（语篇建构）的问题，根据任务的不同既可以让小组合作写，也可以独立写，比如续写故事情节就可以采用接龙的形式合作完成，而书评就应该独立写。“评”就是写后展评，包括自评、组内分享互评，然后推荐组内优秀作品向全班展示，其他同学对照写作要求进行点评等。读写实践课坚持的原则是以读促写，循序渐进，还要发挥好教师的示范作用，坚持师生共同阅读与写作。笔者坚持撰写批注和阅读日记，与同学一起分享读后感受，只有这样才能更好地驾驭课堂教学，指导学生，解决学生的问题，与学生一起享受阅读带来的乐趣和收获，进而提升精神生活，实现自我发展。

教学效果：写是一种高层次的语言学习活动，可以说它是语言学习的落脚点，新形势下的语言教学必定越来越重视读写结合，该课型改变了传统语言课上语言学习讲授和练习的比重，把更多的机会留给学生在阅读的基础上通过各种形式来创意表达，这必将体现教学的灵活性和开放性，给学生的思维能力的培养提供更大的空间。

第五节 研究的主要成果和特色

目前新一轮的课改和课标的修订都指向各科的核心素养，高中英语学科的核心素养主要由语言能力、思维品质、文化意识和学习能力四方面组成（王蔷，2015）。文学名著的阅读正是以主题意义探究为目的，以语篇为载体，在理解和表达的语言实践活动中，发展语言能力，在自主阅读和探究活动中发展学习能力，在分析问题和解决问题的过程中发展思维品质，在潜移默化、理解共情中培养文化意识。文学阅读的重点还是发展语言能力，在发展语言能力的同时也提升了学生的思维品质和学习能力，而长期浸润在阅读中毫无疑问也培养了学生的文化意识。下面就本研究在提升学生学科核心素养方面的成果(重点以提升学生的语言读写能力为例)进行说明。

1. 文学阅读对提升学生语言读写能力的实践

语言能力是个广泛的概念，包括很多深层因素。语言能力是语言表达能力、交际能力、分析能力的综合体(Chomsky，1965)。因此，无论是语言学习还是语言教学都应该全方位、多角度培养学生综合运用语言的能力，即语用能力。然而目前高中英语教学中，学生大多局限于学习课本知识，教师在课堂也普遍采用传统的教学方式，侧重于对语言知识的传授，缺乏对学生语言运用能力的培养。在教学中仍存在教师"一言堂"现象，学生通常被动接受老师的讲解，较少采用"发现式"学习，造成学、用脱节，综合运用语言的能力无法得到提高。

培养语言能力必须转变学习方式(黄远振，2015)。基于"文学圈"模式的教学不同于目前传统的教学方式，它对学生的自主性学习和合作性学习提出了更高的要求，学生的学习方式也由原先的被动接受变成了主动探究。另外，《普通高中英语课程标准(实验)》(教育部，2003)对高中生文学赏析能力的培养作出了明确要求：八级目标要求学生能够在教师的帮助下欣赏浅显的英语文学作品；九级目标要求学生能够阅读一般英文原著，抓住主要情节，了解主要人物。目前大多数学校所使用的人教版教材的阅读材料鲜有原汁原味的文学作品，因此有必要整合一些课外资源，把文学阅读作为高中阅读的补充。文学作品往往运用丰富的想象力、多彩的语言和修辞手法等，是人类精神文化的宝库，是优质语言学习的重要资源。由于文学语言是语言应用的最高层次，所以阅读文学作品时，学生不再是单调乏味地学习单词或句型，而是在作者基于现实生活、经艺术加工所创造的世界里，亲临语言环境，感受不同场合中不同语言的运用。因此，笔者认为基于“文学圈”模式的英语文学作品教学有助于培养学生的语言能力。下面主要以 *The Secret Garden* 为例，谈谈教师如何基于“文学圈”模式开展英语文学作品教学中的语言教学。

(1)借助语境学习词汇，积累惯用语

语境是语言交际所依赖的环境。有这样一句教育名言：“每个孩子都可以学会100种语言，关键是他有没有100种语言的环境。”(李琳，2012) 因此让学生借助文学作品所创设的语境学习词汇能帮助他们更好地理解并学会正确运用词汇。

在教学过程中，笔者要求“文学圈”小组中的“语言大师”从文中找出自己认为比较优美的词句在全班进行分享，并简单陈述挑选这些词句的原因。

学生A的分享： Mary felt her spirits sink even lower.

So Mary's days took shape.

For once, Colin was lost for words.

The eyes gave it away. He had Lilias' beautiful eyes.

分享理由： 句子中有很多优美词组，即词块，如take shape，be lost for words，give away等。

学生B的分享： No wonder you are so pale.

If only she could find the door.

It was the first time Colin had talked of what he would do in the future.

Picking up a sharp stick, Mary began prodding in the earth.

She found herself surrounded by four high walls.

分享理由： 这些句子涵盖很多常用句型，如No wonder(难怪)，If only(要是……就好了)，It was the first time somebody had done something(这是某人第一次做某事)。另外还有两句包含了较复杂的结构，也就是非谓语动词。

收集、整理惯用词语搭配对英语语言学习起着非常重要的作用。在词汇学习中，学生不仅要有丰富的词汇量，还要掌握词汇之间的搭配关系，这样才能掌握真实地道的英语。

(2)“发现式”语法教学，提升语法教学有效性

目前的语法教学中，往往存在教师“一言堂”现象，学生在课堂上通常被动接受老师的讲解，教师也只是通过学生做大量的语法选择题来检测其对所学语法的掌握情况。学生感觉学习语法非常枯燥，渐渐地对学习语法失去了兴趣。因此转变传统的语法教学方式非常有必要，在教学中教师可以尝试“发现式”语法教学。在教学《典范英语 10》第 2 本 *White Fang* 时，笔者发现文中有很多倒装句，尤其是完全倒装。于是笔者抓住这一契机，让学生找出文中的倒装句，并归纳总结倒装句的基本规则。文中的倒装句有：

Chapter 2：Running with her was her new mate, an old battle-scarred wolf with one eye.

Then came a warning snarl from his mate.

Snuggled between She-wolf's legs were five tiny, whimpering bundles.

Then came a time when there was no food for the little family.

There would come a time when She-wolf would again take the left fork tothe lynx's lair.

Chapter 4：Little could he know that his mother had taken the left fork by the stream, by the lair of the lynx and stolen a kitten.

In front of him were five, live creatures.

Chapter 12：Through the open door came a low, anxious whinc, like a sobbing under the breath.

Then came a long sniff, as White Fang looked at his master, checking he was still there.

Then came the day when through the cabin door White Fang

saw his master packing his bags.

From inside came a low whining and sobbing.

Sitting on the deck of the steamship, watching wistfully was White Fang!

以文学作品输入为载体的高中英语语法教学课，是将目标语法复现率高、可理解性强且富有思想内涵的英语文学作品作为语法教学输入的重要载体，在教学中综合考虑语法的形式、意义和语用，把语法课堂生活化，将语法知识的教学与话题情境的创设、语法知识的学习和语言技能的训练、语言输入与语言输出等结合起来，引导学生在发现、体验、探究和归纳的过程中准确、恰当地运用语言结构，以培养学生的综合语言运用能力和自主学习能力。(杨延从、王碧文，2013)

从以上两点可以看出文学作品有着丰富的语境，学生可以通过文学作品学习并掌握一些词汇及句法，从而为培养综合运用语言能力打下扎实的基础。

2. "文学圈"模式为发展学生语言交际能力提供平台

笔者任教学校宁波效实中学把文学作品作为英语辅助教学材料。因课时有限，大量的阅读任务要求学生自主阅读完成。英语小班化教学适合开展"文学圈"小组活动。在文学作品教学中，我们根据构成文学作品的基本要素——人物、情节、主题、语言，设定人物分析师、情节分析师、主题分析师和语言大师等基本角色，另外根据情节内容需要补充绘图小天使等角色。在教学之前，先让学生形成4~5人为单位的"文学圈"小组，小组中每位成员都要认真、独立地阅读选定的材料，然后结合自身特点选择自己能够胜任或者希望尝试的角色，并完成相应学案。自主选择角色给学生提供了一个发现、发掘自身潜力的机会，赋予了学生特定的责任感与使命感，也能逐步培养学生的自主阅读能力。在各自完成相应学案之后，小组成员会聚在一起，相互分享并讨论。虽然学生阅读能力参差不齐，但"文学圈"阅读模式为有困难的学生提供了很好的同伴学习机会，在相互讨论的时候获得启发；期间，阅读能力稍强的学生促进了“文学圈”小组其他成员学习的责任感，同时也学会了理解与尊重小组中每位成员的观点与意见。心理语言学家维果茨基(Vygotsky)的“最近发展区”观念就有力地说明了“文学圈”中学生互相合作的重要性，指出了同伴影响与合作学习对儿童心理发展的重要意义。小组成员之间的讨论形成了一个“潜在可能发展区”，给不同阅读能力的学生们提供了互动、交流、合作学习的机会，提升了学生的合作学习能力。这种分享式的合作学习还给予了学生充分的锻炼口头表达能力的机会，体现了语言的交际作用。

3. 利用文学作品语言输入提升语言表达能力

语言表达能力通常包括口头表达能力和书面表达能力。学生只有吸收足够多的语言材料，才能形成有效的语言输出。教师要积极拓展教学资源，努力通过各种渠道为学生提供真实有效的教学资料，增加语言输入，以便促进学生语言输出的能力。英美经典文学作品中的语言是英语中的精华，阅读英美文学作品有助于提高学生的英语语言能力，这既包括对文学作品语言的感受能力，又包括对文学作品内容的欣赏能力。因此教师要努力让学生充分汲取作品中的精华。

(1)通过朗读，提升口头表达能力及语感

朗读在英语中的作用是不容忽视的，对提高英语教学质量和学生的口语能力、语感及记忆力有很大的促进作用。《典范英语》每本书都有配套的音频资料，学生可以通过听录音来模仿变化丰富的语音语调，听文本录音其实也是一种听觉输入，通过大量的听觉输入，再让学生大声朗读进行口头输出，有助于学生形成良好的语音、语调。在朗读过程中，学生能发现并及时纠正自己的语音错误，也就是说，朗读能改进发音。如果学生能将英语文章准确、流利地读出来，就会产生成就感，养成乐学的心态。而且反复朗读课文后，许多语言现象会在脑海中留下深刻的印象，能脱口而出很多句子，因此，诵读对于语感的培养具有特别重要的意义。英语朗读训练就是在学习中自己创造英语氛围，通过反复朗读，把书面文字还原成口语，把语言知识转化为使用技能。在长期接触真实、地道的语言材料的过程中，学生的语感潜移默化地得到了提高。

在对 *The Secret Garden* 进行教学的过程中，笔者还设计了以小组为单位的朗读比赛，每个小组自行选择感兴趣的某个章节，小组成员分角色进行有感情的朗读，该活动深受学生喜爱。

(2)通过多角度语言输入，提升书面表达能力

① 语言输入

A. 语块化输入，为写作积累素材

文学作品语言的特点之一就是“语块化”。根据这一特点，笔者布置了这样一个任务：找出描写花园的词组或句子。

学生从书中找到下列句子：

There was a large pool with a fountain in the middle. But the flowerbeds were bare and wintry and the fountain was not working.

At the far end of the path she noticed a wall covered in ivy.

Instead the ivy grew wild here, trailing like a waterfall down to the ground.

(P13)

Rose trees had taken over the garden. They had climbed over urns and arbours and other trees, spreading thorny tendrils across to each other, as if holding hands. The branches were all either grey or brown.

She was amazed to find tiny green shoots beneath the dead vegetation.

(P23)

Mary told him about the garden. About how it was turning from grey to green. About all the birds that felt it was a place so safe, they could build their nests there. About the buds beginning to show on the rose trees.

(P56)

The plum tree was about to burst with white blossom and it formed a canopy under which Colin sat in wonder.

(P62)

The place was a feast of autumn yellow and purple, and flaming scarlet. Late roses climbed and hung and clustered. The afternoon sun shone down on the leaves and made everything appear like a temple of gold.

(P75)

以上所有画横线的表达都是描写花园或景色的，学生可以在自己的写作中借鉴这些语块，以提高自己的写作能力。

B. 欣赏文学作品中的修辞

修辞手段的运用是文学语言的又一特点。文学作品通常运用大量的修辞，使语言更具感染力，增强作者情感的表达，凸显文章的生动性及形象性，将文章中描述的真实情境展现给读者，引起读者的共鸣。针对文学作品的这一特征，笔者在教学 *The Secret Garden* 时，布置给“语言大师”的另一个任务就是找出文中所用的修辞，并对各种修辞进行简单的分析，如表 2-1 所示。

表 2-1 *The Secret Garden* 所用修辞及分析

Rhetorical devices	Examples
Simile	P6: as sour as a crab apple P15: trailing like a waterfall down to the ground
Metaphor	P24: wrapped in a warm blanket
Personification	P23: as if holding hands
Exaggeration	P21: her heart beating faster than a galloping horse P65: eyes nearly popped out of his head
Repetition	P56: I can see it. I can see it.

通过教师的分析和引导，学生可以逐步体会并学会运用这些语言技

巧，从而提高欣赏文学作品的能力。

②语言输出

基于上述两个方面的语言输入，笔者让学生描写公园或校园的一角。以下是其中一个学生写的文章。

Walking through the beautiful park, I can see the afternoon sun shining on the falling leaves and it makes everything look like a temple of gold.

There are many kinds of flowers blooming in the corner of the park—even in autumn. I smell the fresh scent with cool breeze. How sweet! Birds fly here to build nests because of the coming season. The cascading ivy turns into yellow, whose leaves are like soldiers protecting the wall.

If you have enough free time, you'll find it surprising with a feast of colors created by nature. Maybe a naughty kid has taken the last flaming scarlet rose, or you can meet a canopy with greenery. Every nook and cranny is as attractive as a fairy tale.

Now let's find the clustered purple blossom surrounded by reedy sounds. Enjoy the "paradise".

从学生习作中不难看出，经过教师引领下的归纳、分析，学生能够恰当运用一些词组和句型，也能在写作时尝试一些修辞手法，以此来美化自己的作文。

语言学习最重要的是输入，高质量的输入是保证学生英语优质学习的基础。在写作教学过程中，教师不能仅仅只是教授写作技巧，更重要的是告诉学生如何积累和运用写作的素材。而文学语言正为教师开展"以读促写"教学模式提供了良好契机。

(3)设计探究类活动，提升学生语言分析能力

在"文学圈"模式中，还有一个必不可少的角色，那就是人物分析

师。在 *The Secret Garden* 的教学任务中，人物分析师主要的任务是找出文中主要角色，并用思维导图的形式呈现人物关系，然后分析人物性格，并从文中找出依据来支撑自己的观点，

如学生在分析 Colin 这个主要人物时，先从文中找到能反映 Colin 性格的一些语言，如第 50 页"throw a tantrum"，第 54 页"a spoilt brat"，由此推断他是一个脾气暴躁的男孩。再如文中提到"Colin didn't want others to see him"，由此推断他是一个自卑的男孩。到后文，如第 67 页，学生会读到"a proud grin on his face"，由此得出结论：Colin 成了一个有自信心的阳光男孩。分析完了 Colin 的性格变化后，教师再设问"What led to his change?"，引导学生从多个角度去分析、推断造成 Colin 性格变化的原因，以此来培养学生的推理、分析能力。

在分析完人物性格的基础上，笔者尝试让学生用诗歌来描写自己最喜爱的人物。以下是部分学生的诗歌作品。

学生作品 1

Colin

He was a weak boy in the past
Lying in the bed during the whole day
He thought he had no time left
Every day he was lonely, shouting "I'm going to die"
Never show his love, his dad
His mother, died when he was born
No wonder his temper was so bad
Until he met Mary because of the crying
The secret garden, which Mary was saying
Give him lots of energy
Colin himself was also changing
With his friend's help

He put in effort walking
At present, Colin is a handsome and strong boy
It is so amazing.

学生作品 2

Dickon

Humble person in the manor,
Dickon, a born nature lover
Reliable companion Mary always prefer,
True adventure should take adventure
Brought a newborn lamb and courage and warmth
Reclaim barren land in heart as a gardener.
All the passion and love he gathered
Made the garden alive and everybody happy together.

基于人物分析的写诗体现了较强的综合性，没有简单停留在直接信息的获取与理解上，而是注重了综合语言交际的完整过程，可以对考生的概括能力、逻辑推理能力、创新思维能力、谋篇布局能力进行全方位、多视角的考察。

4. 自主探究、合作分享，养成学习能力

学生的学习能力，尤其是自主学习的能力在文学阅读中得到了充分的培养。自主学习是一种学生在教师的科学指导下，通过自身能动的、富有创造性的学习，实现自主性发展的教育实践活动。文学圈阅读模式充分激发了学生的自主学习能力，从他们组建小组、小组合作完成任务到小组展示，无不体现了自主、合作、探究的学习能力的提升。下面几位同学阐述了“文学圈”这种阅读模式如何培养他们的学习能力，这些能力不仅包括自主、合作、探究等能力，而且还包括思维等能力。

“‘文学圈’不仅可以提高我们的阅读能力，而且还可以增强团队合作能力和同学间交流的能力，因为每位同学分享出几个自己的观点，汇集起来，总会有自己不曾想到的点，这可以开拓我们的思维，开拓视野，我们阅读这本书时会有更加深入的了解，同时在阅读其他名著时也可以思考得更深更广。”

“‘文学圈’这种阅读模式对我来说是全新的，却也是值得尝试的。这让阅读变得更像个集体的狂欢，而非个人进行的一项任务。与同伴的分享可以让自己对文学作品的了解有个新的视野与方向，能更全面地解读、体悟一部作品，是愉快的。在读 *Wuthering Heights* 时，错综复杂的人物关系以及不一样的叙述风格让阅读这部作品变得格外困难，但通过课后与同学的交流，同学分享的人物关系图让这部作品的线索清晰了不少。”

5. 分析推断、批判创新，提升思维品质

高中英语文学阅读在我国现行高中英语课程标准中属于选修系列Ⅱ“欣赏类”课程，但目前正在修订中的高中英语课程标准将英语文学阅读列为选修Ⅱ的“拓展类”课程，旨在奠定学习者英语文学素养基础，与思维品质(分析与比较、综合与分类、抽象与概括、批判与创新)等要素共同构成英语学科核心素养。这反映了高中英语文学阅读与思维发展对英语学科教与学的重要意义(兰春寿，2015)。国内外研究表明文学阅读对英语学习者的思维能力发展有深远影响，在英语教学中，英语文学阅读因为其丰富的英语教育文化内涵而体现了英语课程工具性和人文性的统一，在学习者思维培育方面具有其他任何阅读无可比拟的优势。文学阅读是读者结合已有知识和经验使用一定的阅读策略在文本的各部分之间，在文本与个人经验之间积极构造意义，在这样的释义过程中，学生对文本内容的推理、评价和其个人的判断反映了他们对文本本身所蕴含的信息进行认知、理解与加工的高层次思维。

在阅读文学名著的过程中，思维的培养是渗透在整个阅读过程中的。读前以文学基本要素(人物、情节、主题、文体、主题等)的分析为抓手初读，着手打造思维的底层框架。读中讨论问题的思维化：问题的设置从理解到应用、从分析到评价、从联想到推断、从比较到质疑等思维活动层层深入、循循善诱、激趣引思。读中活动的探究化(Exploring and evaluating)：探究结构和情节(Exploring the structure and the plot)、探究主题思想(Exploring the theme and the writer's ideas)、探究象征意义(Exploring the symbolic meanings)、探究人物特征(Exploring the character)等(戴军熔，2015)。还可以运用可视化思维(thinking maps)降低读本理解难度，带动学生与文本发生多重对话。这些活动不仅有利于学生内化文学作品的语言和内容，更能培养其批判性思维能力，也为读后的创意表达与综合评价做好铺垫。

6. 潜移默化、理解共情，培养文化意识

《普通高中英语课程标准(征求意见稿)》明确把文化意识作为基础教育阶段英语课程的总体目标之一，倡导一种具有文化视野的英语教育。文化是一个人类群体的生活方式和形态。同时也指出："语言有丰富的文化内涵。在外语教学中，文化是指所学语言国家的历史地理、风土人情、传统习俗、生活方式、文学艺术、行为规范、价值观念等。"而文学作品的阅读是浸润在异域文化的精神之旅，文学作品饱含作者所处的时代，以及作者所在国家的风土人情、历史地理、生活方式、价值观念等信息，长期阅读文学作品不论对培养显性的文化还是隐形的文化都具有潜移默化的作用。有些文化是隐性的，如价值观、社会制度、宗教信仰等，该文化的大部分内涵只能在该文化语境中理解。还有文化是显性的，如历史文化、节庆活动、日常生活方式等，可以在其他文化语境里理解(E，T. Hall，1959，转引自 Patrick R. Moran，2003，鲁子问导读)。对显性文化的教学容易在学生中引发共情，而学生对隐形文化的敏感度则需要教师的启发和引导(施丽华，2015)。

例如《简爱》是反映维多利亚时代(Victorian Era)生活的典型作品，维多利亚时代是英国工业革命和大英帝国的顶峰时期，作品中描写了当时社会面貌，特别是寄宿制学校的生活，以及女性作为家庭教师职业的特殊性、爱情观等，而这些在同时代的小说《呼啸山庄》《大卫·科普菲尔》等小说中也集中反映出来，这些隐性的文化只有通过教师的启发和引导，学生才能对于维多利亚时代，特别是工业革命时期的社会面貌和文学特征形成了一个整体的概念，而这些文化知识不仅有助于加深学生对作品的理解，更有助于提升其对相关时期作品的解读能力。

第六节 结 语

基础教育的基本任务是素质教育，而素质教育的核心是人的教育。外语(英语)教育作为基础教育的一部分，其目的应该是使学生通过外语(英语)来学习文化，认识世界，培养心智，为终身学习和发展打下基础。这是外语(英语)素质教育的核心内容，也是许国璋先生多年前提出的观点(韩宝成，2008)。开展英语文学阅读的根本原因也在此。文学阅读不仅能让学生接触更多真实的语言，丰富学生的文学读写体验，培养语感，而且还具有特殊的思想、人文等诸方面的课程价值，能提高学生的文化意识和思维能力。更为重要的是，它能改变教学方式，变接受学习为自主学习、合作学习、探究学习，提高学生课堂生活质量，促进学生精神的成长，实现从英语教学到英语教育的转变(何泽，2016)。

◎ 参考文献

1. Chomsky, N.. *Aspects of the Theory of Syntax*. Cambridge, Mass.: MIT Pres, 1965
2. Collie, J. & Slater, S.. *Literature in the Language Classroom* [M]. Cambridge: Cambridge University Press, 1987.
3. Daniels H.. *Literature Circles: Voice and Choice in the Student-Centered Classroom* [M]. York, Marine: Stenhouse Publishers, 1994.
4. Daniels, H.. *Literature Circles: Voice and Choice in Book Clubs and Reading Groups*. (2nd ed.) [M]. York, Marine: Stenhous Publishers, 2002.

5. Frances Hodgson Burnett.. *The Secret Garden* [M]. New York, NY: Oversea Publishing House, 1995.

6. Goodman, K.. *On Reading*. [M]. New York, NY: Reed Elsevier Incorporated, 1996.

7. Rubin, D.. *The Teacher Handbook of Reading/Thinking Exercises*. [M]. New York, NY: Hott, Rinehart and Winston, 1980.

8. 程岚. 面向全体学生引导自主阅读——高中英语文学阅读七步法探索与研究[J]. 英语学习(教师版), 2015 (10).

9. 童庆炳. 文学概论[M]. 北京：北京大学出版社, 2006.

10. 韩宝成. 关于我国中小学英语教育的思考[J]. 外语教学与研究(外国语文双月刊), 2010(4).

11. 韩宝成, 刘润清. 我国基础教育阶段英语教育回眸与思考(一)——政策与目的[J] 外语教学与研究(外国语文双月刊), 2008: 150-155.

12. 黄瑞贤. 基于学生体验的高中英语文学阅读导读 [J]. 中小学外语教学(中学篇), 2015(6).

13. 黄远振, 兰春寿, 黄睿. 英语文学体验阅读 READ 教学模式建构研究[J]. 外语界, 2013(1).

14. 黄远振, 兰春寿, 黄睿. 为思而教：英语教育价值取向及实施策略[J]. 课程. 教材. 教法, 2014(4).

15. 黄远振. 培养学生的语言能力必须转变学习方式[J]. 英语学习(教师版), 2015 (11).

16. 何泽. 在高中英语阅读教学中采用英文原著的实践 [J]. 中小学外语教学(中学篇), 2016(3).

17. 中华人民共和国教育部. 普通高中英语课程标准(实验)[M]. 北京：人民教育出版社, 2003.

18. 中华人民共和国教育部. 义务教育英语课程标准(2011 版)[M]. 北京：北京师范大学出版社, 2012.

19. 兰春寿. 基于思维过程的高中英语文学阅读思维型课堂教学构架

[J]. 课程·教材·教法, 2015 (12): 82-89.

20. 施丽华. 也谈中学英语教育和学生文化意识培养[J]. 英语学习, 2015(12).

21. 王初明. 学相伴用相随——外语学习中的学伴用随原则[J]. 中国外语, 2009(5).

22. Alfred North Whitehead. 教育的目的 [M]. 徐汝舟, 译. 上海: 三联书店, 2014.

23. 王蔷. 从综合语言运用能力到英语学科核心素养——高中英语课程改革的新挑战[J]. 英语教师, 2015(16).

24. 杨延从, 王碧文. 基于文学作品的语言输入强化在高中英语语法教学中的运用 [J]. 中小学外语教学(中学篇), 2013(10).

25. 周成平. 高中新课程给教师的 100 条新建议[M]. 南京: 江苏人民出版社, 2007.

26. 郅庭瑾. 教会学生思维[M]. 北京: 教育科学出版社, 2001.

附 件

【附件一】 课题研究大事记

1. 2014 年 11 月，该课题参与浙江省教科院课题立项网上申报并立项成功。
2. 2015 年 3 月 11 日，宁波市教科所张立新老师等四位专家到我校进行开题指导。
3. 2015 年 6 月 19—20 日，课题组成员去浙江师范大学外国语学院就课题查阅相关资料，并得到外国语学院郑志恋等老师的指导。
4. 2015 年 11 月，该课题在宁波市教科所接受中期检查，得到相关专家的指导。
5. 2015 年 12 月，课题组成员陈晓红在宁波效实中学就课题研究上回报展示课，参与听课的有福建省师范大学教授黄远振、特级教师林枫和工作室成员以及宁波市部分骨干教师。
6. 2016 年 3 月，课题部分成果发表于中文核心期刊《中小学外语教学》。
7. 2016 年 4 月 1 日，课题组成员郑朝霞、何泽在宁波效实中学就课题成果向全校老师和部分专家上课题成果汇报课。
8. 2016 年 5 月，宁波市教科所专家来我校就该课题进行结题检查和指导。
9. 2016 年 6 月，《如何提高读写综合能力——基于英美名篇的高中英语阅读》在上海教育出版社出版。
10. 2016 年 7 月，该课题顺利结题。2016 年 9 月，该课题获得宁波市教学成果一等奖，浙江省教学成果三等奖。

【附件二】 导学案与小组合作活动表

一、导学案

(一) *The Secret Garden*

Ⅰ. How much do you know about literary elements of a novel?

* Setting　　* Plot　　* Character　　* Theme

* Symbol　　* Point of view/perspective

Ⅱ. What do you know the book of *The Secret Garden*?

◆**Setting**

1. What do you know about the author?
2. When & where did the story happen?

◆**Characters**

1. Besides Mary, what other characters are involved in the story? Who are they?
2. Is Robin one of the characters? (*Character: an imaginary person represented in a work of fiction (or play or film or story)*)

◆**Plot**

A. Identify the main idea for each chapter

Such as: Chapter 1 *Mary was taken into her uncle's manor after her parents were killed by cholera, receiving no welcome.*

Chapters 2~11...

B. Try to use plot mountain to show the development of the story.

◆ **Character analysis**

About Mary

1. What kind of family background does Mary come from? (supporting details)
2. What do you think has changed Mary? (appearance, personality)

◆**Theme, Symbol and Others**

A. About *The Secret Garden*

a. There are some nice and subtle descriptions of different scenes about the secret garden in the book. Can you find them?

b. Illustrations-sharing

B. About Robin(How many times does it turn up? Function? Symbol?)

C. Theme

1. What is the theme of the story?
2. What is the underlying theme of the story?
3. Making connections between the author's background and the underlying theme by giving supporting facts.

Ⅲ. Clips of the movie

Ⅳ. Presentation

(*G1*) *Present your favorite part*

(*G2*, 3) *Analyse one of your chosen characters*

(*G4*, 5) *Activities in The Secrect Garden*: *with the help of Robin*, *Mary discovered it*; *began to do gardening and explore it with Dickon*; *Colin was led into the garden and stood up.*

You're expected to share with each other in class on Nov. 20 (*Friday*)

Ⅴ. Which part of the story do you like best? Why?

Ⅵ. Read/Listen to the story of *The Secret Garden* for the third time and discuss and finish the following missions in groups.

1. Make improvements of the main ideas for all chapters that you've done on summer vacation.
2. There are some nice and subtle descriptions of different scenes about the secret garden in the book. Make a sketch (illustration) of one of the scenes based on the description with your imagination please! You are expected to share on Thursday's class. (on A3 Paper)
3. What is your puzzlement or confusion in understanding the story while reading?

(二) *The Gift of the Magi* (Individual Study)

1. Read the short story for two and three times and read aloud at least once if possible.
2. Consider the literary elements in the novel: setting, plot, character, conflict, theme, symbol, and point of view.
3. Answer the following questions on your own. (Write your answers on the back of the paper)
   (1) How much money did Della have each week to run the house after paying the rent?
   (2) How did she manage to save money? And why did she want to save the money?
   (3) How did she find the gift for Jim?
   (4) What were Jim's reactions toward Della's hair-cut?
   (5) What gift did Jim buy for Della? How could he afford it?
   (6) Why did Della scream ecstatically and then suddenly cry hysterically when seeing the gift given by her husband?
   (7) What did Jim do at seeing Della's gift for him?
4. How many parts will you divide the story into and why will you have this

division?

5. Which is your favorite part? And state the reason why you like it.

6. After reading alone, what's impressed you most, the theme, the language, the writing style or else?

7. How do you understand the title "<u>The Gift of the Magi</u>"?

二、小组合作活动表

Reading and Sharing Response

Novel: ________________ Name: ________ Date: ________

Share your reading experience with your partners and enjoy your sharing!

1. The setting of the book:

____

2. Try to draw the plot mountain or flow map:

3. Character analysis (Bubble Map is encouraged!):

4. Theme: central idea or insight of the story.

(Strategies kept in mind while seeking the theme: ①The title of the story; ②Write down some important statements by the author and the character, especially the protagonist(主角); ③Details repeated several times, and make sure whether they are of any symbolic meaning.)

5. Connections: background information about the author and the story.

A diagram for reference:

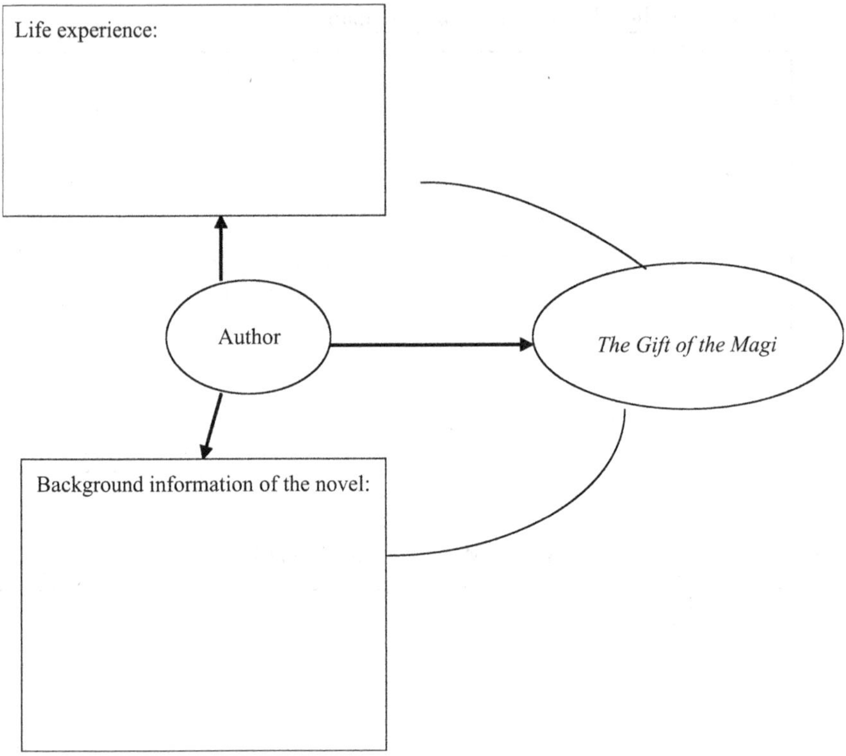

6. Language features (chewing and digesting):
(simile/metaphor/hyperbole/personification/repetition/alliteration/ellipsis/irony/parallelism/allusion/...)

7. "I can ask questions!" (based on your reading and sharing experience)

三、文学圈阅读模式学生用表格

Discussion Director/Summarizer

Date: ________

Novel you're reading: ____________________

Pages read to prepare for this discussion: ________

As the Discussion Director, it is your job to be in charge of your group discussion and also write down some good questions that you think your group would want to talk about. List a minimum of five thoughts provoking questions below. (Think of these starters: Why..., If..., What..., Who..., and How...)

(1)

(2)

(3)

(4)

(5)

Summary

Language Master/ Literary Luminary/Passage Person

Date: ________

Novel you're reading: ______________________

Pages read to prepare for this discussion: ________

As the Language Master/Literary Luminary, it is your job to read aloud some sentences or paragraphs in order to help your group members remember some interesting, powerful, puzzling, or important sections of the text. You decide which passages or paragraphs are worth reading aloud, and justify your reasons for selecting them. Write the page numbers and paragraph numbers on this form along with the reason you chose each passage. You must choose a minimum of 3 passages.

Language selected and page # where found	Reasons why the language was selected

Connector/Theme Analyst

Date: ________

Novel you're reading: ______________________

Pages read to prepare for this discussion: ________

As the Connector, it is your job to find connections between the novel your group is reading and the outside world. This means connecting the reading to:

* Your own life
* Happenings at school or in the neighborhood
* Similar events at other times and places
* Other books or stories
* Other writings on same topic
* Other writings by the same author

Think about a minimum of two connections today's reading reminded you of. List the connection and explain how the events are similar.

1)

2)

Character Captain/Character Analyst

Date: ________

Novel you're reading: ______________________

Pages read to prepare for this discussion: ________

As the Character Captain, it is your job to share observations you have about the main character(s). Select three adjectives that describe one or more of the characters in your novel, and support your selection with an example taken from your reading assignment.

Character	Specific example of behavior/action
Character Adjective	Page ________ Paragraph ________
Character Adjective	Page ________ Paragraph ________
Character Adjective	Page ________ Paragraph ________

Plot Analyst

Date: ________

Novel you're reading: ______________________

Pages read to prepare for this discussion: ________

As the Plot Analyst, it is your job to read the novel carefully and fill in the blanks using some key events or some words.

Setting
Beginning
Development plot
Turning point(s)
Climax
Ending

Artistic Adventurer (Optional)

Date: ________

Novel you're reading: ____________________

Pages read to prepare for this discussion: ________

As the Artistic Adventurer it is your responsibility for sharing an artistic representation of the material you read for today's Literature Circle. Some ideas for sharing may include: a character, the setting, a problem, an exciting part, a surprise, a prediction, or anything else. Examples of genres for expression may include:

* Artwork * Music * Poetry * Collage * Mobile

Have fun! Let your imagination soar!

What I shared: ____________________

In the space below please provide a written description of what you shared and explain how it represents a facet of the assigned reading.

【附件三】 终结性评价(卷面测试)

Test for Extensive Reading of Good English

Ⅰ. 语块

根据句意用书中所学词汇填空

1. After several days of discussion, our plans began to become more complete and organized.

   After several days of discussion, our plans began to ________ ________.

2. Seeing his daughter coming back safe, he sat down in a relaxing way.

   Seeing his daughter coming back safe, he sat down ________ ________.

3. Just when we thought we had the problem settled, Alan came in hurriedly and angrily, claiming the vote was unfair.

   Just when we thought we had the problem settled, Alan ________ ________, claiming the vote was unfair.

4. Police believe that the same man is responsible for three other murders in the area.

   Police believe that the same man ________ ________ ________ ________ three other murders in the area.

5. She changed into old clothes in order to stay comfortable.

   She changed into old clothes ________ ________ ________ ________ comfort.

6. Robb found it hard to choose between becoming a doctor and a career in athletics.

   Robb ________ ________ between becoming a doctor and a career in athletics.

7. She tried to control her inner emotion before the guests but without success.

   She tried to control her inner emotion before the guests but ________ ________.

8. Why don ' t you negotiate directly with him and solve this issue forever?

   Why don 't you negotiate directly with him and solve this issue ________ ________ ________ ________?

9. We arrived on the platform just as the train was leaving the station.

   We arrived on the platform just as the train was ________ ________ ________ the station.

10. I'll never tell you another secret if you let this one out.

    I'll never tell you another secret if you ________ this one ________.

Ⅱ. 文学元素

A. 看看自己对文学元素了解多少，请把找到的相应序号填入横线中。

1. ________ Characters
2. ________ Plot
3. ________ Climax
4. ________ Conflict
5. ________ Narrator
6. ________ Point of view
7. ________ Theme
8. ________ Setting

a. The relationship of the narrator to the story

b. The person who tells a story

c. A struggle between opposite sides or forces

d. The time, place, and other background of a story—when, where, and under what circumstances the story takes place

e. An imaginary person represented in a work of fiction (play or film or story)

f. The moment of greatest emotional tension (a turning point from the rising action to the falling action) in a story

g. An author usually writes a story in order to communicate a general message about life. The message may be a moral truth, or a general observation about nature, society, or human behavior

h. The sequence of events that occur in the story

B. 作者通过人或动物的外貌、言语、行为、心理活动等元素来刻画文学形象，请从方框中选出与各描述相匹配的形象。

a. Colin	b. White Fang	c. Mary	d. Mrs. Medlock
e. Dickon	f. Ben Weatherstaff	g. Mr. Craven	h. She-wolf
i. Beauty Smith	j. Lip-lip	k. Scott	

1. I've been going from person to person for weeks, like the booby prize in pass the parcel.
2. Running with her was her new mate, an old battle-scarred wolf with one-eye.
3. Her tone changed immediately. Her voice was soft and smarmy.
4. At first he thought it an honor to be leader- but he soon found it was the worst place to be.
5. He teased and taunted him until the dog went into a rage. Then he beat him without mercy.
6. If anyone in this house was as sour as a crab apple it was her!
7. What didn't follow him, for once, was the dark shadow he had carried around for ten years. The shadow that clung to him like an ice-cold fog.
8. He was never one for orders and the latest one was plain daft. Not do any gardening mid afternoon? With all the work he had to do? Nonsense.
9. From his mother, he had a dog's size and cleverness, and from his father, the cunning and strength of a wolf.
10. He took a knife from his belt and cut deep into some of the branches. "A few are," he said, "But not all. See these green bits? They'll shoot up if we cut'em reet back and give'em some space."
11. Scott was determined to use kindness to awaken White Fang's need to love and be loved.

12. He flung himself over so his face was buried in the pillow. He continued to wail and began banging his stick-like arms and legs.

C. 根据故事内容，完成以下故事梗概，首字母已给出。

The Summary of *The Secret Garden*

The Secret Garden is a best-selling novel w ________ (1) by FrancesHodgson Burnett w ________ (2) was one of the most famous E ________ (3) authors on child literature.

The opening chapter in *the Secret Garden* finds Mary Lennox an ugly and d ________ (4) girl. A ________ (5) her parents died in an o ________ (6) of Cholera, this lonely girl is s ________ (7) to live with her uncle, Archibold Craven, at Misselthweite Manor, in Yorkshire moor, England.

There, out of c ________ (8) and with the help of the r ________ (9), Mary discovers a garden which has been s ________ (10) up for ten years. Under the care of Mary and Dickon, who lives on the moor, the dead garden is turned into a flourishing garden f ________ (11) of vigor and vitality.

In the garden, Colin tries to restore his heath and g ________ (12) happiness. At the end of the book, Mr. Craven r ________ (13) to the garden and eventually Mr. Craven, Mary and Colin are reunited h ________ (14) in the beautiful garden.

Ⅲ. 实践演练

The Necklace

Guy de Maupassant

Part 1

Matilda was one of those pretty and charming girls born, as though fate had blundered over her, into a family of artisans. She had no marriage portion, no expectations, no means of getting known, understood, loved, and wedded by a man of wealth and distinction; and she let herself be married off to a little clerk in the Ministry of Education. Her tastes were simple because she had never been able to afford any other, but she was as unhappy as though she had married beneath her; for women have no caste or class, their beauty, grace, and charm serving them for birth or family. their natural delicacy, their instinctive elegance, their nimbleness of wit, are their only mark of rank, and put the slum girl on a level withthe highest lady in the land. She suffered endlessly, feeling herself born for every delicacy and luxury. She suffered from the poorness of her house, from its mean walls, worn chairs, and ugly curtains. All these things, of which other women of her class would not even have been aware, tormented and insulted her. The sight of the little Breton girl who came to do the work in her little house aroused heart-broken regrets and hopeless dreams in her mind. She imagined silent antechambers, heavy with Oriental tapestries, lit by torches in lofty bronze sockets, with two tall footmen in knee-breeches sleeping in large arm-chairs, overcome by the heavy warmth of the stove. She imagined vast saloons hung with antique silks, exquisite pieces of furniture supporting priceless ornaments, and small, charming, perfumed rooms, created just for little parties of intimate friends, men who were famous and sought after, whose homage roused every other woman's envious longings.

When she sat down for dinner at the round table covered with a three-days-old cloth, opposite her husband, who took the cover off the soup-tureen, exclaiming delightedly: "Aha! Scotch broth! What could be better?" She imagined delicate meals, gleaming silver, tapestries peopling the walls with folk of a past age and strange birds in faery forests; she imagined delicate food served in marvellous dishes, murmured gallantries, listened to with an inscrutable smile as one trifled with the rosy flesh of trout or wings of asparagus chicken.

She had no clothes, no jewels, nothing. And these were the only things she loved; she felt that she was made for them. She had longed so eagerly to charm, to be desired, to be wildly attractive and sought after. She had a rich friend, an old school friend whom she refused to visit, because she suffered so keenly when she returned home. She would weep whole days, with grief, regret, despair, and misery. One evening her husband came home with an exultant air, holding a large envelope in his hand. Here's something for you, he said. Swiftly she tore the paper and drew out a printed card on which were these words: "The Minister of Education and Madame Ramponneau request the pleasure of the company of Monsieur and Madame Loisel at the Ministry on the evening of Monday, January the 18th." Instead of being delighted, as her-husband hoped, she flung the invitation petulantly across the table, murmuring: "What do you want me to do with this?"

"Why, darling, I thought you'd be pleased. You never go out, and this is a great occasion. I had tremendous trouble to get it. Every one wants one; it's very select, and very few go to the clerks. You'll see all the really big people there." She looked at him out of furious eyes, and said impatiently: "And what do you suppose I am to wear at such an affair?" He had not thought about it; he stammered: "Why, the dress you go to the theatre in. It looks very nice, to me...." He stopped, stupefied and utterly at a loss when he saw that his wife was beginning to cry. Two large tears ran slowly down from the corners of her eyes towards the corners of her mouth. "What's the matter with you? What's the matter with you?" he faltered. But with a violent effort she overcame her grief and replied in a calm voice, wiping her wet cheeks: "Nothing. Only I haven't a dress and so I can't go to this party. Give your invitation to some friend of yours whose wife will be turned out better than I shall." He was heart-broken. "Look here, Mathilde," he persisted.: "What would be the cost of a suitable dress, which you could use on other occasions as well, something very simple?"

She thought for several seconds, reckoning up prices and also wondering for how large a sum she could ask without bringing upon herself an immediate refusal and an exclamation of horror from the careful-minded clerk. At last she replied with some hesitation: "I don't know exactly, but I think I could do it on four hundred francs." He grew slightly pale, for this was exactly the amount he had been saving for a gun, intending to get a little shooting next summer on the plain of Nanterre with some friends who went lark-shooting there on Sundays. Nevertheless he said: "Very well. I'll give you four hundred francs. But try and get a really nice dress with the money." The day of the party drew near, and Madame Loisel seemed sad, uneasy and anxious. Her dress was ready, however. One evening her husband said to her: "What's the matter with you? You've been very odd for the last three days." "I'm utterly miserable at not having any jewels, not a single stone, to wear," she replied. "I shall look absolutely no one. I would almost rather not go to the party." "Wear flowers," he said. "They're very smart at this time of the year. For ten francs you could get two or three gorgeous roses." She was not convinced. "No... there's nothing so humiliating as looking poor in the middle of a lot of rich women."

"How stupid you are!" exclaimed her husband. "Go and see Madame Forestier and ask her to lend you some jewels. You know her quite well enough for that." She uttered a cry of delight. "That's true. I never thought of it." Next day she went to see her friend and told her trouble. Madame Forestier went to her dressing-table, took up a large box, brought it to Madame Loisel, opened it, and said: "Choose, my dear."

First she saw some bracelets, then a pearl necklace, then a Venetian cross in gold and gems, of exquisite workmanship. She tried the effect of the jewels before the mirror. Suddenly she discovered, in a black satin case, a superb diamond necklace; her heart began to beat covetously. Her hands trembled as she lifted it. She fastened it round her neck, Then, with hesitation, she asked in anguish: "Could you lend me this, just thisalone?"

"Yes, of course."

She flung herself on her friend's breast, embraced her frenziedly, and went away with her treasure. The day of the party arrived. Madame Loisel was a success. She was the prettiest woman present, elegant, graceful, smiling, and quite above herself with happiness. All the men stared at her, inquired her name, and asked to be introduced to her. All the Under-Secretaries of State were eager to waltz with her. The Minister noticed her. She danced madly, ecstatically, drunk with pleasure, with no thought for anything, in the triumph of her beauty, in the pride of her success, in a cloud of happiness made up of this universal homage and admiration, of the desires she had aroused, of the completeness of a victory so dear to her feminine heart. She left about four o'clock in the morning. Since midnight her husband had been dozing in a deserted little room, in company with three other men whose wives were having a good time. He threw over her shoulders the garments he had brought for them to go home in, modest everyday clothes, whose poverty clashed with the beauty of the ball-dress. She was conscious of this and was anxious to hurry away, so that she should not be noticed by the other women putting on their costly furs. Loisel restrained her. "Wait a little. You'll catch cold in the open. I'm going to fetch a cab." But she did not listen to him and rapidly descended-the staircase. When they were out in the street they could not find a cab; they began to look for one, shouting at the drivers whom they saw passing in the distance. They walked down towards the Seine, desperate and shivering. At last they found on the quay one of those old nightprowling carriages which are only to be seen in Paris after dark, as though they were ashamed of their shabbiness in the daylight. It brought them to their door in the Rue des Martyrs, and sadly they walked up to their own apartment. It was the end, for her. As for him, he was thinking that he must be at the office at ten.

She took off the garments in which she had wrapped her shoulders, so as to see herself in all her glory before the mirror. But suddenly she uttered a cry. The necklace was no longer round her neck! "What's the matter with you?" asked her husband, already half undressed. She turned towards him in the utmost distress. "I... I... I've no longer got Madame Forestier's necklace..."

A. 根据上下文意思，选择能替换句中画线部分词汇的选项。

1. She had no way of meeting a rich and distinguished man, so she married a clerk. The word "distinguished" means

   A. famous and respected.　　B. strong and handsome.

   C. kind and helpful.

2. She dressed simply because she could not afford to dress well. When you can afford to dress well, you

   A. must wash your expensive clothes all by yourself.

   B. have to buy expensive clothes.

   C. have enough money to buy expensive clothes.

3. She was wondering how much she could ask for without frightening her thrifty husband. People who are thrifty

   A. are very rich.

   B. don't care how much money they spend.

   C. try to save money by spending very carefully.

4. He had saved just that amount to buy a rifle so that he could go on a hunting trip. Here "a rifle" is probably

   A. a pair of gloves.　　B. a hunting gun.

   C. a tent for camping.

5. This did not convince her. "No," she said... Here the word "convince" means

   A. persuade.　　B. annoy.

   C. trust.

6. At the end of the day, they went wearily back to their apartment. The word "wearily" means

A. very cold.　　B. very tired.

C. very excited.

7. She longed for a beautiful house with servants. She imagined herself talking to rich and famous people. When you long for something, you

A. wait for it.　　B. want it very much.

C. hate it.

8. After a few minutes, they found a cab and headed for home. When you head for a place, you are

A. leaving the place.　　B. going to the place.

C. looking for the place.

B. 请根据故事的发展，给以下情节排序。

1. ________ a. Mr. Loisel agreed to give Matilda money to buy a new gown.
2. ________ b. The Loisels found a cab and went home.
3. ________ c. Matilda threw the invitation onto the table.
4. ________ d. Matilda was upset because she didn't have any jewelry.
5. ________ e. Mrs. Forester let Matilda borrow a diamond necklace.
6. ________ f. Mr. Loisel gave Matilda an envelope.
7. ________ g. Matilda said that the necklace was gone.
8. ________ h. Many men danced with Matilda at the party.
9. ________ i. Mr. Loisel received an invitation to the party
10. ________ j. Matilda went to her friend's house and explained the situation.

C. 根据课文回答下列问题。

1. Who are the major characters in Part 1?
2. How did Matilda always feel when she returned from her friend Jeanne's

house?

3. What did Matilda do with the invitation her husband showed her?
4. What dress did Mr. Loisel think his wife could wear to the party?
5. How much did Matilda think a new gown would cost?
6. What did Matilda realize when she took off her coat in front of the mirror?

【附件四】　调查问卷

1. 关于选材的调查表

高一(　　)班 组别________ 成员：____________________

亲爱的同学们：

《典范英语 10》共 14 本，皆为文学经典名著简写读本，语言材料地道、真实自然，语言知识复现率高，符合语言学习规律；涵盖内容广博，人物活灵活现，人文内涵丰富，是一套真正意义上的中学生必读作品，也是高中三年的泛读教材。受课时所限，我们计划选择其中的 9 本作为课内精读，其余几本由同学们在教师导读之下完成自读。请同学们根据自己的阅读经历或者浏览书中扉页简介后，选择精读读本，并简单陈述选择理由。

这些小说按内容大致分为以下几类：

a. Animal & human & nature：(1)秘密花园　(2)白牙　(4)黑骏马

b. Sci-fiction：(5)海底两万里　(6)失落的世界　(8)弗兰肯斯坦

c. Travel & adventure：(3)格列佛游记　(11)鲁滨逊漂流记　(13)金银岛

d. Biography：(7)大卫·科普菲尔　(9)简·爱　(12)呼啸山庄　(14)麦克白

e. Detective story：(10)福尔摩斯故事集

我的选择和理由（请写书的序号和简单理由）：

例如：

1. (1)喜欢本书话题，神秘诱人……
2. (2)希望了解动物世界以及人与动物的关系……

1. ________

2. ________

3. ________

4. ________

5. ________

6. ________

7. ________

8. ________

9. ________

高一备课组

2015 年 9 月

2. 给教师的调查表

文学阅读教学中教师的困惑和角色

1. 你在处理教材前后遇到的问题或困惑

- Before the reading：

- While the reading：

- After the reading：

2. 你认为你在文学阅读中的作用如何？

3. 简要反思自己在文学阅读中的地位和作用？

3. 部分学生访谈实录

(1)你觉得现在的文学名著阅读对你英语学习(听说读写)的什么方面有帮助?(试具体举例说明)

S1. 阅读名著让我收获颇多，尤其在读和写方面。在阅读名著的过程中会碰到大量的词汇，遇到不懂或不理解的我就会去查字典、查资料。久而久之，我积累了大量的词汇，也提高了写作能力。

S2. 在听的方面，每一本《典范英语》都有录音，有时候我会边看边读、边听，帮助纠正发音，目前语感方面和考试听力方面都有了极大的提高。

S3. 了解语言环境及具体词汇的应用，不断积累和巩固所学到的词汇，如 develop 在不同语境中的不同含义。

S4. 文学阅读对我的写作有一定的帮助。比如《老人与海》语言很地道，让我能够感受到真正文学的魅力和写作方法。

S5. 阅读文学名著可以提高我的读写能力和扩大词汇量。比如，很多叙述性、描写性的词汇通常会在一部文学作品中反复出现，并且一义多词，这无疑会拓展一些关联性词汇。例如 Frankenstein 中的 thrilled, marveled, grief, agitated 等有关心情描写的词汇。当熟练掌握这些词汇后，你就会自然而然地将它们运用到写作中去。

S6. 掌握了一些较为书面的词汇和一些高级词汇。

(2)除了提高语言能力外，你觉得文学阅读对提高人文素质和培养思维方面有帮助吗?请举例说明。

S1. 文学经典之所以成为经典，是因为它所塑造的人物能给人树立榜样，能够让读者从中汲取能量，催人向上。例如高尔基的自传体小说中的人物，虽身处逆境，但他们不丧志、不气馁，顽强地与命运抗争，最终实现了人生的超越，体现了生命的价值，还有经典作品给人以信仰的力量，如伏尼契的《牛虻》、奥斯特洛夫斯基的《钢铁是怎样炼成的》，保尔·柯察金爱憎分明，和牛虻一样有着钢铁般的意志和不屈不挠的精神，激励了一代又一代青年人，为理想而奋斗终生。

S2. 文学阅读不仅有助于我们对小说人物的理解，而且也有利于我们塑造自身更优秀的品格。

S3. 文学阅读能促使我思考亲情和道德的关系。阅读名著就像和作者面对面交流。

S4. …… 对于文学作品的深入解读可以拓展我们的知识面，提高人文素养和思辨能力。

S5. ……大量阅读英语小说会加深语言的理解和运用，我们会逐渐习惯于从英语的角度理解英文而不是用中文去强行翻译，……会自然而然地理解了英语作为语言的魅力。

（3）你喜欢文学圈这种阅读方式吗？你和同伴的分享中有哪些收获？请举例说明。

S1. 这种阅读方式使人受益匪浅，不仅能提高自身的阅读水平，还通过阅读提高自身的文学修养。在与同学的分享和探讨中，加深了对作品的理解。

S2. 我认为文学圈不仅可以提高我们的阅读能力，而且还可以增强团队合作能力和同学间交流的能力，因为每位同学都有自己的观点，总能补充自己的不足。

S3. 可能因为是外国文学，没有中文文学情感那么直接强烈，我与同伴的分享仅限于小说情节。

S4. 这种阅读模式对我来说是全新的，却也是值得尝试的。这让阅读变得更像个集体的狂欢，而非个人进行的一项任务。与同伴的分享可以让自己对文学作品的了解有个新的视野与方向，能更全面地解读、体悟一部作品，我觉得是一件愉快的事情。在读 *Wuthering Heights* 时，错综复杂的人物关系以及不一样的叙述风格让阅读这部作品变得格外困难，但通过课后与同学的交流，对这部作品的线索清晰了不少。

S6. 谈不上喜欢也谈不上不喜欢。一方面在完成小说阅读的同时又要准备课内知识自然是一大挑战；另一方面当阅读成为作业，平时因为没空阅读的一些经典作品得以补全，并能与同学交流分享，着实是一大幸运。至于收获，就是更增强了自身的逻辑思维。

S7. 不是很喜欢。因为没有好的阅读同伴，我所属的文学圈里大多数人都在敷衍了事，我只能寻找其他的同伴。在文学圈中有些同学浮躁，加上每个人喜好不同，如果将每个人强行容纳在一本书下会产生厌倦的。比如说我对 *Jane Eyer* 这本书就不如 *Macbeth*，*Treasure Island*，*Wuthering Heights* 看得津津有味，笔记也记得密密麻麻，喜欢这些书，就有了学习的动力，就会克服一切困难。其实很多人根本没好好读，收效甚微。然而我也不敢保证每个人各读各的就一定好。但从我的角度出发我觉得文学阅读的方式需要改进和调整。

S8. 文学圈阅读方式从本质上说是比较好的，它可以给学生提供更为丰富的学习经验和更多的机会去接触一些课外读物。至于和同学分享和交流自己的观点之类的事，自然是为了能够更好地扫清不同的知识漏洞。我们目前将文学圈大致分为 Language，Plot，Character，Theme，Discussion Leader 五个方面，然后小组来进行综合性表达。这种表达模式能够完善每个人的思维结构、提高制作 PPT 的能力和整合文本的概括能力。

（4）结合你个人的阅读和学习经历，你对文学名著阅读有何建议？

S1. 青少年时期多读名著，读好名著，是一生受用的。但高中生学习时间毕竟是紧张的，因此要根据学生的时间和阅读经验，制定好合理的阅读顺序，循序渐进地安排。比如在假期可多读几本名著，因平时课时作业及考试已充斥了学生的所有时间，如再想抽空去读名著，不太现实，就是读了也是草草地阅读，效果不佳。

S2. 引导学生积累好词佳句，学习运用巧妙的语法，了解文章背后的主题内涵。名著篇目的选择可以根据学生的喜好来定。也可组织同学观看电影片段，以激发阅读兴趣；在课堂上可以给学生更多的讨论时间，还可随时检查同学们的阅读情况，防止偷工减料。

S3. 建议选取适合学生、与学生阅读水平能力相当的或者高一个层次的作品，在内容上有思想，但不枯燥；给予学生足够的阅读时间，并适时做适当的引导、促进与梳理；结合文选内容，对知识性要点与课内学习内容结合进行教学讲解，对涉及的思想内容进行拓展。

S4. 从阅读中汲取语言并将之消化是一个艰难的过程，不妨以默写形式将其巩固，另外与课内内容结合可能会使同学们加强记忆，使阅读效果更佳。

S5. 个人认为，文学圈有不足之处。首先，对于成员的分工上，比如绘图小天王，如果一个组中的确有喜爱绘画或者绘画水平高的人，那么这是一份美差。但是如果没有，这就是沉重的负担。的确，原来分工十分“摆得上台面”，作为公开展示的时候很精美。但是对于实际学习来说，这样的分工太过繁琐，需要精简。最好的分工是人人都能做，都愿意做。其次是时间。这是一个大问题，也是应试教育和素质教育最不相容地方。刷几张试卷只需要一个晚上，但是读完一本书呢？那就遥遥无期了。另外，学业压力使学生很难挤出时间来看书。在“温饱问题”都还没解决的情况下，读名著这样的“精神享受”根本做不到。最后是学习劲头的问题，也是一切教育都要面临的问题。如果做完当天作业，你会选择看英语名著，还是拿起手机刷动态、看视频、玩游戏？我想绝大多数人会选择后者。时代的发展，手机的泛滥，人们更偏向于快而俗的文化。清茶回味无穷，对身体也好，但是却被颜色绚丽口感甜腻的饮料所打败。的确，在一天高强度的学习之后，我们更想获得简单快捷的欢乐。这就使得主动学习的人很少。不主动怎么办？那就强制实施，被动学总比不学好。这是大多数老师的答案，也是看似较好的解决方案。如果一门科目的作业少了，减负了，对于整天的作业量来说，其实并没有少很多。所以我觉得有时候适当的强迫也是必须的，毕竟有压力才有动力。

S6. 文学名著阅读教学首先可以给大家看看由名著翻拍的电影，让大家初步了解名著内容，这样也会增加同学的学习兴趣。另外，必要的听写与默写也是重要的，不然很多东西学过之后就会遗忘；增加同学上台演讲的次数和增加表演等；边看电影边分析文学作品；在课外可增加自习课来阅读文学作品等。

【附件五】 优秀教案选

Teaching Plans for *The Secret Garden*

Period 1　Setting & Plot Analysis

Ⅰ. A brief introduction to the author

What do you know about Frances Hodgson Burnett?

An American-English playwright and novelist

Be famous for children's literature

A little Princess　　　Little Lord Fauntleroy

Ⅱ. Story setting

When and where: Story setting.

Read Page 4 and find clues for when and where the story is set.

When: the late 1800's and the early 1900's, British India(1858-1947).

Where: Misselthwaite Manor in the middle of the Yorkshire moors. (bleak black wilderness)

—An idea of time and space

Ⅲ. Plot

1. Story line: What's one of the best ways to get to know the book? Read the CONTENTS. What's included in contents? (an event, a person, a place, etc.)
2. Compare the contents: Ss compare the contents of the adapted edition with those of the original work(See PPT).

   Highlight the chapters in common. ①Why are these chapters chosen for the adapted book? (main characters and events)

   ②Who might have said the words in the titles of Chapter 6, 12, 18, 19, 20 in the original book? Why? —Interest in the original work

3. Main characters and their relationship

Complete the sentences with the names and then put the sentences in a correct order—Plot mountain

4. Ss work in groups and read the contents of the book. With the help of the chapter titles, each group gives a short summary for two to three chapters. The numbers can be decided by drawing lots. —A whole scenario

5. Which part is the climax of the story?

6. Which part do you like best? Why?

Period 2　Characters Analysis

1. Character web

2. Character analysis

1) Ben

Unruly/unconstrained(P64)

Bad-tempered/irritable (P65)

Allegiant/devoted/faithful

Responsible/hard-working (P66)

Q: Why was Ben furious when seeing the kids?

2) Martha

Q1: What's it in Martha that draws Mary close to her?

Friendly/warm-hearted: smile(P9), introduce Dickon to Mary(P25)

Encouraging(P10/P16)

Communicative:

Q2: Why didn't Mary tell Martha about the secret garden? (P25)

(P11, P40, P42) A little timid (be afraid of gettiing involved in the trouble /might report the secret to Mrs Medlock)

3) Mrs. Medlock

Cold/indifferent/as sour as a crab apple(P6, P8, P31) (usual scowl)

Smarmy/snobbish(P31, P45) (tone changed immediately)

Bossy(P16)

4) Mr. Craven

Q: What's your first impression of Mr. Craven?

Indifferent/strange/odd/as sour as a crab apple

In fact: gentle/kind(P33)

Loving(P72)

Q: Why did he always go away and not seem to care much about his son? Did he love his son? Evidence? (P38)

5) Mary

Appearance: plain-looking, pale, yellow... sick(P6)

Personality

Spoiled(P9)

Rude/impolite

Proud/self-conceited/arrogant/ A great sense of self-esteem: stubborn pride (死要面子)(P8)

Q: Who should be responsible for that? (P6)

Father: always at work

Mother: beautiful, always at some party or other

In order not to annoy her mother, Mary's servants would let her do things at will / never go against Mary's will.

(P16)The fresh air put colour in her cheeks and she grew stronger.

Curious(P11, P13, P15, sensitive/smart)

Brave(P35)

Straight-forward(P43, P50, PP52-54)

Easy-going

Sympathetic/Understanding(P45: she has a soft part deep down her heart.)

Have a better control of herself(P27)

6) Dickon

Appearance: (P27) glorious rust-coloured hair and blue eyes the colour of the sky

Personality:

nature lover/adventurous//energetic

Friendly/helpful: help Mary with gardening

Reliable/trustful: tell him the secret(P28)

Understanding/sympathetic(PP51-57)

Encouraging(P59)

Knowledgeable: Green fingers

Q: Why did Mary trust Dickon?

7) Colin:

Appearance: huge, dark eyes that seemed too big for thin, pale face(P36)

stick-like arms and legs(P54)

Selfish: some stupid boy, be jealous(P50)

Ⅲ-tempered/capricious(任性的，变化无常的): throw a tantrum (P50)

hysterics hysterical (P51), a spoilt brat(P54)

Gloomy/self-abandoned: I'm going to be a hunchback. (P54)

Self-abased: not want others to see him

His arms grew stronger. His legs grew stronger. (P69)

tall/ handsome(P74)

A great sense of self-esteem: My legs aren't gammy. (P66)

Confident/optimistic: a proud grin on his face(P67)

Q: What led to his change?

3. Who is your favorite character? Why?

Write a poem about your favorite character.

Period 3　Theme Analysis

1. Q: What led to Colin's change?

inner: positive thinking

a desire to go outside/ to have companions / to get love from parents

Evidence:

P38: "Tell me about India."

P42: "Look, I've been finding pictures of some of the things you told me."

P39: You must come again, "Come again soon."

P68: "He'll want to see me when I am awake as well as asleep."

outer: support from others

the magic of the secret garden

2. Share part of the last chapter of the original novel & part of the movie.

What's your understanding of the sentence in the original novel "Where you tend a rose, a thistle cannot grow."

Similar expressions in the movie: You must pull the weeds up to give flowers the room.

3. About the title.

Sentence from the book:

"It was the magic of this place. The magic of the secret garden."

"While the secret garden was coming alive and two children were coming alive with it, Lord Craven was coming back to life."

(1) Make a list of the words and expressions describing the garden.

P14: bare/wintry

P23: grey, brown, dead vegetation

P18: tiny green shoots

P48: green shoots everywhere

P75: a feast of autumn yellow and purple, and flaming scarlet

(2) Why is the novel entitled "The Secret Garden"?

(3) What does the secret garden serve as in the story?

The secret garden serves as—

a magical paradise to heal pains;

fountain of life and happiness;

a perfect background with warm and booming atmosphere for a story about love;

a mirror of people and their lives (positive attitude);

...

4. What is the underlying theme of the story?

positive auto-suggestion

(You can heal yourself by thinking yourself well.)

the power/magic of nature

love

...

5. Making connections between the novel and the author:

Experience: move to America to live with a relative.

Environment: a lovely rose garden.

Expectation (belief): You can heal yourself by thinking yourself well.

Period 4　Language Analysis

1. Share beautiful phrases or sentences in the story and state your reasons.

e. g. Mary felt her spirits sink even lower.

So Mary's days took shape.

For once, Colin was lost for words.

The eyes gave it away. He had Lilias' beautiful eyes.

No wonder you are so pale.

If only she could find the door.

It was the first time Colin had talked of what he would do in the future.

Picking up a sharp stick, Mary began prodding in the earth.

She found herself surrounded by four high walls.

2. Choose your favorite part of the story and read it in groups

3. Find expressions about showing one's anger

P27 fly into a rage

P31 Mrs Medlock stormed in, the usual scowl nailed to her face.

P38 growl + P46 Colin growled, puffing himself up

P40 Master Colin's probably in one of his paddies now!

P49 He's working his way up to a right tantrum.

P49 Mary felt a wave of anger sweep over her.

P50 Mary's face turned to thunder.

P51 She was still furious.

P51 He is having hysterics.

P52 The sound set her teeth on edge.

P54 Mary fumed.

P64 yell at

P65 shake his fist at

4. Appreciating rhetorical devices

simile: P6: as sour as a crab apple

P15: trailing like a waterfall down to the ground

metaphor: P24: wrapped in a warm blanket

personification: P23: as if holding hands

exaggeration: P21: her heart beating faster than a galloping horse

P65: eyes nearly popped out of his head

repetition: P56: I can see it. I can see it.

Teaching Plan for *The Gift of the Magi*

Step 1　Warming up

A free talk about Christmas and Christmas gifts.

Step 2　Dipping into the short story *The Gift of the Magi*

Characters; setting; thread of the story

Step 3　Diving into the story

A discussion and sharing among the group (3 minutes)

Tasks for group work

①Plot Analyst:

As the Plot Analyst, it is your job to read the story carefully and draw the plot mountain or flow chart of the story.

②Character Captain/Character Analyst

As the Character Captain, it is your job to share observations you have about the main characters. Select at least three adjectives that describe the two main characters in your story, and support your description with evidence taken from the novel. (Bubble map is encouraged here.)

③Theme Analyst

As the Theme Analyst, it is your job to make connections between the story and the following aspects:

* Your understanding of the title

＊ Meaning of Christmas stories

＊ Your own life (the similar story you've seen, heard around you)

Think about a minimum(最少) of two connections the novel reminds you of. List the connections and explain how the events are similar.

④Connector

As the Connector, it is your job to search the information about the author, find some connections between the author's life experience and the novel, and learn the background information about the novel! We hope the job will help your fellow students understand the novel better!

⑤Language Master/ Literary Luminary

As the Language Master/Literary Luminary, it is your job to read aloud some sentences or paragraphs worth reading and help your group members decide the highlight sections of the text.

Step 4　A mini-presentation after group discussion

Step 5　Assignments after class

＊ Read and appreciate the language

＊ "I can ask questions!" (based on your reading and sharing experience)

【附件六】 学生作业选

1.《秘密花园》概要及书评

概要：

[A Summary is a brief statement that presents the main points in a concise form]

The Secret Garden is a story about Mary's discovery of a locked garden.

Mary's family are killed by cholera, and she is sent to her uncle's manor which has several gardens. One has been locked for years because of her aunt's death. Mary finds the buried key with the Robin's help and enters. And at the same time, she gets to know Dickon who's good at gardening and her cousin Colin who has trouble walking. They share the secret of that garden. Days pass, the garden comes alive and Colin is able to walk and run. The happiness spreads.

Remember to keep a curious heart. Remember to be kind and warm-hearted because happiness is an attitude. (Lucy, Class 3)

书评：

[A Book Review is a statement of what the author has tried to do, evaluates how well the author has succeeded, and presents evidence to support this evaluation. It is written from the reviewer's perspective.]

Book Review 1

This is an amazing story about growth, love and nature, written by an English author Frances Hodgson Burnet. Over 100 years passed, but we can still be deeply moved.

Mary was a weak and negative girl before she arrived at her uncle's manor. However, upon finding the secret garden which was associated with a sad story, she fell in love with nature. She made friends with Martha and Dickon who were siblings. She became healthier and happier. They enjoyed themselves a lot in the garden. One day, Mary came across Colin who was her cousin by chance and found that he was so weak just as she used to be, so she shared the secret of the garden with him and tried her best to help him become gentle and positive. She and Dickon even asked him to go out and had a wonderful time in the secret garden. A miracle happened at last, Mary's uncle Mr. Craven came back home and everything turned out OK—Colin learned to walk and became much healthier.

Through the wonderful story, the author shows us: attitude counts. Being positive towards life can help you overcome all kinds of difficulties. As teenagers, from my perspective, it is very beneficial to read the book. We are going through similar pains as the main characters. What we can learn from them is also the attitude. And in conclusion, I highly recommend the book, and hope you can read it again and again! (Tracy, Class 4)

Book Review 2

The Secret Garden is a wonderful book written by Frances Hodgson Burnett and the topic of it is changes of Mary and Colin. The "magical" garden is a place where the people heal themselves and become better: Mary used to be rude and always depend on others and seldom went outside, then she changes into a proper country nature-lover girl who is kind and independent; Colin always in a bad mood in the past and was very thin, then he becomes a healthy and confident boy; Mr. Craven begins to face the knot in his mind bravely; the garden was brought to life by Mary and Dickon... The author tries to characterize many different characters linked with the garden. And it is a chance and also a key, showing its 'magic'to make people change.

So, the main idea is that you can heal yourself by thinking yourself better, just like what the author believes. Never give up and try to face the problem bravely. Sometimes you'll need a person to wake you up like Mary to Colin.

What's more, the author is really good at describe the scenes in the beautiful garden, which is full of life and energy. They make me learn that Everyone has a secret garden, everyone tries to become better. (Cherry, Class 4)

2. 基于《秘密花园》人物分析的诗歌作品

根据 *The Secret Garden* 的人物分析，请你为你所喜爱的一个人物写首诗。

Colin

The small master of the manor,
The owner of a pair of beautiful eyes.
It's him, Colin.
A weak and thin boy,
With bad temple and sensitive mind
Filled with loneliness and hopelessness.
But everything changes
At his age of ten
When he met the girl, Mary.
Getting inside the secret garden,
Growing stronger and healthier,
Who is it tall and handsome boy?
It's a new Colin who finally get happiness.

(Lisa 1810)

Colin

A boy of ten, he thinks no one loves him.
Ill-tempered and weak, stay in bed all day.
At a night rain began again, Colin has his life turned.
Mary came in his life, and talked with him.
After an unreasonable tantrum, Colin became sensible.

When Mary told him about the secret garden,
Colin for the first time to be trusted.
With the help of Mary and Dickon,
Colin felt stronger and was able to stand up.
He is as healthy as other boys.
It was the magic of the place,
The magic of the secret garden

(Linda 1811)

Colin

He was a weak boy in the past
Lying in the bed during the whole day
He thought he had no time last
Every day he was lonely, shouting "I'm going to die"
Never show his love, his dad
His mother, died when he was born
No wonder his temper was so bad
Until he met Mary because of the crying
The secret garden, which Mary was saying
Give him lots of energy
Colin himself was also changing
With his friend's help
He put in effort walking
At present, Colin is a handsome and strong boy
It is so amazing.

(Kelly 1810)

Dickon

Humble person in the manor,
Dickon, a born nature lover
Reliable companion Mary always prefer,

True adventure should take adventure
Brought a newborn lamb and courage and warmth
Reclaim barren land in heart as a gardener.
All the passion and love he gathered
Made the garden alive and everybody happy together.

(Sindy 1811)

Come Alive—For Colin

I remember tears streaming down your face
When you felt the lumps on your back
When all those shadows almost killed your light
I remember you said, don't leave me here alone
But all that's dead and gone and passed tonight
Just open your eyes
The sun is rising up
You'll be all right
Come morning light
You and I, with the secret garden will come alive

(Lily 1811)

The Friendly Robin

Robin, Robin, Robin!
Black and beady eyes
Perched near a wall
Chirruping in a tree
Hopped towards the wall
Pulling juicy worm
So lovely a bird was
Without you, everything won't happen
Helping Mary find the key
And showing her the door

How friendly a bird was

You'll be remembered by us all!

(Jack 1810)

【附件七】　英文原著选修课课程纲要

英文原著阅读与欣赏：《相约星期二》

课程纲要

课程名称：英文原著阅读与欣赏：《相约星期二》

开发者：浙江省宁波效实中学　何泽

课程类型：知识拓展类校本选修课程

授课对象：高一、高二学生

课时安排：16 课时

一、前言

传统的英语教学大多遵循"教学—考试"的路径，这样的教学往往过度重视语言的工具性而忽略语言的人文性。该选修课就是针对语言教学中的这一弊端尝试在高中英语教学中引进英文文学原著作为教学内容，旨在凸显语言的工具性的同时，更加注重挖掘语言的人文性。

《相约星期二》讲的是一个真实的故事：年逾七旬的社会学教授莫里在 1994 年罹患肌萎性侧索硬化症（ALS，俗称"渐冻人"），一年以后与世长辞。作为莫里早年的得意门生，米奇在老教授缠绵病榻的十四周里，每周二都上门与他相伴，聆听他最后的教诲，并在他死后将老师的醒世箴言缀珠成链，冠名《相约星期二》。这是一本进行人生教育和生命教育的绝佳教材。高中学生逐渐步入成年期，对生活中家庭、情感、金钱、死亡等已经有自己的思考，《相约星期二》正是人生教育和生命教育的绝佳教材。可以说这本书直视青少年成长的过程中遇到的困惑和烦恼，在英美国家该书被广泛选为文学阅读教材，并被改编成为电影、话剧等艺术形式。这本书于 2013 年被宁波外国语学校的高一年级选为必读的英语读物，在学生中引起了强烈的共鸣，很多学生说这本书是目前为止他们最喜欢阅读的一本书。

二、课程目标

1. 语言知识和语言技能

- 通过阅读和理解该小说的内容，提高学生的词汇量和阅读理解能力。
- 通过课堂的讨论和分享，提高学生的文学鉴赏能力和思维能力。
- 通过写书评，提高学生的写作技能。

2. 文化意识和情感态度

- 了解小说中美国文化现象，培养学生的国际视野和对异域文化的判断和融合能力。
- 探讨小说中有关社会、人生等方面的问题，能批判性地接受和理解作者的观点并能从不同的角度思考这些重大问题，进而培养学生的评判性思维能力和独立思考的能力。
- 通过发掘小说中积极的人生观和价值观，让学生反思自己的人身观和价值观，进而帮助学生形成正确的人生观和价值观。
- 激发学生对英文原著阅读的兴趣，为今后的英语学习和终身发展打好坚实的基础。

3. 学习策略和方法

- 通过阅读、讨论、诵读、话题讨论等课堂活动，培养学生对文学作品的阅读和欣赏能力。
- 通过小组活动，培养学生的实践和探究的能力，找到最适合自己的学习方式。

三、课程内容

1. 课程构成

本课程以英文原著 *Tuesdays with Morrie* 为教材，在 16 节课(40 分钟一节课)内完成全书的阅读教学任务。全书的阅读分为导读、主题阅读、总结提升等几部分。在导读部分共安排 2 节课，主要是为学生阅读小说做好铺垫，内容包括小说的写作背景、人物、主要情节等。主干阅读共安排10节课，包括小说的主干内容——莫里教授和学生的14周的谈话，这些谈话的主题涉及世界、死亡、爱情、人性等，通过阅读和欣赏旨在引发学生的思考。总结部分包括整本小说阅读的任务展示和书评写作等。

2. 课程安排

该小说主体部分共14章，每节课大概可完成一章的阅读和教学任务，根据小说的情节和内容在具体教学中可采用不同的课型，具体的课型如下：

任务展示课：阅读前把阅读任务分配给各小组（通常是周末或假期前，以确保学生有充足的阅读时间），这些任务包括小说的情节(plot)、人物的分析(character analysis)、精彩语句或段落赏析(good paragraphs)等，每个小组可以选择一个主题做好展示作业(大多是PPT形式)，然后发到指定的邮箱，在学生展示前，老师会批阅学生的作业，提出修改意见，最后集中在某个教学时段让学生展示他们的作业，其他同学可以根据同学的展示做好笔记并就同学的展示提出问题。

读写实践课：学生在课外的阅读时间是有限的，课堂上也要留足学生阅读的时间和阅读的量，课堂上的阅读形式以精读和出声朗读为主，主要是让学生阅读一些重点章节、重点段落，要给学生读出声的机会，让学生展示出优美的语音和语调，诵读出经典文学作品的魅力；还可以结合一些主题来读，比如让学生读人物对话、人物描写、景物描写、心情描写、最喜欢的段落等。学完每个章节后，教师以Reading Comprehension Check的形式设置4~5个经典问题来抽查学生，或让学生任选角度写一个小书评(book review)。

综合分析课：综合分析课以讨论、分享为主。讨论是以小组合作的方式针对所读作品某一问题或信息展开，小组成员在讨论中交流看法、交换意见。分享是个体与群体的互动，分享的内容包括人物和情节分析，解析难懂的语句和段落，谈论阅读心得、体会和经验，换位思考，预测下章等活动。综合分析课的课堂组织形式有师生互动式分析、生生互动式分析、小组互动式分析等形式。

欣赏表演课：阅读完部分章节或整本书后，教师根据具体情况让学生观看该书的电影版、电视版或者话剧等，然后让学生选取部分章节尝试表演。同学们排练后集中表演所选章节或精彩片段。学生还可以通过手机或相机拍摄表演过程，在课堂上和同学们一起分享。

附：课时安排

授课内容	课时数
Introduction+ pp. 1-41	1
The First Tuesday pp. 48-54	1
The Second Tuesday pp. 55-61	1
The Third Tuesday pp. 62-80	1
The Fourth Tuesday pp. 81-89	1
The Fifth Tuesday pp. 90-99	1
The Sixth Tuesday pp. 100-113	1
The Seventh Tuesday pp. 114-121	1
The Eight Tuesday pp. 123-128	1
The Ninth Tuesday pp. 130-141	1
The Tenth Tuesday pp. 142-151	1
The Eleventh Tuesday pp. 152-P163	1
The Twelfth Tuesday pp. 163-170	1
The Thirteenth Tuesday pp. 171-180	1
The Fourth Tuesday pp. 181-192	1
Conclusion	1
总课时	16

四、课程实施

1. 本课程教学遵循的基本原则

(1)以学定教的原则。学是教学的关键，可根据学生的实际情况以学定教，最大限度发挥学生的主观能动性，并尊重个性差异，尽力让每位学生都有所收获。

(2)阅读和思考相结合的原则。这本小说充满了哲理，处处有值得思考的名言警句，阅读中尽量打开学生的思维，让学生结合自己的生活经历去思考一些重大问题，培养学生的独立阅读能力和评判性思维能力。

2. 教学评价的原则和要求

(1)成绩评定

本课程的成绩评定由四部分组成：课堂活动(30%)+出勤率(10%)+作业(20%)+测试(40%)。其中课堂活动包括任务展示、讨论等，作业包括小论文、回答问题等；测试以书评形式进行。

(2)学分认定

缺勤不超过两次，成绩60分以上均给予1个学分。

◎ 本章小结

本章以“文学圈”阅读模式为理论框架，尝试在高中英语教学中嵌入文学作品的阅读。

在本轮实践中，文学阅读的选材是以《典范英语 10》系列文学名著简写本为主，这些文学名著简写本共 14 本，按主题和体裁分类进行阅读和教学，高一以人与自然，科幻小说类为主；高二以旅游、探险和人物传记类为主。

本轮实践中采用了文学圈阅读模式，这种阅读模式是把学生分成若干个小组，按章节和阅读内容以小组形式轮流分享阅读成果，除了运用上轮实验中采用的几种文学阅读课型外，还重点讨论教师如何引领、学生如何自主阅读等常见问题。教学中教师的引领策略主要有：以文学要素为支架载体，铺设思维的底层框架；以思维导图为图表支架，使思维可视化；多种对话中不断追问，培养学生的申辩性思维。学生的自主阅读主要包括阅读前的自主选材、导学案引领下的自主阅读、自建文学圈后的自主阅读、合作中的自主阅读，以及分享自主阅读成果、自主阅读中的自主创作等。

第三部分　中小学英语文学阅读实践探索：读写结合

第一节　引　　言

现行初高中英语教学已逐步从英语教学过渡到英语教育的层面。英语作为一门工具学科，其人文涵养和育人功能越来越显现。《普通高中英语课程标准(2017 版)》的颁布标志着英语教学已进入核心素养培养阶段，传统的过分注重语言知识和英语技能的英语教学理念已经不能满足时代发展的要求；英语作为一门语言，其本身的美感、蕴含的思想精华、传播的优秀文化、传递的人文力量越来越受到重视，而现行英语教材因不同地域的教育发展不均衡等因素，所选材料不能满足不同学习程度的学生；此外，现行教材所选材料多是事实性文本，主要是根据学生的语言程度改写的，也使得很多教材很难经受时间的检验，缺乏深度解读的张力，不具备经典性和人文性。鉴于此分析，教学中我们可根据当地教学实际选择文学阅读文本来拓展现有语言学习，培养学生的语言学习兴趣，奠定良好的人文根基。本章从童话导读、文学阅读和核心素养、整本书阅读，基于英美文学名著的阅读实践等继续探讨文学阅读，聚焦学生读写素养的逐步养成。

第二节　童话导读：体验、想象与审美意蕴的构建①

《义务教育语文课程标准》(2011)(以下简称《课标》)中指出：阅读是运用语言文字获取信息、认识世界、发展思维、获取审美体验的重要途径。要重视培养学生广泛的阅读兴趣，提倡“少做题，多读书，好读书，读好书，读整本的书”；应加强阅读方法的指导，让学生逐步学会精读、略读和浏览。应培养学生广泛的阅读兴趣，扩大阅读面，增加阅读量，提高阅读品位。要求语文教师加强对学生课外阅读的指导，开展各种课外阅读活动，创造展示与交流的机会，营造人人爱读书的良好氛围。《课标》中这些关于阅读教学的要求和建议是语文阅读教学的行动纲领，但当前中小学语文阅读教学碎片化、功利化、应试化的现象普遍存在，虽然《课标》中对中小学学生的阅读量、阅读内容和阅读素养有明确的指导和规范，但实际教学中大多教师缺乏对阅读教学的深度研究，缺乏对阅读教学的科学指导，中小学中好读书、读好书的风气并未养成，无论是教师的阅读教学还是学生的自主阅读大多依然处于盲目和跟风的状态，因而科学认识中小学语文阅读教学的地位，探讨科学规范的阅读教学方法依然迫在眉睫。

为了更深刻地理解义务教育阶段中小学语文阅读教学的要求、阅读内容和阅读素养的培养等具体内容，笔者仔细研读《课标》后，以表格的形式呈现义务教育(小学段)语文阅读教学目标和内容，如表3-1所示：

①　本节是2019年1月笔者和中国民族师范教育研究中心专家一行受民革中央邀请赴贵州省威宁彝族回族苗族自治县第三小学参加义务支教活动时给全县小学语文教师做的同题讲座，虽然话题是语文童话导读，但对英语文学阅读同样有启发，故收录。

表 3-1　义务教育(小学段)语文阅读教学目标和内容

年级段	课外阅读量(不少于)	阅读内容	阅读素养
1~2 年级	积累自己喜欢的成语和格言警句。背诵优秀诗文 50 篇(段)。课外阅读总量不少于 5 万字。	浅显的童话、寓言、故事；诵读儿歌、儿童诗和浅近的古诗；认识课文中常出现的标点符号。	正确、流利、有感情地朗读课文；喜欢阅读、感受阅读的乐趣。养成爱护图书的习惯。学习默读；展开想象，获得初步的情感体验，感受语言的美。
3~4 年级	积累课文中的优美语段、精彩段落，以及在课外阅读和生活中获得的语言材料。背诵优秀诗文 50 篇(段)。课外阅读总量不少于 40 万字。	叙事性作品、优秀的诗文、读书看报。在理解语句的过程中体会句号与逗号的不同用法，了解冒号、引号的一般用法。	初步学会默读，做到不出声、不指读。学习略读，粗知文章大意；诵读优秀诗文，注意在诵读过程中体验情感，展开想象，领悟诗文大意；养成读书看报的习惯，收藏图书资料，乐于与同学交流。
5~6 年级	背诵优秀诗文 60 篇(段)，课外阅读总量不少于 100 万字。	叙事性作品、诗歌、说明性文章、优秀诗文、简单非连续性文本。	默读要有一定的速度(每分钟不少于 300 字)；学习浏览，推想课文中有关词句的意思，辨别词语感情色彩；体会作者思想感情，初步领悟文章的表达方法；在讨论和交流中，敢于提出自己的看法，做出自己的判断；领会不同体裁作品的阅读要求。

根据表格可以看出，义务教育小学段语文阅读教学既重视基本的阅读方法、阅读习惯的养成，又重视阅读内容契合儿童的心理认知。阅读方法的养成指学会略读、学会积累、学会运用工具书等阅读方法。阅读习惯包括读书看报、爱惜图书、收藏图书、乐于分享读后感等。阅读内容可涉及童话、寓言、故事、儿歌、儿童诗等具有童趣的作品。《课标》还对所有学段提出了具体课外阅读量的要求，整个小学段课外阅读总量不少于150万字。结合以上分析，笔者以2019年1月参加中国民族阅读中心专家组去往贵州威宁彝族回族苗族自治县第三小学开展的童话导读为案例，探讨小学童话的导读，期望对中小学的阅读教学有所启发。

一、童话和童话导读

童话作为一种历史悠久的儿童文学文体，不同学者对其解释略有差异。有观点认为，童话是儿童文学的一种，通过丰富的想象和夸张来塑造艺术形象，反映生活，增进儿童思想性格的成长。一般童话故事神奇曲折，内容和表现形式浅显生动，对自然物的描写常用拟人化手法，符合儿童的接受能力。也有观点认为，童话是“为儿童读者而采记、复述、加工、再创作和创作的荒诞性与真实性有机结合、协调统一的奇妙故事，是最容易具有历史和人类的共同性的文学样式之一”。尽管对童话的定义有所差别，但我们可以认为童话是一种以幻想、拟人、夸张和象征为主要表现特征的儿童文学样式，并常以故事为主要叙述形式。童话通常故事性强，具有幻想、童言童语等特征，如童话《丑小鸭》中丑小鸭可以变成小天鹅，鳄鱼可以爱上长颈鹿，这样离奇而又充满幻想的情节契合了儿童的童心，满足了他们的童趣。根据不同的体裁或表现形式，小学生阅读的童话通常有文学童话、科学童话、拟人体童话、常人体童话和超人体童话等。

导读在阅读学中即阅读指导。导读的核心意义只能是对具体阅读方法和具体难点、重点的点拨和启导。离开这一核心意义，导读就是抽象的，并没有实际意义。导读通常具有以下特征：被导者已经形成一定的或较强的独立阅读能力，而导读者则比被导者更胜一筹。某本书与被导者可能发生的积极关系是导读有效性的前提。导读本质上是非技术的。导读是复杂的(伴有社会因素)、高级的精神活动，也是高度个性化的活动。笔者认为导读是成熟的阅读者(通常是教师)先为一群阅读水平差不多的阅读者精心挑选一份文本，然后导读者和读者共同确定阅读中需要关注的“关键内容”，并就阅读方法给予指导，以便帮助读者熟练掌握文本，进行有效阅读。

童话导读“关键的内容”就是要让儿童体会到童话的乐趣。童话的乐趣很多，比如，满足心愿的乐趣、扮演角色的乐趣、经历奇异幻境的乐趣、想象的乐趣、游戏的乐趣、感受曲折故事情节的乐趣、获得悲喜交加情感共鸣的乐趣、冥思默想体悟诗意的乐趣，等等。让学生感受到童话阅读的乐趣和美好，是引领他们踏上阅读之旅的最佳方法。而且童话导读的意义不仅仅在于导读者导读了一篇或数篇童话，而是在童话的导读中激发学生的阅读兴趣，使其养成良好的阅读习惯，丰富其阅读体验，并在他们的生命中撒播下文学的、诗意的、情感的种子。这才是童话导读的精髓所在。

二、《小王子》导读实践

《小王子》是一篇经典的童话故事。故事以一位飞行员作为叙述者，他由于飞机故障迫降在撒哈拉沙漠，遇见一个来自外星球的小王子。小王子向他讲述了生平和经历，对旅途中遇见的形形色色的“古怪的”人表示不可理解，最后为了对一朵玫瑰花尽责而返回了自己小小的星球。这篇童话以其生动的情节、丰富的想象和富有诗意的形象而保持经久不衰的魅力，仅中国大陆就有上百种版本。但这本书哲理性强，内涵丰富，虽然广为传播，但儿童要读懂、读出乐趣并非易事。所以，这本经典童话的导读具有深刻的意义。笔者导读的是六年级学生，他们具备初步的阅读能力，部分学生阅读过该书。结合该书的特点，笔者将导读的中心任务确定如下：首先，通过唤醒学生已有的阅读经历让学生熟悉故事，体验小王子游历的乐趣；其次，引领他们运用思维和想象理解童话中丰富意象的内涵，并将自己的生命体悟融入其中，感受这篇童话中诗的味道与情感的丰富。阅读的最终意义不仅仅是阅读别人的故事，而且要返身照看自己的镜像，乃至自己的生命。让学生在童话阅读中超越文本本身获得审美的享受才是阅读的终极目的。限于篇幅，本节例举导读中的几个关键活动做简要说明。

1. 唤起儿童的体验

导读前简单介绍《小王子》这本书的影响和特点：这本书一个多世纪以来经久不衰，发行量居世界第二位，被誉为“不仅写给小孩，也写给大人”的童话，书中有作者亲手绘制的精美插图，绘图和文字巧妙地交融在一起，读起来令人兴趣盎然，赏心悦目。《小王子》其实是一部旅行日记，小王子从B612号小行星出走，他访问了不同的星球，认识了形形色色、奇奇怪怪的人，作者记录了小王子参观不同星球后的感受。进行这类童话的阅读时，如果能让儿童置身于这些特定的生活场景，进行一次次愉快的探险、旅行，这样的阅读过程似乎是进入一个充满魅力的游戏场，产生一种强烈的参与感，从而从阅读中获得极大的快乐。儿童喜欢看“历险”类的作品，即是体现了这一心理，因此导读前让小读者回顾他们已经读过的这类童话，当同学们说出《洋葱头历险记》《吹牛大王历险记》《丁丁历险记》《小布头奇遇记》《尼尔斯骑鹅历险记》《爱丽丝漫游奇境记》《泰迪熊火车历险记》等耳熟能详的童话时，不仅激发了同学们的阅读欲望，也建立了一定的阅读支架，从而降低了阅读的难度。接下来让同学们根据插图快速寻找小王子去过的地方，整本书的脉络和轮廓就清楚了。

2. 激发儿童想象

唤醒儿童阅读体验后，如何抓住学生阅读中可能遇到的难点进行导读是导读的核心。笔者在阅读中发现很多话题值得讨论，如“小王子和大人们”“小王子和他的玫瑰花”“小王子和狐狸”“小王子和‘我’”。在一节课的时间里，笔者把导读的重点放在三个关键问题上：分析不同形象的象征意义；对童话中反复提到的“大人和小孩”的理解；对“驯服”的理解。

首先，通过第一个活动让学生们找出六个星球不同的主人、地球上的蛇、三瓣花、回声、玫瑰花园、狐狸、扳道工和商人等不同形象，这些不同的形象又是丰富的意象，都有不同的象征意义。每一个意象象征了一种不同的生活状态，导读中重点引导同学们通过表 3-2 分析六个星球上不同形象的象征意义。

表 3-2　小王子六个星球游历记

星球	人物	性格特点	你的评价
325 号星球			
326 号星球			
327 号星球			
328 号星球			
329 号星球			
330 号星球			

其次是小说关于“大人和小孩”这一主题，导读中让学生分组找出书中描写大人和小孩特点的句子，然后共同分享，当读到“大人们劝我别再画什么蟒蛇了，而是把兴趣放到地理、历史、算术和语法上”“大人喜欢谈论桥牌、高尔夫球、政治、领带什么的”“那些大人喜欢数字”“如果你交了一个朋友，他们只会问你‘他几岁啦’‘有几个兄弟?’‘他父亲挣多少钱’”等句子时，同学们忍俊不禁，被这些充满童趣和哲理的句子深深打动。

书中的“驯养”也是阅读难点。笔者将“驯养”解释为“建立联系”，然后让学生阅读相关章节，就大大降低了难度。小王子来到沙漠，碰到会说话的狐狸。狐狸首先道出了人与人关系的重点在于“被驯养”，“驯养”的过程是一个慢慢深入，形成习惯、依赖，最终“建立感情联系”的过程。“如果你驯养了我，那该有多么美妙啊！

小麦也是金黄色的，能让我想起你来，而且我也会爱上那吹拂麦穗的风声……”“人只能用心去观察。本质的东西，眼睛是看不见的”……通过追溯文本，同学们可以深刻领会“驯养”就是建立友谊和情感，为自主阅读奠定基础。

这部分是导读的主干，旨在聚焦文本的关键点，激发学生的形象思维。学生经过思维主体的感受、创造，逐步形成自我的审美感受。

3. 引领儿童成长

阅读说到底是一种精神加工，阅读教学应引导学生钻研文本，在主动积极的思维和情感活动中，加深理解和体验，有所感悟和思考，受到情感熏陶，获得思想启迪，享受审美乐趣。可见体验和思考最终只要上升到审美的高度才能体味阅读的魅力。《小王子》经久不衰也是因为它的精神魅力，挖掘它的精神魅力，引领儿童的成长是阅读这本书的终极价值。以童话中的语言为例，童话中充满哲理的语言像皇冠上的钻石一样熠熠生辉，如，“本质的东西眼睛是看不见的”“星星美丽，因为里面有一朵看不见的花”“沙漠美丽，因为沙漠的某处隐藏着一口井”“人都缺乏想象力，只会重复别人对他们讲的话”“看见麦子的金黄色，我就有感触”，这些充满诗意和哲理的语言让我们感受到了一个不同于现实的美好、纯真的世界。通过阅读我们可以感受生活的美好，通过想象我们可以感受小王子的纯真，所有的这些阅读体验都超越了心理的现实性，从而达到一种审美的意蕴。《小王子》一书总显得那么与众不同，它用一颗童心唤醒了人们内心逝去或沉睡的童真，从而引导儿童珍惜童年，健康成长。

三、童话导读的反思

此次导读是笔者的一次尝试，通过学习，笔者认识到近几年在我国导读已逐渐受到重视，并且多是民间自发组织进行的。其实在国外，导读已是阅读指导常见的一种形式，它对培养儿童终身阅读习惯，提升儿童阅读素养意义重大。美国阅读推广专家卡尔金斯通过大量的实证研究总结出导读的特点(见表 3-3)：

表 3-3　指导性阅读的特点

指导性阅读不是……	指导性阅读是……
教师的导读是通过一系列问题引导学生了解文本。这些问题可能掩盖图书本身，引出一大堆口头阐述，反而偏离了对书本的关注。	教师的导读概括了文章的主要内容，引导学生留意有难度的页码。
针对在共享阅读时段全班已经阅读的文本，学生再次阅读。	学生初次阅读他们不熟悉且通常具有一定挑战性的文本。他们从教师的导读中获得帮助。
学生轮流阅读或齐声朗读或唱读的时段。	小组所有成员都拿着自己的书，同时开始进行默读，通常每个学生都要读完所有的内容。
阅读是断断续续、不连贯的，学生读一小段后就要停下来，听教师集中提示下一部分的内容，比如："读一读，找出安德鲁发疯的原因"。	没有停顿，一口气读完。读完的学生可以再次阅读，或回头找出自己喜欢的内容，等待其他同学读完。
分数是长期的，以学生的能力为依据。	基于学生的能力分组，但是是短期的、临时的。
一次小组活动需 20~40 分钟。	一次小组活动需 10~15 分钟。
阅读活动结束后，要进行字卡学习、句子配对、拼写游戏、练习题等活动。	阅读活动结束后，教师通常会指出一个教学点，即难点，可利用白板或者带磁性的字母卡做些指导。

从上表可以看出导读关注的是主要内容，导读中笔者并不是让学生回答一系列问题或者读后完成各种练习，导读过程只是围绕几个核心问题逐步展开，如请学生说说关于这本书他/她知道些什么，找找

这本书的精彩部分，想想作者为什么写这本书，议议如何读这一整本书。导读后布置给学生的阅读任务也以活动任务单的形式呈现，并没有以练习的形式加重学生的负担。活动任务单的主要任务是：让学生想象自己是书中的某个星球，向同学作自我介绍；创作一首诗歌、歌曲或一个故事来表现童话的主题；根据书中的情节画一张画或图表，并进行相应解释；分组（5～6位同学为一组）为本书设计一张板报，组员包括图画小能手、性格分析师、摘要小神童、文本大神探、平面设计师等。这些活动趣味性和互动性强，有利于激发学生的阅读兴趣。

当然这次导读也有值得改进的地方，如导读中并没有关注一些阅读方法的指导。针对《小王子》这本书，教师可指导学生通过阅读前言、目录、图片和内容提要等获得整体感知；教会学生一章一章地读，适当做一些批注；精彩章节或读不懂的章节可反复读，对于书中精彩部分可做摘记；读完整本书后，结合自己的实际写写读后感，还可以制作好书推荐卡；可以观看该作品的动画片，等等。阅读方法的指导有利于养成良好的自主阅读习惯，从而提升学生的阅读素养。

四、结语

这次导读让笔者深刻体会到，好的童话不是用教条化的理论对读者进行约束和说教，而是用温暖的故事、奇妙的想象和丰富的意蕴来感动人，从而激发读者心中真、善、美的品质。这些好童话如同我们的精神食粮，在我们内心扎根，成为我们成长的养料，让人隔一段时间就从心底里渴望重温它。当前的小学语文教材精心选择了一批经典、优美的童话故事，如《小猫钓鱼》《卖火柴的小女孩》《皇帝的新衣》《咕咚》《小鹿的玫瑰花》《丑小鸭》等，教师在带领孩子们阅读这些童话时应该克服普遍存在的突出教育性、工具性等弊端，从情感与审美体验的角度出发，让儿童读出童话的诗意、幻想、快乐、游戏等特征，从而激发儿童对童话的原初情感，以达到培养儿童爱阅读、会阅读的良好习惯。作为成年读者我们应该牢记，每个成年人曾经都是儿童，我们都有颗童心，带着童心指导儿童阅读是我们每个教育工作者义不容辞的职责。

◎ 参考文献

1. 中华人民共和国教育部. 义务教育语文课程标准：2011 版[M]. 北京：北京师范大学出版社，2012：1-34.
2. 辞海[M]. 上海：上海辞书出版社，1999：5071.
3. 现代汉语词典：第五版[M]. 北京：商务印书馆，2005：1369.
4. 韦苇. 外国童话史[M]. 南京：江苏少年儿童出版社，1991：3.
5. 樊百华. "导读"辨义[J]. 江苏图书馆学报：1996(5)：9-10.
6. 周益民. 造梦课堂：创意语文 13 节[M]. 桂林：广西师范大学出版社，2017：291.
7. 圣-埃克苏佩里. 小王子[M]. 李玉民，译. 西安：西安交通大学出版社，2017.
8. 卡尔金斯. 如何有效运用阅读教学策略[M] 林玲，译. 吴海玲，校. 北京：教育科学出版社，2018：71-72.

第三节　高中英语文学名著阅读和学科核心素养

英语文学阅读摒弃了传统英语阅读中的工具性和实用性倾向，阅读的旨向是人的素养的提高，因为文学阅读主要以故事情节、人物特征、优美语言等为核心，而围绕故事、人物、语言等文学元素的阅读不仅是生动、活泼的而且与阅读者的生活紧密相关，它在培养语言能力的同时，也在不断影响着读者的成长，让读者反思自己的生活，努力提升生活品质和塑造人格。文学阅读的过程是自主的，对作品的理解又是个性化的，这种自然习得英语的过程，更加有利于培养语言综合运用能力和思维能力，也能够让广大读者感受异域文化，培养文化意识。

一、细读鉴赏、学用结合，培养语言能力

文学作品是优美语言的宝库和人类文化的结晶，学生通过阅读、听读、讨论、角色扮演、书评等多种形式达到学用结合，在多种形式的语言运用中实现读写听说能力的自然整合。当学生阅读完文本后进行小组分享时，这个过程本身就是对陈述性知识的内化加工，可以不断提高学生的思考、分析、推理、归纳的能力。例 1 是某小组在阅读 *David Copperfield* 后整理的表达方式：阅读中的这种鉴赏和归纳能力对提高学生的综合语言能力意义深远。

例 1　小说中有关不同情感的表达方式

got up in a rage (P5), light up (P6), a very heavy heart (P8), shivered with fear (P9), full of gloom and cruelly (P9), shook with terror (P12), dragged my spirits down farther (P12), Terror gripped me (P17), with a roar (P17), My stomach tightened with anxiety (P18), nodded glumly (P20), overjoyed with (P23), stayed downhearted (P25), It felt as if my whole world had just been shattered (P26), choking back sobs of fury and desperation (P33), I was now in a pit of total despair (P34), A wave of relief flooded over me (P39), My spirits sank (P40), A flush anger and embarrassment spread across one's cheeks (P41)

例 2　学生完成 *Jane Eyre* 阅读后所整理的人物描写段落

St. John was, I think, nearly thirty, tall, fair, and slender and very handsome with an earnest, intense way of speaking. I was aware of his careful observation, as if no detail should ever be missed. (c87)

A man in black, who with his great height, dark clothes and grim face, looked like a black pillar of stone. (Mr. Brocklehurst)

> She was tall, pale and dark-haired, and for some minutes she surveyed us gravely and silently, I saw kindness in her eyes and dignity in her bearing.

通过对文学名著的阅读，学生在语言语境中学习表达更加自然，许多表达方式经常会出现在学生的作文和口语中。学生的学习兴趣越来越浓厚，有的学生还养成了良好的语言摘录和做批注的习惯，有的学生能非常自然地撰写简短的英文小评论，所有这些都对提高学生的语言运用能力有极大的帮助。

一位学生说文学名著阅读在读和写的方面确实对他影响颇深。首先，很多叙述性、描写性的词汇通常会在一部文学作品中反复出现，并且一义多词，这无疑对词汇量有一个关联性拓展。例如 *Frankenstein* 中的 thrilled，marveled，grief，agitated 等一系列有关心情描写的词汇，当熟悉掌握这些词汇后，会自然而然地运用到写作中，同时也会借鉴与学习作品中出现的语法与句型，丰富原有文章。

二、自主探究、合作分享，养成学习能力

文学圈阅读模式充分激发了学生的自主学习能力，从他们组建小组、合作完成学习任务到小组展示无不体现了学生自主、合作、探究的学习能力的提高。下面是学生对文学阅读模式的阐述。

> “文学圈不仅可以提高我们的阅读能力，而且还可以增强团队合作能力和同学间交流的能力，因为每位同学分享的观点汇集起来，总会有不曾想到的点，这可以开拓大家的思维，开拓视野，对于我们阅读这本书会有更加深入的了解，同时在阅读其他名著时也可以思考得更深更广。”
>
> “文学圈的这种阅读模式对我来说是全新的，却也是值得尝试的。这让阅读变得更像个集体的狂欢，而非个人进行的一项任务。与同伴的分享可以让自己对文学作品的了解有了新的视野与方向，

当能更全面地解读、体悟一部作品时，我感觉自己是愉快的。在读*Wuthering Heights*时，错综复杂的人物关系以及不一样的叙述风格让阅读这部作品变得格外困难，但通过课后与同学的交流，让自己对这部作品的人物线索清晰了不少。"

三、分析推断、批判创新，提升思维品质

"高中英语文学阅读旨在奠定学习者英语的文学素养基础，与思维品质(分析与比较、综合与分类、抽象与概括、批判与创新)等要素共同构成了英语学科核心素养。这反映了高中英语文学阅读与思维发展对英语学科教与学具有重要意义"。在文学名著阅读的过程中，思维的培养是渗透在整个阅读过程中的。读前以文学基本要素(人物、情节、主题、文体、主题等)的分析为抓手粗读，着手打造思维的底层框架。读中讨论问题的思维化：从问题的设置到理解应用、从分析到评价、从联想到推断、从比较到质疑等层层深入，循循善诱，激趣引思。读中活动的探究化：探究结构和情节；探究主题思想；探究象征意义；探究人物特征(戴军熔，2015)。还可以运用可视化思维(thinking maps)降低读本理解难度，引导学生与文本发生多重对话。这些活动不仅有利于学生内化文学作品的语言和内容，更能培养学生批判性思维能力，也为读后的创意表达与综合评价做好铺垫。可以说阅读文学名著关键在于培养联想思维、视觉化能力和想象他们内心的能力。

四、潜移默化、理解共情，培养文化意识

《课程标准》明确把文化意识作为基础教育阶段英语课程的总体目标之一，倡导一种具有文化视野的英语教育。文化是一个人类群体的生活方式和形态。同时也指出："语言有丰富的文化内涵。在外语教学中，文化是指所学语言国家的历史地理、风土人情、传统习俗、生活方式、文学艺术、行为规范、价值观念等。"而文学作品的阅读是浸润在异域文化的精神之旅，文学作品饱含作者所处的时代、所在国家的风土

人情、历史地理、生活方式、价值观念等信息，长期阅读文学作品不论对培养显性的文化还是隐形的文化都具有潜移默化的作用。有些文化是隐性的，如价值观、社会制度、宗教信仰等，该文化的大部分内涵只能在该文化语境中理解。还有一些文化是显性的，如历史文化、节庆活动、日常生活方式等，可以在其他文化语境里理解。对显性文化的教学容易在学生中引发共情，而学生对隐形文化的敏感度则需要教师的启发和引导(施丽华，2015)。

例如《简爱》是反映维多利亚时代(Victorian Era)生活的典型作品，维多利亚时代是英国工业革命和大英帝国的顶峰时期，作品中描写了当时社会面貌，特别是寄宿制学校的生活，女性作为家庭教师职业的特殊性、爱情观等，而这些在同时代的《呼啸山庄》《大卫·科普菲尔》等小说中也集中反映出来，这些隐性的文化只有通过教师的启发和引导，学生才能对维多利亚时代特别是工业革命时期的社会面貌和文学特征形成一个整体的概念，而这些文化知识的熏陶不仅有助于学生对作品的深刻理解，更有助于提升今后对相关时期作品的阅读的解读能力。

五、结语

基础教育的基本任务是素质教育，而素质教育的核心是人的教育。文学原著阅读不仅让学生接触更多真实的语言，丰富学生的文学读写体验，而且原著的阅读还具有特殊的思想以及人文等诸方面的课程价值，能提高学生的文化意识和思维能力。更为重要的是它能改变教学方式，变接受学习为自主学习、合作学习和探究学习，提高课堂教学质量，促进学生成长，实现从英语教学到英语教育的转变。

◎ 参考文献

1. 韩宝成. 关于我国中小学英语教育的思考[J]. 外语教学与研究(外国语文双月刊)，2010(4).
2. 黄瑞贤. 基于学生体验的高中英语文学阅读导读 [J]. 中小学外语教学(中学篇)，2015(6).

3. 中华人民共和国教育部. 普通高中英语课程标准(实验)[M]. 北京：人民教育出版社，2003.
4. 黄远振，兰春寿，黄睿. 为思而教：英语教育价值取向及实施策略[J]. 课程·教材·教法，2014(4).
5. Daniels H.. Literature Circles：Voice and Choice in the Student-Centered Classroom [M]. York，Marine：Stenhouse Publishers.
6. 斯蒂芬·克拉申. 阅读的力量[M]. 李玉梅，译. 乌鲁木齐：新疆少儿出版社，2012.
7. 黄远振，兰春寿，黄睿. 英语文学体验阅读 READ 教学模式建构研究[J]. 外语界，2013(1).
8. 何泽. 在高中英语阅读教学中采用英文原著的实践 [J]. 中小学外语教学(中学篇)，2016(3).
9. 兰春寿. 基于思维过程的高中英语文学阅读思维型课堂教学构架[J]. 课程·教材·教法，2015(12).
10. 戴军熔. 区域高中英语文学欣赏选修课程群的教材开发：实践与探索，2015(11).
11. 施丽华. 也谈中学英语教育和学生文化意识培养[J]. 英语学习，2015(12).

第四节　在中学英语阅读教学中采用整本英文原著的实践与反思

在我国英语教学史中，整本书阅读是有良好的传统的，如许国璋先生在回忆自己的中学英语学习时说，“在中学时……英文课是怎样进行的，我已经忘记了。我只记得课程是《泰西五十轶事》、《天方夜谭》、《莎士乐府本事》(*Tales from Shakespeare*)”(李良佑，1988)，而当今信息时代人们的阅读大多呈现碎片化、快餐化等特点，中小学生也深受影响(何泽，2016)。《义务教育英语课程标准(2011 版)》指出阅读是运用语言文字获取信息、认识世界、发展思维、获得审美体验的重要途径

(教育部，2012)。语文教育前辈叶圣陶在20世纪40年代就提出要读“整本的书”，在他看来“单篇短章”的教材“将会使学生眼花缭乱，心志不专，仿佛走进热闹的都市，看见许多东西，可是一样也没有看清楚”。“并且，读惯了单篇短章，老是局促在小规模的范围之中，魄力就不大了；等遇到规模较大的东西，就说是两百页的一本小书吧，将会感到不容易对付”。“试问，要养成读书习惯而不教他们读整本的书，那习惯怎么养得成?”他认为“以整本的书”为教材，虽然在短短数年读不了几部，但“心志可以专一，讨究可以彻底”。正是认识到整本书阅读的重要性，语文教学中整本书阅读已经写进了课程标准，“要重视培养学生广泛的阅读兴趣，扩大知识面，增加阅读量，提高阅读品位。提倡少做题，多读书，好读书，读好书，读整本书”(教育部，2012)。整本书阅读和研讨已经成为高中语文学习任务群的必修课程之一(教育部，2018)。就课程性质而言，语文和英语均属语言和文学的学习领域，都具有工具性和人文性的特性，教学中理应相互借鉴和相辅相成。而现行不同版本的英语教材中阅读教学仍然是以围绕功能或者话题为主的短文阅读，近些年来，为了改进英语阅读教学内容，国内学者如胡春洞、黄源深、王初明、黄远振等大力倡导加强英语文学名著整本书阅读教学，在基础教育界中越来越多的教师在课堂教学中也尝试文学阅读教学，但这些尝试主要集中在选修课中，选材也大多集中在美文或者少量的短篇小说，实践的时间也多是短期，在中学英语阅读教学中长期、系统地采用整本文学作品进行阅读教学的实践仍显不足(何泽，2017)。本节就近年来笔者在中学英语阅读中尝试整本书的阅读教学实践谈谈整本书阅读教学的基本理念、操作策略和实践反思。

一、整本书阅读的基本理念

笔者先后在两所中学带领学生读完了《典范英语(10)》(英国牛津大学出版社)。《典范英语(10)》是名著简写本，共14本，包括《简爱》《呼啸山庄》《秘密花园》等，整本原著有《彼得·潘》《夏洛的网》《老人与海》《相约星期二》《了不起的盖茨比》等，笔者实践整本书阅读的基本理念如下：

1. 依托课程标准，认识文学阅读的教育价值

《义务教育英语课程标准(2011 年版)》、新修订的《普通高中英语课程标准(2017 版)》都提出英语课程具有工具性和人文性的双重性质。英语教学要实现这双重性质，需要重新定位和梳理英语教育的核心价值、重新建构英语学习的目标。英语教育要体现人文性，应设立"多元目标"即"语言交流""思维认知"和"社会文化"三个目标(龚亚夫，2012)。提高语言技能只是外语教学的结果之一，认知发展和对现实世界的深刻理解才是最终目标，也就是"学以致知"(程晓堂、岳颖，2011)。可见当前英语教育的目标正在发生重大变革，英语作为一门必修学科必须完成属于自己分内的"培养什么样的人"的重任，就英语学科而言，英语教育的目标将从培养"综合语言运用能力"转变为"发展英语学科核心素养"。英语学科作为人文学科，它无疑承载着育人的重任，育人是核心素养的核心组成部分，这是传统的应试教育无法完成的(王蔷，2015)。文学是语言的艺术，文学是一个民族文化的精华部分，要真正学会一门外语，真正理解一个民族的优秀文化，阅读文学作品是必不可少的。历史和现实中大量的事实证明，阅读文学作品特别是文学经典，不仅可以促进一个人思维和感情的发展，也是推动一个人语言能力发展的最重要的渠道。词典家陆谷孙认为现在的教材"缺少对我们情感的打动"，从头念到尾可以不掉一滴眼泪，这算不上好教材。他认为外语输入应该加大"能打动人"的文学经典的比例。(束定芳，2017)。可见动人的整本文学原著的阅读是实现课标中的工具和人文兼具的课程目标和发展英语学科核心素养的必经之路。

2. 综合多种因素选材，激发阅读兴趣是阅读成功的关键

要从卷帙浩繁的外语文学世界中选择适合高中生阅读的作品，毫无疑问选材是关键。所选的文学作品不仅要符合学生的语言认知水平，力求语言优美、地道，而且作品的内容要具有吸引力、主题要积极向上，这样既能保证学生浸润在原汁原味的语言中学习地道的语言，又能保证对青少年的心理成长和思维发展有积极的推动作用。有关选材原则的论述很多，如选材应考虑五项原则：语言难度、语体特点、文学作品的内容和背景、作品的主题、该文学作品在文学史中的地位。(黄睿，2011)；还有教师认为选材要突出欣赏、适合学生、适合教师等特点。(2012，马丽)，除考虑以上因素外，笔者认为还要考虑学生的心理特征、现实条件、教育价值的引领等因素(2016，何泽)。

阅读兴趣是阅读成功的关键，要保持学生的阅读兴趣，首先要找到学生的心理需求并满足他们的心理需求，比如高一阅读的《夏洛的网》，是一首关于生命、友情、爱与忠诚的赞歌，符合高一学生当时的心理需求。

3. 探寻规律，学习阅读方法，提升阅读素养

美国学者莫提勒·J·艾得勒和查尔斯·范多伦在《如何阅读一本书》中提出：读者面对一本书，要先自己在心里提出四个要回答的问题：(1)整体来说，这本书到底在谈些什么？(2)作者细部说了什么，怎么说的？(3)这本书说得有道理吗？是全部有道理还是部分有道理？(4) 这本书跟你有什么关系？实际上这四个问题基本贯穿了整本书阅读的始终，这四个问题大体上可以概括为整本书阅读的三个方面：文本内容，由整体到部分读懂文本的内容；文体特点，即通过分析文本的结构特点、表达方式等赏析文本的写作特点和语言特色；读者立场，即通过分析、评判、探究等方式与文本和作者交流，最后读出自己的观点，并与自己的生活建立链接，从阅读中获得生活的道理。依据这四个问题，《如何阅读一本书》的作者有提出了阅读的四个层次：基础阅读、检视阅读、分析阅读、主题阅读。这四个层次由浅入深，基础阅读和检视阅读主要解决前两个问题，聚焦于文本的整体内容和细节，而分析阅读和主题阅读主要解决后两个问题，贯穿于文本的始终。整本英文原著的阅读同样也是由浅入深、层层递进、相互关联的，即解读作者写了什么、作者为什么写、作者是如何写的，以及你认为作者写得如何，最后进行迁移与运用(张献臣，2018)。

4. 读写结合，固化阅读成果

外语学习不仅需要可理解的输入，更需要可理解的输出，近年来在以读促写、读写结合成为外语教学中研究的热点，高考综合改革试点省份浙江省和上海市对于写作都做了大幅改革，其中浙江写作任务增加至两篇，其中第二篇是读后续写或概要写作，上海市的写作任务是概要写作，新题型的改革也彰显了读写结合的重要性。整本书阅读过程中将阅读和写作结合起来，阅读的内容给写作提供了丰富的语言素材、内容素材、语篇素材和人文素材等，如在基础阅读和检视阅读中对一些优美的语句的赏析，然后进行变式写作，对部分章节的情节进行联想和续写，对某些章节或真本书的概括写作等，在分析阅读过程中的读后书评、角色评析等，在主题阅读过程中的对主题的挖掘等，在读写结合阶段，学生的思维更多是迁移和创新，用英语进行理解和表达的过程不仅有利于学生培养通用的思维能力(如识别、理解、判断)，而且有利于形成英语使用者独有或擅长的思维方式和思维能力(程晓堂、赵思奇，2016)。

二、整本书阅读的教学实践

整本书阅读的理念是教师对于阅读活动整体的理性思考，是阅读的整体设计，而要进入阅读的具体操作层面，需要阅读活动这一载体实现理念和实践的融合，即上述的阅读意义、阅读方法和阅读成果的落实都要通过具体的多样化活动来落实。本节结合《夏洛的网》的阅读，通过展开的活动来展示整本书阅读的实践。整个阅读过程分为初读和理解、细读和分享、研读和表达三个阶段。第一阶段初读和理解历时四周左右，基本利用课外时间完成。第二阶段细读和分享和第三阶段的研读和表达历时一周左右，在课内完成。总体计划如表 3-4 所示：

表 3-4　整本书英文原著阅读整体计划

阅读步骤	主要活动	阅读目的
初读和理解	感知与注意、获取与梳理、概括与整合等（教育部，2018）。具体活动形式主要有梳理故事的故事结构、故事的主要人物及其关系、故事的语言特征、章节阅读卡填写等。	学习理解
细读和分享	描述与阐释、分析与判断、内化与运用等（教育部，2018）。具体活动形式主要有课内单元主题式精读，阅读圈交流等。	应用实践
研读和表达	推理与论证、批评与判断、内化与运用等（教育部，2018）。具体活动形式有报告撰写、续写、表演等。	迁移创新

1. 初读和理解

《夏洛的网》是一部动物小说，全书共 22 章，每章 500~800 字，全书大概在 10 万字，每天需 20~30 分钟阅读原著，建议阅读时间主要安排在课外，周末和假期可以适当增加阅读时间，按阅读速度每分钟 50 词左右，一个月可以轻松地完成 10 万~12 万词左右的原著阅读。本阶段的主要任务是通读《夏洛的网》，了解全书的人物关系、主要内容、重要细节，把握作者的基本观点等，这阶段的阅读目的是通过初读和理解形成本书的概貌。这阶段即回答上文基础阅读和检视阅读中提出的两个问题：(1)这本书到底在谈些什么？(2)作者细部说了什么，怎么说的？因此这一环节的阅读旨在把握全书和章节情节、理清人物关系等，从而为下一步的整体分析人物和情节打下基础，对全书的理解可从粗览全书填写表 3-5 入手：

表 3-5 *Charlotte's Web* 基本信息概览

Title	*Charlotte's Web*	Author	E. B. White
Main characters	Charlotte, Wilbur, Fern, Templeton		
Main structure	(1)a rescue of a runt (2) Wilbur's danger (3) Charlotte's plan of saving Wilbur (4) Charlotte's death		
Features of language	Narration, dialogues		
Theme of the story	Friendship, life and death		

对每章节的检查是以章节阅读卡 Question List 进行的，问题的设计以 WH 问题为主，如 Chapter 1 设计的问题是：(1) Why did Mr. Arable have an axe? (2) How did Fern care for the runt? (3) Why did she do that way? 通过回答这些问题，可以对每章节的大意和细节有初步的理解。初读和理解阶段即从整体上概览整本书，提取关键信息，又通过章节细节进一步感知全书，获取关键内容和细节，总之这阶段阅读的目的主要是感知文学语篇，重点是对故事要素结构进行梳理，包括故事的结构特征、故事的主要人物及其关系以及故事的语言特征。(苏克银，2019)

2. 细读和分享

本阶段主要采用小组合作的形式，每组由 4~5 人组成，学生自由组成文学圈阅读小组，文学圈阅读小组选择的任务通常有组长(discussion leader)、总结员(summerizer)、联系员(connector)、词汇员(word master)、文本员(passage person)、文化员(culture collector)等，每小组选择所读章节的人物、情节、语言、主题等任务，在仔细阅读的基础上，组内分工合作，可通过课件、板书文字、表演或者微视频等形式展示(何泽，2016)。读书报告会也是分享的过程，它是阶段性阅读成果的集中展示，也是不同观点和丰富阅读收获的良机，读书报告会以学生为主体，教师为主导，学生自定展示主题、内容以及展示的方式，教师主要对展示内容进行指导，确定展示报告会时间和场地，设计好评价单。评价包括报告内容、演讲质量、合作程度、展示效果等方面。如有一小组就以 *Wilbur's loneliness* 为主题分享阅读成果，该小组通过整理

书中描写 *Wilbur* 孤独的例句作为例证来阐述 *Wilbur* 对友谊的渴望。以下为该组引用的部分例句：

For a while he stood gloomily indoors.

Suddenly Wilbur felt lonely and friendless.

He groaned, "I'm young, I have no real friend here in barn."

Wilbur was crying again, for the second time in two days.

Wilbur didn't want food, he wanted love. He wanted a friend—someone who would play with him.

Sadly, Wilbur lay down and listened to the rain.

Friendless, dejected, and hungry, he threw himself down in the manure and sobbed.

This was certainly the worst day of his life. He didn't know whether he could endure the awful loneliness any more...

这阶段的阅读和分享以主题和内容为主线、以语言为暗线设计教学活动。学生在理解文本内容、探究主题意义的过程中体验语言的使用，感知语言结构，为运用所学语言奠定基础。(程晓堂，2018)

3. 探究和表达

本阶段的教学活动是在学生完成整本书的阅读后展开的。根据每本书的阅读学习的不同价值，教师可引领学生理解和复述作品、撰写读书报告、总结作品主题、分析人物形象、解析艺术特色、探究创作背景、评价作品等，从而从语言能力、思维品质、文化品格、学习能力等方面全面地关注学生英语学科核心素养的培养(王丽梅、李旭争，2019)。要让整本书阅读达到应有的深度，离不开教师的恰当引导，教师要善于找准切入点和落脚点，带领学生开创更多深层次的活动(刘建，2018)，如在撰写读书报告过程中笔者让学生围绕这三个基本问题来撰写：(1) Give the title, author, and a brief summary of the book's plot. (2) How does this book compare with other books you have read so far in this course?

(3) Would you recommend this book to a friend? Why or why not? 后两个问题就体现了深度和高度，有利于激发学生的好奇心和探究欲望。

整本书读完后还可以让学生围绕以下问题反思自己的阅读体会：(1) What are you noticing about yourself as a reader that is different from the way you read at the beginning of this course? (2) Are your interests, skills, or habits changing in any way? (3) Did you meet any of the reading goals you set for yourself? Which ones? Why do you think that is so? 读后的反思有助于培养良好的阅读兴趣，提升阅读素养和阅读品质，从而达到阅读的最终目的，做一个终身热爱阅读并有良好阅读习惯的读者。

三、实践反思

阅读实践，既充满欣喜也充满挑战，挖掘它在外语教学中的意义还有很长的路要走，本节笔者结合自己的整本英文原著阅读实践谈几点感想。

1. 整本书阅读和阅读素养

阅读素养作为公民核心素养之一，在各国国际学业质量评价中均受到重视，国际阅读素养进展研究项目(Progress in International Reading Literacy Study，简称 PIRLS)将阅读素养定义为“理解和运用社会所需要的或个人认为有价值的书面语言形式的能力。年轻阅读者能够从各种文本中建构意义，他们通过阅读来学习、参与学校和日常生活中的阅读团体，享受阅读的快乐”。国际学生评估项目(Programme for International Student Assessment，简称 PISA)指出，阅读素养是理解、运用、反思并积极参与阅读书面篇章，以增进知识，发挥潜能，参与社会，实现个人目标。由此可见阅读素养包含多个元素，如形成阅读理解能力，参与阅读群体活动，体验阅读乐趣等。阅读素养是对阅读能力的进一步发展，它不仅包含阅读能力所涉及的各要素，如解码能力、语言知识、阅读技巧和策略、阅读流畅度，还包涵了阅读的动机、态度、习惯等促成个体参与社会活动、促成其全人发展所需要的综合素养。经过实践证明整本书阅读有助于学生阅读兴趣和阅读能力的提升，有助于学生学科核心素养的培养(王丽梅、李旭争，2019)。

2. 整本书阅读与育人价值

英语学科的育人价值很大程度上是通过阅读人类历史上的优秀文化成果，培养对于传统文化的美好感情来实现的。文学阅读是所有阅读的核心，具有发展语言和思维的特殊功能(黄远振等，2014)。可见，通过阅读来提升语言能力的同时，阅读，特别是基于整本书的文学阅读在提升思维和发展健全的人格方面具有重大的意义。下面是访谈部分学生的摘录：

> 学生一：我最崇拜的人是 *Tuesdays with Morrie* 里的那个老教授。*Tuesdays with Morrie* 是我读得最认真的一本小说，这本书中具体的事例现在想不起来很多，但是阅读的影响一直都是潜移默化的，这本书让我很有感触，它让人去思考人生，解决了很多纠结的事，Morrie 那种洒脱乐观的态度是我一直都很欣赏也很想拥有的。
>
> 学生二：我读得比较认真的是 *The Great Gatsby*，作者的文笔真的很好啊，相比较于以前读的《傲慢与偏见》，我感觉 *The Great Gatsby* 通俗易懂但语言很巧妙，让人惊喜的 point 很多，笔调很辛辣也透露着悲哀，反正我很喜欢……这本书更多地其实是让我了解了美国那个年代的氛围和生活，还有也让我看到了那种浮华生活下的人物状态其实是很空虚也很愚蠢的，总结起来就是应更多地去提高自己的修养、充实内心，正确的人生观比什么都重要。

从上面的摘录中可见整本书的力量，这种源于生命感悟的阅读无疑会成为读者身上的一种素养。前苏联著名教育家苏霍姆林斯基曾说，“学校教育的缺点之一，就是没有那种占据学生的全部理智和心灵的真正的阅读。没有这样的阅读，学生就没有学习的愿望，他们的精神世界就会变得狭窄和贫乏”。著名的英语教育专家刘润清结合自身经验告诫我们，“读原著才是英语教育的开始”。因此，中学英语教育应创造条件把整本文学原著作为阅读教学的材料，在阅读中习得语言的同时，引导学生与伟大的心灵对话，滋养学生的心灵，从而克服当前各类快餐文化和功利思维的影响，这样才有利于通过提升学生的阅读素养来实现英语教学的育人重任。

3. 整本书阅读与阅读指导

整本书篇幅过长、词汇量要求与大纲要求也不一致，因此受阅读时间和生词过多等因素的限制，整本书英文原著的阅读阻力很大。这就要求老师主动引导并且给学生提供阅读指导。语文教学界有学者提出的整本书阅读的三个原则同样值得我们借鉴：这三条原则是“连滚带爬地读”“绞尽脑汁地想”和“挖空心思地用”（余党绪，2016）。“连滚带爬地读”主要是指阅读过程中应该重整体理解，不必苛求字字落实、句句较真。“绞尽脑汁地想”是强调思考的价值，阅读中的思考不仅包括对作者选词造句的斟酌，更包括对书中精神世界的深度思考，没有思考的阅读依然是浅层次的，这就需要批判性阅读。“挖空心思地用”是指尝试把阅读转化为自己的表达资源，“读以致用”。“用”可以深化对读的理解，阅读也由此走向深入。“用”也不限于写作，日常说话、交际和生活中都可以有意识、创造性地使用，特别是新高考中读写结合题型的出现，整本书阅读过程中对部分章节的赏析、借鉴、模仿、缩写、改写、续写等活动对于提高读写综合技能都大有裨益。

四、结语

国内的教育专家朱永新教授认为：一个人的精神发育史就是阅读史。可见阅读在人生发展中的地位和作用。本节倡导的整本书阅读目的是推动阅读教学的进一步发展，从而让更多学生在人生发展的基础阶段养成良好的阅读习惯，形成阅读素养，更好地发挥英语学习在教育中的作用。令人欣喜的是近年来外语教育界也有学者提出整本书阅读的理念，学者王初明认为英语学习者读英文小说帮助大，读英文长篇小说帮助更大，一部长篇小说会反复出现某些词语和句型，作品越长，其复现率就越高，从而不仅提供了依赖于文字创造、促进外语学习必不可少的丰富的情境语境，而且还为加速掌握外语语言结构提供了高效平台（王初明，2009），但整本书阅读在英语教学中的研究仍然处于起步阶段，希望在这方面的研究和实践更加深入。

◎ 参考文献

1. OECD. Assessment Framework Key Competencies in Reading, Mathematics and Science[M]. Paris: OECD Publishing, 2010.
2. 程晓堂，岳颖. 语言作为心智发展的工具——兼论外语学习的意义[J]. 中国外语，2011(1).
3. 程晓堂，赵思奇. 英语学科核心素养的实质内涵[J]. 课程 · 教材 · 教法，2016(5).
4. 程晓堂. 基于主题意义探究的英语教学理论与实践[J]. 中小学外语教学(中学篇). 2018(10).
5. 龚亚夫. 英语教育新论：多元目标英语课程[M]. 北京：高等教育出版社，2015.
6. 何泽. 在高中英语阅读教学中采用英文原著的实践[J]. 中小学外语教学(中学篇)，2016(3).
7. 何泽. 高中英语文学名著阅读教学实践探索[J]. 福建教育学院学报，2016(12).
8. 何泽. 高中英语文学阅读教学行动研究[D]. 华东师范大学博士论文，2017.
9. 黄睿. 外语教学中如何选用课外文学作品[J]. 现代教育科学，2011(5).
10. 黄远振，兰春寿，黄睿. 为思而教：英语教育价值取向及实施策略[J]. 课程 · 教材 · 教法，2014(4).
11. 中华人民共和国教育部. 义务教育英语课程标准(2011 版)[M]. 北京：北京师范大学出版社，2012.
12. 中华人民共和国教育部. 普通高中英语课程标准(2017 版)[M]. 北京：人民教育出版社，2018.
13. 李良佑. 中国英语教育史[M]. 上海：上海外语教育出版社，1988.

14. 刘润清. 漫长的学习道路[J]. 外国语，2003(4).
15. 刘建. 基于深层阅读的初中英语课外名著阅读欣赏课的实践与思考[J]. 中小学外语教学，2018(7).
16. 马丽. 浅谈高中英语文学欣赏选修课的选材[J]. 中小学外语教学(中学篇)，2012(5).
17. [美] 莫提默·J·艾德勒，查尔斯·范多伦. 如何阅读一本书[M]. 北京：商务印书馆，2004.
18. 束定芳. 中国特色外语教学理论的深厚实践基础——陆谷孙先生的外语教学理念与主张[J]. 外语界，2017(1).
19. [苏] 苏霍姆林斯基. 给老师的建议[M]. 杜殿坤，译. 北京：教育科学出版社，2001.
20. 苏克银. 高中英语主题阅读教学：探索与思考[J]. 中小学英语教学与研究，2019(1).
21. 王丽梅，李旭争. 基于学科核心素养的高中英语整本书阅读教学探析[J]. 中小学英语教学与研究，2019(2).
22. 王初明. 学相伴用相随——外语学习的学伴用随原则[J]. 中国外语，2009(5)
23. 王蔷. 从综合语言运用能力到英语学科核心素养——高中英语课程改革的新挑战[J]. 英语教师，2015(5).
24. 叶圣陶. 叶圣陶语文教育论集[M]，北京：教育科学出版社，2015.
25. 余党绪，叶开. 为什么我们都主张"整本书阅读"？[J]. 语文教学通讯(高中版)，2016(7-8).
26. 张献臣. 基于英语学科核心素养的中学英语阅读教学[J]. 中小学外语教学(中学篇)，2018(8).

第五节　提升读写综合素养

——基于英美名篇的高中英语文学阅读

该部分是作者在教学中开发的文学阅读材料举例，所选材料注重经典性，(如《秘密花园》原著节选，这是学生阅读该书简写本后的补充和升华；注重教育性，如海伦·凯勒的经典名著《假如给我三天光明》关于生命教育和挫折教育；注重时代性，如比尔·盖茨在哈佛大学的演讲。相信类似的文学阅读材料对开拓学生的视野、提高学生的人文素质，培养健全的人格、提升综合语言运用能力具有无与伦比的功用。所选材料和针对材料编写的练习不一定成熟，但希望其中蕴含的理念能起到抛砖引玉的作用。

Lesson 1　*The Secret Garden*

Frances Hodgson Burnett

(Excerpts)

In each century since the beginning of the world wonderful things have been discovered. In the last century more amazing things were found out than in any century before. In this new century hundreds of things still more **astounding** will be brought to light. At first people refuse to believe that a strange new thing can be done, then they begin to hope it can be done, then they see it can be done—then it is done and all the world wonders why it was not done centuries ago. One of the new things people began to find out in the last century was that thoughts—just mere thoughts—are as powerful as electric batteries—as good for one as sunlight is, or as bad for one as poison. To let a sad thought or a bad one get into your mind is as dangerous as letting a scarlet fever germ get into your body. If you let it stay there after it has got in you may never get over it as long as you live.

So long as Mistress Mary's mind was full of disagreeable thoughts about her dislikes and sour opinions of people and her determination not to be pleased by or interested in anything, she was a yellow-faced, sickly, bored and wretched child. Circumstances, however, were very kind to her, though she was not at all aware of it. They began to push her about for her own good. When her mind gradually filled itself with robins, and moorland cottages crowded with children, with queer **crabbed** old gardeners and common little Yorkshire housemaids, with springtime and with secret gardens coming alive day by day, and also with a moor boy and his "creatures," there was no room left for the disagreeable thoughts which affected her liver and her digestion and made her yellow and tired.

So long as Colin shut himself up in his room and thought only of his fears and weakness and his **detestation** of people who looked at him and reflected hourly on humps and early death, he was a hysterical half-crazy little hypochondriac who knew nothing of the sunshine and the spring and also did not know that he could get well and could stand upon his feet if he tried to do it. When new beautiful thoughts began to push out the old **hideous** ones, life began to come back to him, his blood ran healthily through his veins and strength poured into him like a flood. His scientific experiment was quite practical and simple and there was nothing weird about it at all. Much more surprising things can happen to any one who, when a disagreeable or discouraged thought comes into his mind, just has the sense to remember in time and push it out by putting in an agreeable determinedly courageous one. Two things cannot be in one place.

"Where, you tend a rose, my lad,

A **thistle** cannot grow."

While the secret garden was coming alive and two children were coming alive with it, there was a man wandering about certain far-away beautiful places in the Norwegian **fiord**s and the valleys and mountains of Switzerland and he was a man who for ten years had kept his mind filled with dark and heart-broken thinking. He had not been courageous; he had never tried to put any other thoughts in the place of the dark ones. He had wandered by blue lakes and thought them; he had lain on mountain-sides with sheets of deep blue **gentian**s blooming all about him and flower breaths filling all the air and he had thought them. A terrible sorrow had fallen upon him when he had been happy and he had let his soul fill itself with blackness and had refused **obstinately to allow any rift** of light to pierce through. He had forgotten and deserted his home and his duties. When he traveled about, darkness so brooded over him that the sight of him was a wrong done to other people because it was as if he poisoned the air about him with gloom. Most strangers thought he must be either half mad or a man with some hidden crime on his soul. He was a tall man with a **drawn** face and crooked shoulders and the name he always entered on hotel registers was, "Archibald Craven, Misselthwaite Manor, Yorkshire, England."

He had traveled far and wide since the day he saw Mistress Mary in his study and told her she might have her "bit of earth." He had been in the most beautiful places in Europe, though he had remained nowhere more than a few days. He had chosen the quietest and remotest spots. He had been on the tops of mountains whose heads were in the clouds and had looked down on other mountains when the sun rose and touched them with such light as made it seem as if the world were just being born.

But the light had never seemed to touch himself until one day when he realized that for the first time in ten years a strange thing had happened. He was in a wonderful valley in the Austrian Tyrol and he had been walking alone through such beauty as might have lifted, any man's soul out of shadow. He had walked a long way and it had not lifted his. But at last he had felt tired and had thrown himself down to rest on a carpet of moss by a stream. It was a clear little stream which ran quite merrily along on its narrow way through the **luscious** damp greenness. Sometimes it made a sound rather like very low laughter as it bubbled over and round stones. He saw birds come and dip their heads to drink in it and then **flick** their wings and fly away. It seemed like a thing alive and yet its tiny voice made the stillness seem deeper. The valley was very, very still.

As he sat gazing into the clear running of the water, Archibald Craven gradually felt his mind and body both grow quiet, as quiet as the valley itself. He wondered if he were going to sleep, but he was not. He sat and gazed at the sunlit water and his eyes began to see things growing at its edge. There was one lovely mass of blue forget-me-nots growing so close to the stream that its leaves were wet and at these he found himself looking as he remembered he had looked at such things years ago. He was actually thinking tenderly how lovely it was and what wonders of blue its hundreds of little blossoms were. He did not know that just that simple thought was slowly filling his mind—filling and filling it until other things were softly pushed aside. It was as if a sweet clear spring had begun to rise in a **stagnant** pool and had risen and risen until at last it swept the dark water away. But of course he did not think of this himself. He only knew that the valley seemed to grow quieter and quieter as he sat and stared at the bright delicate blueness. He did not know how long he sat there or what was happening to him, but at last he moved as if he were awakening and he got up slowly and stood on the moss carpet, drawing a long, deep, soft breath and wondering at himself. Something seemed to have been unbound and released in him, very quietly.

Excerpts From *The Secret Garden*

A Author and Background

Frances Eliza Hodgson Burnett (November 24 1849-October 29 1924) was an American-English playwright and author. She is best known for her children's stories, in particular *Little Lord Fauntleroy* (published in 1885-1886), *A Little Princess* (1905), and *The Secret Garden* (1911).

Burnett liked plants since the childhood, and there were several walled garden around her British home, one of which was her outdoor study. She wrote in the garden every day. In 1909, when she was in her garden of New York Long Island, she got the inspiration of "secret garden". The novel first came out in 1911, which is popular in her two countries- the UK and the USA and has become her most famous and successful works.

B Vocabulary and Discrimination

B1. New Vocabulary

生词释义

astounding	*adj.* 使人震惊的
crabbed	*adj.* 脾气坏的
detestation	*n.* 憎恶，嫌恶
hideous	*adj.* 可怕的
thistle	*n.* 蓟属植物；蓟
fiord	*n.* (尤指挪威的)峡湾
gentian	*n.* 龙胆属的植物，龙胆根
obstinately	*adv.* 顽固地，固执地
rift	*n.* 裂缝，裂口
drawn	*adj.* 疲惫的，憔悴的；
luscious	*adj.* 满足感官的
flick	*v.* 轻弹，轻击
stagnant	*adj.* 不流动的，停滞的

B2. Difficult Sentences

长难句译注

1. One of the new things people began to find out in the last century was that thoughts—just mere thoughts—are as powerful as electric batteries—as good for one as sunlight is, or as bad for one as poison. To let a sad thought or a bad one get into your mind is as dangerous as letting a scarlet fever germ get into your body. If you let it stay there after it has got in you may never get over it as long as you live.

   上个世纪，人们开始发现的新事物之一即思想——只是思想本身——和电池一样强有力——跟阳光一样对人益处多多，抑或是跟毒药一样对人害处多多，让一个阴暗的或邪恶的念头腐蚀你的思想，就犹如让猩红热的病菌潜入你的体内一样危险。如果你一直放任它存在于你的思想，那么你的寿命有多长它就能毒害你有多久。

2. So long as Colin shut himself up in his room and thought only of his fears and weakness and his detestation of people who looked at him and reflected hourly on humps and early death, he was a hysterical half-crazy little hypochondriac who knew nothing of the sunshine and the spring and also did not know that he could get well and could stand upon his feet if he tried to do it.

只要柯林还把自己关在房间里，一心想着他的恐惧和懦弱，憎恨着那些窥探自己、不时地揶揄自己驼背和早夭的人们，他就会一直是个歇斯底里、处于半癫狂状态的抑郁症患者，对阳光和春天一无所知，也不知道自己有可能会好转，更不知道如果自己努力，有一天还会重新站起来。

3. Much more surprising things can happen to any one who, when a disagreeable or discouraged thought comes into his mind, just has the sense to remember in time and push it out by putting in an agreeable determinedly courageous one. Two things cannot be in one place.

如果一个人当不为人喜或令人气馁的念头涌上心头时，就是有意识地及时把它们排除体外，换之令人愉悦和欢欣鼓舞的念头，那么将会有更加惊人的新变化发生在这个人身上，这两种念头不可能同时出现。

4. A terrible sorrow had fallen upon him when he had been happy and he had let his soul fill itself with blackness and had refused obstinately to allow any rift of light to pierce through. He had forgotten and deserted his home and his duties. When he traveled about, darkness so brooded over him that the sight of him was a wrong done to other people because it was as if he poisoned the air about him with gloom.

当他一度沉浸在幸福中时，可怕的悲痛降临到他身上，从此他的灵魂便充斥着黑暗，并且固执地抵制丝丝亮光的刺入。他已经遗忘了他的家园，丢弃了自己的责任。当他四处旅行时，黑暗的氛围弥漫在他的左右，任何人看到他都不觉得是件好事，因为他用阴郁的情绪污染着周围的空气。

5. He had been on the tops of mountains whose heads were in the clouds and had looked down on other mountains when the sun rose and touched them with such light as made it seem as if the world were just being born.
他曾在直插云霄的山顶，俯瞰其他山头，当时旭日初升，每个山头都染上了金色的光芒，就仿佛整个世界都是初生的一般。

B3. Essential Words

在例句中选出与文本中画线词汇同义的句子。

1. … The valley was very, very still.
   A. A hot still day makes everyone in the hall uncomfortable and upset.
   B. We stood still and watched as the deer came closer.
   C. The house was completely still.
2. He had forgotten and deserted his home and his duties.
   A. Mike's confidence seemed to have deserted him.
   B. Helen was deserted by her husband.
   C. This area of the country is mostly desert.
3. There was one lovely mass of blue forget-me-nots growing so close to the stream that its leaves were wet and at these he found himself looking as he remembered he had looked at such things years ago.
   A. They were sitting close together on the couch.
   B. It was close to 1：15 a. m..
   C. The two countries are close to signing a peace agreement.
4. He was actually thinking tenderly how lovely it was and what wonders of blue its hundreds of little blossoms were.
   A. The sight of the Taj Mahal filled us with wonder.

B. No wonder you've got a headache, the amount you drank last night.

C. A few moments of relaxation can work wonders.

C Understanding and Thinking

C1. Understanding the Text

根据文章内容回答下列问题。

1. What once made Mistress Mary yellow-faced, sickly and tired?
2. What happened to Colin when new beautiful thoughts got into his mind?
3. Did Mr. Craven really enjoy traveling? Then why had he traveled far and wide?
4. What actually awakened Mr. Craven to the darkness that he was once trapped in?

C2. Critical Thinking Based on the Text

根据文章内容思考下列问题。

1. What's the function of the first paragraph of this reading part? Is it related to the theme of this passage?
2. This reading part is aimed to tell us the wonders worked on the three characters. So what actually changed them? Does this part have any relationship with the theme of the whole book "the secret garden"?

D Extension and Usage

D1. Language in Use

阅读下列材料，在空白处填入适当的内容(一个单词)或括号内单词的适当形式。

The singular calmness remained with him the rest of the evening and he __1__ (sleep) a new reposeful(平稳的) sleep; __2__ it was not with him very long. He did not know that it could be kept. By the next night he had opened the doors wide to his dark thoughts and they had come trooping and

___3___ (rush) back. He left the valley and went on his wandering way again. But, strange as it seemed to him, there ___4___ (be) minutes—sometimes half-hours—when, without his knowing why, the black burden seemed ___5___ (lift) itself again and he knew he was a living man and not a dead one. Slowly-slowly-for no reason that he knew of—he was "coming alive" with the garden.

As the golden summer changed ___6___ the deep golden autumn he went to the Lake of Como. There he found the loveliness of a dream. He spent his ___7___ (day) upon the crystal blueness of the lake or he walked back into the soft thick verdure of the hills and tramped until he was tired so ___8___ he might sleep. But by this time he had begun to sleep ___9___ (good), he knew, and his dreams had ceased to be a terror to ___10___ (he).

Excerpts from *The Secret Garden*

D2. Literary Bank

朗读从文中摘录的文字，尤其是画线部分，注意感受文字描写的环境、景色，你的心境是否因而转变。尝试翻译画线部分！

He was in a wonderful valley in the Austrian Tyrol and he had been walking alone through such beauty as might have lifted, any man's soul out of shadow. He had walked a long way and it had not lifted his. But at last he had felt tired and had thrown himself down to rest on a carpet of moss by a stream. (1) It was a clear little stream which ran quite merrily along on its narrow way through the luscious damp greenness. Sometimes it made a sound rather like very low laughter as it bubbled over and round stones. He saw birds come and dip their heads to drink in it and then flick their wings and fly away. It seemed like a thing alive and yet its tiny voice made the stillness seem deeper. The valley was very, very still.... He sat and gazed at the sunlit water and his eyes began to see things growing at its edge. (2) There was one lovely mass of blue forget-me-nots growing so close to the stream that its leaves were wet and at these he found himself looking as he remembered he had looked at such things years ago. He was actually thinking tenderly how lovely it was and what wonders of blue its hundreds of little blossoms were.

Lesson 2 *Three Days to See*

(Excerpts)

Helen Keller

All of us have read thrilling stories in which the hero had only a limited and specified time to live. Sometimes it was as long as a year; sometimes as short as twenty-four hours, but always we were interested in discovering just how the doomed man chose to spend his last days or his last hours. I speak, of course, of free men who have a choice, not **condemned** criminals whose **sphere** of activities is strictly **delimited**. Such stories set up thinking, wondering what we should do under similar circumstances. What associations should we crowd into those last hours as mortal beings? What happiness should we find in reviewing the past, what regrets?

Sometimes I have thought it would be an excellent rule to live each day as if we should die tomorrow.

Such an attitude would **emphasize** sharply the values of life. We should live each day with a gentleness, a **vigor**, and a keenness of appreciation which are often lost when time stretches before us in the constant **panorama** of more days and months and years to come. There are those, of course, who would adopt the epicurean motto of "Eat, drink, and be merry," but most people would be chastened by the certainty of impending death.

In stories the doomed hero is usually saved at the last minute by some stroke of fortune, but almost always his sense of values is changed. He becomes more appreciative of the meaning of life and its permanent spiritual values. It has often been noted that those who live, or have lived, in the shadow of death bring a mellow sweetness to everything they do.

Most of us, however, take life for granted. We know that one day we must die, but usually we picture that day as far in the future, when we are in **buoyant** health, death is all but unimaginable.

We seldom think of it. The days stretch out in an endless **vista**. So we go about our petty task, hardly aware of our listless attitude towards life.

The same **lethargy**, I am afraid, characterizes the use of our faculties and senses. Only the deaf appreciate hearing, only the blind realize the manifold blessings that lie in sight. Particularly does this observation apply to those who have lost sight and hearing in adult life. But those who have never suffered impairment of sight or hearing seldom make the fullest use of these blessed faculties. Their eyes and ears take in all sights and sound hazily, without concentration, and with little appreciation. It is the same old story of not being grateful for what we have until we lose it, of not being conscious of health until we are ill.

I have often thought it would be a blessing if each human being were stricken blind and deaf for a few days at some time during his early adult life. Darkness would make him more appreciative of sight; silence would teach him the joys of sound.

Now and then I have tested my seeing friends to discover what they see. Recently I was visited by a very good friend who had just returned from a long walk in the woods, and I asked her what she had observed. "Nothing in particular," she replied. I might have been incredulous had I not been accustomed to such responses, for long ago I became convinced that the seeing see little.

How was it possible, I asked myself, to walk for an hour through the woods and see nothing worthy of note? I who cannot see find hundreds of things to interest me through mere touch. I feel the delicate **symmetry** of a leaf. I pass my hands lovingly about the smooth skin of a silver birch, or the rough shaggy bark of a pine. In spring I touch the branches of trees hopefully in search of a bud, the first sign of awakening Nature after her winter's sleep I feel the delightful, velvety texture of a flower, and discover its remarkable convolutions; and something of the miracle of Nature is revealed to me. Occasionally, if I am very fortunate, I place my hand gently in a small tree and feel the happy quiver of a bird in full song. I am delighted to have cool waters of a brook rush through my open fingers. To me a lush carpet of pine needles or spongy grass is more welcome than the most **luxurious** Persian rug. To me the pageant of seasons is a thrilling and unending drama, the action of which streams through my finger tips.

At times my heart cries out with longing to see all these things. If I can get so much pleasure from mere touch, how much more beauty must be revealed by sight. Yet, those who have eyes apparently see little. The panorama of color and action fill the world is taken for granted. It is human, perhaps, to appreciate little that which we have and to long for that which we have not, but it is a great pity that in the world of light and the gift of sight is used only as mere convenience rather that as a means of adding fullness to life.

Excerpts From *Three Days to See*

A　Author and Background

Helen Keller was an American writer and speaker. She was born in Tuscumbia, Alabama in 1880. When she was nineteen months old she became sick and lost her eyesight and hearing. Her teacher Anne Sullivan helped Helen to learn how to communicate with other people. She taught her the names of things by writing the words on Helen's hand. When she was nineteen years old, Helen went to Radcliffe College in Massachusetts. She graduated from Radcliffe in 1904. She was the first deaf and blind person to earn a Bachelors of Arts degree. In 1903, Helen wrote a book about her life called The Story of My Life. She also wrote a book about Anne Sullivan called Teacher (1955). She also wrote other books. Out of the Dark (1913), and

Three Days to See (1933).

Helen tried to help poor people and other blind people during her life. She traveled to over 39 countries with Anne to talk about her life and experiences. Helen Keller still affects us today. She reminds us that people with disabilities can do great things. In April 1998, the United States magazine TIME included Helen Keller in its list of the 100 most influential people of the 20th century, for "She altered our perception of the disabled and remapped the boundaries of sight and sense."

B　Vocabulary and Discrimination

B1. New Vocabulary

生词释义

condemn　*v.* 谴责
sphere　*n.* 范围
delimit　*v.* 限定
emphasize　*v.* 强调
vigor　*n.* 活力
panorama　*n.* 全景
buoyant　*adj.* 繁荣的
vista　*n.* 景色
lethargy　*adj.* 无精打采的
incredulous　*adj.* 不可信的
symmetry　*n.* 对称
luxurious　*adj.* 奢侈的

B2　Difficult Sentences

长难句译注

1. Such stories set up thinking, wondering what we should do under similar

circumstances. What associations should we crowd into those last hours as mortal beings? What happiness should we find in reviewing the past, what regrets?

这样的故事让我们思考，在相似的情况下，我们该怎么办，作为终有一死的人，在那最终的几个小时内安排什么事件，什么经历，什么交往？在回顾往事时，我们该找到什么快乐？什么悔恨？

2. There are those, of course, who would adopt the epicurean motto of "Eat, drink, and be merry," but most people would be chastened by the certainty of impending death.

当然，也有人愿意按照伊壁鸠鲁的信条"吃、喝和欢乐"地去生活，但绝大多数人还是被即将面临死亡的必然性所折磨。

译注：伊壁鸠鲁是古希腊哲学家，他认为生活的主题是享乐，而最高的享受唯通过合理的生活，如自我控制才能得到。因为生活享受的目的被过分强调，而达到此目的之手段被忽视，所以伊壁鸠鲁的信徒现今变为追求享乐的人。他们的信条是："让我们吃喝，因为明天我们就死亡。"

3. Most of us, however, take life for granted. We know that one day we must die, but usually we picture that day as far in the future, when we are in buoyant health, death is all but unimaginable.

We seldom think of it. The days stretch out in an endless vista. So we go about our petty task, hardly aware of our listless attitude towards life.

但是，我们大多数人把生活认为是理所当然的。我们知道，某一天我们一定会死，但通常我们把那天想象在遥远的将来。当我们心宽体健时，死亡几乎是不可想象的，我们很少想到它。时日在无穷的展望中延展着，于是我们干着琐碎的事情，几乎意识不到我们对生活的倦怠态度。

4. I who cannot see find hundreds of things to interest me through mere touch. I feel the delicate symmetry of a leaf. I pass my hands lovingly about the smooth skin of a silver birch, or the rough shaggy bark of a pine.

我自己，一个不能看见东西的人，仅仅通过触觉，会发现许许多多令我有兴趣的东西。我感触到一片树叶的完美的对称性。我用手喜爱地抚摸过一株白桦那光潮的树皮，或一棵松树的粗糙树皮。

5. It is human, perhaps, to appreciate little that which we have and to long for that which we have not, but it is a great pity that in the world of light and the gift of sight is used only as mere convenience rather that as a means of adding fullness to life.

   或许，这是人性共有的特点：对我们具有的不怎么欣赏，而对我们不具有的却渴望得到。然而，这是一个极大的遗憾，在光明的世界里，视力的天赋仅仅作为一种方便之用，而没有作为增添生活美满的手段。

B3　Essential words：选用方框中的单词并用它的适当形式填空。

thrilling	circumstance	review	emphasize	stretch
appreciate	concentration	delicate	remarkable	gently

1. The ring has a very ________ design.
2. I'd just like to ________ how important it is for people to learn foreign languages.
3. The area is ________ for its scenery.
4. She tries to ________ across the table for the butter.
5. ________ on your studies will result in good grades.
6. Our ________ are so desperate that it is uncertain whether we will ever return alive.
7. ________ your homework before you turn it in.
8. I'd ________ it if you would like to teach me how to use the machine.
9. The breeze is ________ and we really have a good time at the beach.
10. The film is so ________ that we all want to see it.

C　Understanding and Thinking

C1. 根据文章内容回答下列问题。

1. Why does the author think it would be an excellent rule to live each day as if we should die tomorrow?
2. What is the majority's attitude towards life according to the author?
3. How does the author find the interesting things in different seasons?

C2. 根据文章内容思考下列问题。

1. What is the purpose of writing this essay in your opinion?
2. How do you account for the fact that many people with perfect sight often see little, or when they do see, see things inaccurately? In your opinion is there any remedy for this?

D　Extension and Usage

D1. 阅读下列材料，在空白处填入适当的内容(一个单词)或括号内单词的正确形式。

If I were the president of a university I should establish a compulsory course in "How to Use Your Eyes". The professor would try to show his pupils how they could add joy __1__ their lives by really __2__ (see) what passes unnoticed before them. He would try to awake their dormant and sluggish faculties.

Perhaps I can best illustrate by imagining what I should most like to see if I were __3__ (give) the use of my eyes, say, for just three days. And while I am imagining, suppose you, too, set your mind __4__ (work) on the problem of how you would use your own eyes if you had only three more days to see. If with the on-coming __5__ (dark) of the third night you knew that the sun would never rise for you again, how would you __6__ (spend) those three precious intervening days? What would you most want to let your gaze rest upon?

I, naturally, should want most to see the things which have become dear to me through ___7___ (I) years of darkness. You, too, would want to let your eyes rest on the things that have ___8___ (become) dear to you so ___9___ you could take the memory of them with you into the night that loomed before you.

If, by some miracle, I were granted three seeing days, to be followed by a relapse into darkness, I should divide the period ___10___ three parts.

D2. 朗读从文中摘录的文字，注意画线部分的词和短语，并选用文中画线部分的短语翻译后面的句子。

How was it possible, I asked myself, to walk for an hour through the woods and see nothing worthy of note? I who cannot see find hundreds of things to interest me through mere touch. I feel the delicate symmetry of a leaf. I pass my hands lovingly about the smooth skin of a silver birch, or the rough shaggy bark of a pine. In spring I touch the branches of trees hopefully in search of a bud, the first sign of awakening Nature after her winter's sleep I feel the delightful, velvety texture of a flower, and discover its remarkable convolutions; and something of the miracle of Nature is revealed to me. Occasionally, if I am very fortunate, I place my hand gently in a small tree and feel the happy quiver of a bird in full song. I am delighted to have cool waters of a brook rush through my open fingers. To me a lush carpet of pine needles or spongy grass is more welcome than the most luxurious Persian rug. To me the pageant of seasons is a thrilling and unending drama, the action of which streams through my finger tips.

1. 他的新理论值得注意。

2. 你仅仅通过触摸就可以网上购物。

3. 阳光透过窗户倾泻进来。

4. 我很高兴得知你被足球社录取了。

5. 她进了厨房，想找点喝的。

Lesson 3　*The Boys' Ambition*

Mark Twain

When I was a boy, there was but one permanent ambition among my comrades in our village on the west bank of the Mississippi River. That was, to be a steamboatman. We had **transient** ambitions of other sorts, but they were only transient. When a circus came and went, it left us all burning to become clowns; the first negro **minstrel show** that came to our section left us all suffering to try that kind of life; now and then we had a hope that if we lived and were good, God would permit us to be pirates. These ambitions faded out, each in its turn; but the ambition to be a steamboatman always remained.

Once a day a cheap, **gaudy** packet arrived upward from St. Louis, and another downward from Keokuk. Before these events, the day was glorious with expectancy; after them, the day was a dead and empty thing. Not only the boys, but the whole village, felt this. After all these years I can picture that old time to myself now, just as it was then: the white town **drowsing** in the sunshine of a summer's morning; the streets empty, or pretty nearly so; one or two clerks sitting in front of the Water Street stores, with their splint-bottomed chairs tilted back against the wall, chins on breasts, hats slouched over their faces, asleep—with shingle-shavings enough around to show what broke them down; a sow and a litter of pigs loafing along the sidewalk, doing a good business in watermelon rinds and seeds; two or three lonely little freight piles scattered about the "levee"; a pile of "skids" on the slope of the stone-paved wharf, and the fragrant town drunkard asleep in the shadow of them; two or three wood flats at the head of the wharf, but nobody to listen to the peaceful lapping of the wavelets against them; the great Mississippi, the **majestic**, the **magnificent** Mississippi, rolling its mile-wide tide along, shining in the sun; the dense forest away on the other side; the "point" above the town, and the "point" below, bounding the river-glimpse and turning it into a sort of sea, and withal a very still and brilliant and lonely one. **Presently** a film of dark smoke appears above one of those remote "points"; instantly a negro **drayman**, famous for his quick eye and **prodigious** voice, lifts up the cry, "S-t-e-a-m-boat a-comin!" and the scene changes! The town drunkard stirs, the clerks wake up, a furious clatter of drays follows, every house and store pours out a human contribution, and all in a twinkling the dead town is alive and moving.

Drays, carts, men, boys, all go hurrying from many quarters to a common center, the wharf. Assembled there, the people fasten their eyes upon the coming boat as upon a wonder they are seeing for the first time. And the boat is rather a handsome sight, too. She is long and sharp and **trim** and pretty; she has two tall, fancy-topped chimneys, with a gilded device of some kind swung between them; a fanciful pilot-house, a glass and "gingerbread", **perch**ed on top of the "texas" deck behind them; the paddle-boxes are gorgeous with a picture or with gilded rays above the boat's name; the boiler deck, the hurricane deck, and the texas deck are fenced and ornamented with clean white railings; there is a flag **gallantly** flying from the jack-staff; the furnace doors are open and the fires glaring bravely; the upper decks are black with passengers; the captain stands by the big bell, calm, **imposing**, the envy of all; great volumes of the blackest smoke are rolling and tumbling out of the chimneys—a **husband**ed **grandeur** created with a bit of pitch pine just before arriving at a town; the crew are grouped on the forecastle; the broad stage is run far out over the port bow, and an envied deckhand stands **picturesquely** on the end of it with a coil of rope in his hand; the pent steam is screaming through the gauge-cocks, the captain lifts his hand, a bell rings, the wheels stop; then they turn back, **churn**ing the water to foam, and the steamer is at rest. Then such a scramble as there is to get aboard, and to get ashore, and to take in freight and to discharge freight, all at one and the same time; and such a yelling and cursing as the mates **facilitate** it all with! Ten minutes later the steamer is under way again, with no flag on the jack-staff and no black smoke issuing from the chimneys. After ten more minutes the town is dead again, and the town drunkard asleep by the skids once more.

My father was a justice of the peace, and I supposed he possessed the power of life and death over all men and could hang anybody that offended him. This was distinction enough for me as a general thing; but the desire to be a steamboatman kept **intruding**, nevertheless. I first wanted to be a cabin-boy, so that I could come out with a white apron on and shake a tablecloth over the side, where all my old comrades could see me; later I thought I would rather be the deckhand who stood on the end of the stage-plank with the coil of rope in his hand, because he was particularly **conspicuous**. But these were only day-dreams—they were too heavenly to be **contemplated** as real possibilities. By and by one of our boys went away. He was not heard of for a long time. At last he turned up as **apprentice** engineer or 'striker' on a steamboat. This thing shook the bottom out of all my Sunday-school teachings. That boy had been **notoriously** worldly, and I just the reverse; yet he was exalted to this **eminence**, and I left in **obscurity** and misery. There was nothing generous about this fellow in his greatness. He would always manage to have a rusty bolt to **scrub** while his boat **tarried** at our town, and he would sit on the inside guard and scrub it, where we could all see him and envy him and loathe him. And whenever his boat was laid up he would come home and swell around the town in his blackest and greasiest clothes, so that nobody could help remembering that he was a steamboatman; and he used all sorts of steamboat **technicalities** in his talk, as if he were so used to them that he forgot common people could not understand them. He would speak of the "labboard" side of a horse in an easy, natural way that would make one wish he was dead. And he was always talking about "St. Looy" like an old citizen; he would refer casually to occasions when he was coming down Fourth Street, or when he was passing by the Planter's House, or when there was a fire and he took a turn on the brakes of "the old Big Missouri"; and then he would go on and lie about how many towns the size of ours were burned down there that day. Two or three of the boys had long been persons of consideration among us because they had been to St. Louis once and had a vague general knowledge of its wonders, but the day of their glory was over now. They **lapsed** into a humble silence, and learned to disappear when the ruthless cub-engineer approached. This fellow had money, too, and hair oil. Also an ignorant silver watch and a showy brass watch chain. He wore a leather belt and used no suspenders. If ever a youth was **cordially** admired and hated by his comrades, this one was. No girl could withstand his charms. He "cut out" every boy in the village. When his boat blew up at last, it diffused a tranquil contentment among us such as we had not known for months. But when he came home the next week, alive, renowned, and appeared in church all battered up and bandaged, a shining hero, stared at and wondered over by everybody, it seemed to us that the partiality of Providence for an undeserving reptile had reached a point where it was open to criticism.

Excerpts from *Life on the Mississippi*

A Author and Background

Samuel Langhorne Clemens (November 30, 1835-April 21, 1910), better known by his pen name Mark Twain, was an American author and humorist. He wrote *The Adventures of Tom Sawyer* (1876) and its sequel, *theAdventures of Huckleberry Finn* (1885), the latter often called "The Great American Novel".

Life on the Mississippi (1883) is a memoir by Mark Twain of his days as a steamboat pilot on the Mississippi River before the American Civil War, and also a travel book, recounting his trip along the Mississippi River from St. Louis to New Orleans many years after the War.

B Vocabulary and Discrimination

B1. New Vocabulary

生词释义

transient	*adj.* 临时的
minstrel show	黑人说唱团演出
gaudy	*adj.* 花哨的
drowse	*v.* 打瞌睡
majestic	*adj.* 宏伟的
magnificent	*adj.* 壮丽的
presently	*adv.* 不久
drayman	*n.* 运货马车车夫

prodigious	*adj.* 异常的，惊人的
trim	*adj.* 修长的
perch	*v.* 停留
gallantly	*adv.* 大胆地
imposing	*adj.* 威风的
husband	*v.* 节俭地使用
grandeur	*n.* 富丽堂皇
picturesquely	*adv.* 形象地
churn	*v.* 搅动
facilitate	*v.* 促进，助长
intrude	*v.* 闯入
conspicuous	*adj.* 惹人注意的
contemplate	*vt.* 注视，凝视
apprentice	*n.* 学徒
notoriously	*adv.* 恶名昭彰地
eminence	*n.* 显赫，卓越
obscurity	*n.* 晦涩
scrub	*v.* 用力擦洗，刷洗；
tarry	*vi.* 停留
technicality	*n.* 术语
lapse	*vi.* 陷入(into)
cordially	*adv.* 诚挚地

B2. Difficult Sentences

长难句译注

1. … one or two clerks sitting in front of the Water Street stores, with their splint-bottomed chairs tilted back against the wall, chins on breasts, hats slouched over their faces, asleep—with shingle-shavings enough around to show what broke them down.

一两个员工坐在瓦特街商店的门口，藤条椅子翘起来，靠在墙上，下巴顶在胸前，帽子垂下遮着脸，打着瞌睡——他们身边有许多木瓦刨花，这足以说明削木瓦把他们累坏了。

2. ... two or three lonely little freight piles scattered about the "levee"; a pile of "skids" on the slope of the stone-paved wharf, and the fragrant town drunkard asleep in the shadow of them; two or three wood flats at the head of the wharf, but nobody to listen to the peaceful lapping of the wavelets against them.

两三个孤零零的小货物堆在码头上散置着，石头铺的起卸码头的坡上有一堆垫木，镇上的醉汉就在这木堆近旁酣睡着；码头上端有两三只平底木船，可是，水浪拍打着这些船只的柔和声音却没有人倾听。

levee：河堤；skid：（原意）滑道，滚道

wavelet：-let 后缀，意为"小"，如 booklet(a small book)，piglet(a little pig)，applet(a small computer application)，owlet(a young owl)

3. ... the "point" above the town, and the "point" below, bounding the river-glimpse and turning it into a sort of sea, and withal a very still and brilliant and lonely one.

镇子上游的地角和下游的地角划分了河面的景色，把瞬间流淌的河水变成一种大海的景色，而且这海面还是风光明媚、沉寂而幽静。

withal：adv. 此外

4. ... the paddle-boxes are gorgeous with a picture or with gilded rays above the boat's name; the boiler deck, the hurricane deck, and the texas deck are fenced and ornamented with clean white railings...

浆轮壳也漂亮非凡，那上面绘着图画，还在船名之上绘了一些金色的光带；锅炉甲板、顶层甲板和上层甲板周围都配有干净的白栏杆……

5. But when he came home the next week, alive, renowned, and appeared in church all battered up and bandaged, a shining hero, stared at and

wondered over by everybody, it seemed to us that the partiality of Providence for an undeserving reptile had reached a point where it was open to criticism.

但是下个星期他居然活着回家了，并且还出了名，浑身带伤，绑着绷带在教堂出现，成了个出风头的英雄，人人都注视着他，对他感到惊异，这时候我们就觉得老天(上帝)对一个毫无价值的坏蛋的偏爱似乎是到了一种应受批评的地步了。

B3. Essential Words

在例句中选出和文本中画线词汇同义的句子。

1. After all these years I can picture that old time to myself now,...

   A. She's been pictured as a difficult, demanding woman.

   B. She is pictured with her mum Christine and sister Kelly.

   C. Tom, picturing the scene, smiled.

2. Presently a film of dark smoke appears above one of those remote "points";...

   A. A film of oil floated on the surface of the water.

   B. Have you ever seen any good films recently?

   C. The whole incident was recorded on film.

3. Then such a scramble as there is to get aboard, and to get ashore, and to take in freight and to discharge freight, all at one and the same time.

   A. It was a mad scramble trying to get things ready in time.

   B. He broke his leg in his scramble down the wall.

   C. The inexperienced young promising men were pushed aside in the scramble for places.

4. Ten minutes later the steamer is under way again, with no flag on the jack-staff and no black smoke issuing from the chimneys.

   A. Water issuing from the hole in the wall feels cool.

   B. Please issue everyone with a pencil.

C. This brochure on farming was issued by the Department of Agriculture.

C Understanding and Thinking

C1. 根据文章内容回答下列问题。

1. What were once the boys' ambitions although they were transient? And what was their permanent ambition?
2. What happened to the dead town when the steamboat was coming?
3. In what ways can we find the boat is rather a handsome sight?

C2. 根据文章内容思考下列问题。

1. In the reading part, we can find many parts employing contrast and comparison, for example, the changing scenes of the town before and when the boat was coming; the notorious boy turning apprentice engineer was exalted to the eminence while I left in obscurity and misery... What can you infer from those parts with contrast and comparison?
2. What finally did "I" do as my career? And what would occur to me when "I" looked for the job?

D Extension and Usage

D1. 阅读下列材料，在空白处填入适当的内容（1个单词）或括号内单词的适当形式。

So by and by I ran away. I said I never __1__ (come) home again till I was a pilot and could come in glory. But somehow I could not manage __2__. I went meekly __3__ a few of the boats that __4__ (lie) packed together like sardines at the long St. Louis wharf, and very __5__ (humble) inquired __6__ the pilots, but got only a __7__ shoulder and short words from mates and clerks. I had to make the best of this sort of treatment for the time being, but I had __8__ (comfort) daydreams of a future when I should be a great and honored __9__, with plenty of money, and could kill some of these mates and clerks and pay for __10__ (they).

D2. 用括号里所给的单词或短语翻译下列句子。

1. 我禁不住回忆过往。(can't help)

2. 她说得好像她知道整件事件似的。(as if)

3. 尽管她未提任何名字吗，但大家都清楚她在指谁。(refer to)

4. 我有时间和孩子待一天的场合相当少。(occasions... when...)

5. 他对美国历史了解甚少。(have knowledge of)

Lesson 4　*The World as I See It*

Albert Einstein

How strange is the lot of us **mortals**! Each of us is here for a brief **sojourn**; for what purpose he knows not, though he sometimes thinks he senses it. But without deeper reflection one knows from daily life that one exists for other people—first of all for those upon whose smiles and well-being our own happiness is wholly dependent, and then for the many, unknown to us, to whose **destinies** we are bound by the ties of sympathy. A hundred times every day I remind myself that my inner and outer life are based on the labors of other men, living and dead, and that I must **exert** myself in order to give in the same measure as I have received and am still receiving. I am strongly drawn to a **frugal** life and am often oppressively aware that I am **engrossing** an **undue** amount of the labor of my fellowmen. I regard class distinctions as unjustified and, in the last resort, based on force. I also believe that a simple and unassuming life is good for everybody, physically and mentally.

I do not at all believe in human freedom in the philosophical sense. Everybody acts not only under external compulsion but also in accordance with inner necessity. Schopenhauer's saying, "A man can do what he wants, but not want what he wants," has been a very real inspiration to me since my youth; it has been a continual consolation in the face of life's hardships, my own and others', and an unfailing **wellspring** of tolerance. This realization mercifully **mitigates** the easily paralyzing sense of responsibility and prevents us from taking ourselves and other people all too seriously; it is **conducive** to a view of life which, in particular, gives humor its due.

To inquire after the meaning or object of one's own existence or that of all creatures has always seemed to me absurd from an objective point of view. And yet everybody has certain ideals which determine the direction of his endeavors and his judgments. In this sense I have never looked upon ease and happiness as ends in themselves—this ethical basis I call the ideal of a **pigsty**. The ideals which have lighted my way, and time after time have given me new courage to face life cheerfully, have been Kindness, Beauty, and Truth. Without the sense of **kinship** with men of like mind, without the occupation with the objective world, the eternally unattainable in the field of art and scientific endeavors, life would have seemed to me empty. The **trite** objects of human efforts—possessions, outward success, luxury—have always seemed to me **contemptible**.

My passionate sense of social justice and social responsibility has always contrasted **oddly** with my pronounced lack of need for direct contact with other human beings and human communities. I am truly a "lone traveler" and have never belonged to my country, my home, my friend, or even my immediate family, with my whole heart; in the face of all these ties, I have never lost a sense of distance and a need for solitude-feelings which increase with the years. One becomes sharply aware, but without regret, of the limits of mutual understanding and **consonance** with other people. No doubt, such a person loses some of his innocence and unconcern; on the other hand, he is largely independent, of the opinions, habits, and judgments of his fellows and avoids the temptation to build his inner **equilibrium** upon such insecure foundations.

The most beautiful experience we can have is the mysterious. It is the fundamental emotion which stands at the cradle of true art and true science. Whoever does not know it and can no longer wonder, no longer **marvel**, is as good as dead, and his eyes are dimmed. It was the experience of mystery—even if mixed with fear—that **engendered** religion. A knowledge of the existence of something we cannot **penetrate**, our perceptions of the profoundest reason and the most radiant beauty, which only in their most primitive forms are accessible to our minds—it is this knowledge and this emotion that constitute true religiosity; in this sense, and in this alone, I am a deeply religious man. I cannot **conceive** of a God who rewards and punishes his creatures, or has a will of the kind that we experience in ourselves. Neither can I nor would I want to conceive of an individual that survives his physical death; let feeble souls, from fear or absurd **egoism**, cherish such thoughts. I am satisfied with the mystery of the **eternity** of life and with the awareness and a glimpse of the marvelous structure of the existing world, together with the devoted striving to comprehend a **portion**, be it ever so tiny, of the Reason that **manifests** itself in nature.

A Author and Background

Albert Einstein (14 March 1879-18 April 1955) was a German-born theoretical physicist who developed the theory of general relativity, effecting a revolution in physics. For this achievement, Einstein is often regarded as the father of modern physics and one of the most prolific intellects in human history. He received the 1921 Nobel Prize in Physics "for his services to theoretical physics, and especially for his discovery of the law of the photoelectric effect". The latter was pivotal in establishing quantum theory within physics. Einstein's intellectual achievements and originality have made the word "Einstein" synonymous with "genius".

Einstein believed in humanity, in a peaceful world of mutual helpfulness, and in the high mission of science. Intended as a plea for these beliefs, this book, like no other provides a complete key to the understanding of this distinguished man's personality.

This book does not represent a complete collection of the articles, addresses, and pronouncements of Albert Einstein; it is a selection made with a definite object—namely, to give a picture of a man. Today this man is being drawn, contrary to his own intention, into the whirlpool of political passions and contemporary history. As a result, Einstein is experiencing the fate that so many of the great men of history experienced: his character and opinions are being exhibited to the world in an utterly distorted form.

B Vocabulary and Discrimination

B1. New Vocabulary

生词

mortal	*n.* 凡人
sojourn	*n.* 逗留

destiny	*n.* 命运
exert	*v.* 努力
frugal	*adj.* 节俭的
engross	*v.* 使全神贯注
undue	*adj.* 过度的
wellspring	*n.* 源泉
mitigate	*v.* 缓和，减轻
conducive	*adj.* 有助于
pigsty	*n.* 猪圈
kinship	*n.* 亲切感
trite	*adj.* 老生常谈的
contemptible	*adj.* 可鄙的
oddly	*adv.* 怪异地，奇特地
consonance	*n.* 一致，协调
equilibrium	*n.* 均衡
marvel	*v.* 感到惊讶
engender	*v.* 导致，引发
penetrate	*v.* 穿透，渗透
conceive	*v.* 想出
egoism	*n.* 利己主义
eternity	*n.* 永恒，永生
portion	*n.* 一部分
manifest	*v.* 显现，证明

B2. 长难句译注

1. How strange is the lot of us mortals! Each of us is here for a brief sojourn; for what purpose he knows not, though he sometimes thinks he senses it.
   我们这些肉体凡胎是多么奇怪啊！每个人来到这个世上都只作短暂停留，究竟为了什么目的却无从知晓，虽然有时觉得自己好像有所感悟。

2. Without the sense of kinship with men of like mind, without the occupation with the objective world, the eternally unattainable in the field of art and scientific endeavors, life would have seemed to me empty.

如果没有对志同道合者的那种亲近感，如果没有对客观世界——那个艺术和科学研究永远也无法穷极的世界——的孜孜以求，生命对我来说就是一场空。

3. Whoever does not know it and can no longer wonder, no longer marvel, is as good as dead, and his eyes are dimmed.

无论是谁，如果没有感受过它的魅力，如果不再感到好奇，不再发出惊叹，他就无异于行尸走肉，瞎眼盲心。

B3. 在例句中选出和文本中画线词汇同义的句子。

1. But without deeper <u>reflection</u> one knows from daily life that one exists for other people…

   A. A week off would give him time for <u>reflection</u>.

   B. He admired his <u>reflection</u> in the mirror.

   C. Your clothes are often a <u>reflection</u> of your personality.

2. … I must exert myself in order to give in the same <u>measure</u> as I have received and am still receiving.

   A. We must take preventive <u>measures</u> to reduce crime in the area.

   B. Our thanks are due in equal <u>measure</u> to every member of the team.

   C. Is this test a good <u>measure</u> of reading comprehension?

3. I do not at all believe in human freedom in the philosophical <u>sense</u>.

   A. The dog has a very acute <u>sense</u> of smell.

   B. I had the <u>sense</u> that he was worried about something.

   C. In a <u>sense</u> it doesn't matter any more.

4. It is the fundamental emotion which <u>stands</u> at the cradle of true art and true science.

A. Their honesty stands in total contrast to the deceitfulness of their opponents..

B. She couldn't stand being kept waiting.

C. She was standing beside my bed staring down at me.

5. ... which only in their most primitive forms are accessible to our minds...

A. The remote desert area is accessible only by helicopter.

B. He gets along well with everyone because he is accessible.

C. This is a program making science more accessible to young people.

C　Understanding and Thinking

C1. Understanding the Text 根据文章内容回答下列问题。

1. What is a pigsty?
2. Why does the writer regard himself as a lone traveler?
3. Why does the writer say "mysterious" is the fundamental emotion?

C2. Critical Thinking 根据文章内容思考下列问题。

1. Have you ever thought about why you exist in this world?
2. Why can a man do what he wants, but not want what he wants?

D　Extension and Usage

D1. Language in Use 阅读下列材料，在空白处填入适当的内容(一个单词)或括号内单词的适当形式。

I was sitting outside my new home yesterday, ________(watch)(1) the world go by. There were people in cars, in a hurry ________ (get)(2) to their next appointment. There were birds flying by, insects just as busy as the people in cars, plants and weeds thriving in the humid Guam climate. ________(3) the house, my children were also busy, as ever, making a mess of the house, getting into things, their natural ________(curious)(4) overpowering our previous pleas for them ________(not play)(5) with lotion or take things apart.

The sky was ________ (slight) (6) overcast and there was a cool breeze, quite strong and pleasant actually. It's not often that most of us just sit quietly, and allow the world to pass us by.

Why not? What is so important ________(7) it can't wait until later? What email must ________ (answer)(8) right this moment? Do we need to have the television and radio and Internet on all the time? Are we missing out on the beautiful world around us as we constantly think about the ________ (9) and the past.

When was the ________(10) time you just sat, and observed? Why not do it today?

D2. 朗读从文中摘录的文字，注意画线部分的词和短语，并选用文中画线部分的短语翻译后面的句子。

I do not at all believe in human freedom in the philosophical sense. Everybody acts not only under external compulsion but also in accordance with inner necessity. Schopenhauer's saying, "A man can do what he wants, but not want what he wants," has been a very real inspiration to me since my youth; it has been a continual consolation in the face of life's hardships, my own and others', and an unfailing wellspring of tolerance. This realization mercifully mitigates the easily paralyzing sense of responsibility and prevents us fromtaking ourselves and other people all tooseriously; it is conducive to a view of life which, in particular, gives humor its due.

1. 没有人强迫你立刻付款。

2. 我们遵照我父母的意愿行事。

3. 面对危险她表现出了巨大的勇气。

4. 他们认真对待自己的职责。

5. 他喜爱读书，尤其是科幻小说。

Lesson 5　*Bill Gates' Graduation Speech at Harvard*

Bill Gates

I applaud the graduates today for taking a much more direct route to your degrees. For my part, I'm just happy that the Crimson① has called me "Harvard's most successful dropout." I guess that makes me **valedictorian** of my own special class... I did the best of everyone who failed.

What I remember above all about Harvard was being in the midst of so much energy and intelligence. It could be **exhilarating**, **intimidating**, sometimes even discouraging, but always challenging. It was an amazing privilege—and though I left early, I was transformed by my years at Harvard, the friendships I made, and the ideas I worked on.

But taking a serious look back... I do have one big regret.

I left Harvard with no real awareness of the awful **inequities** in the world-

① The Harvard Crimson, the daily student newspaper of Harvard University, was founded in 1873.

the **appallingdisparities** of health, and wealth, and opportunity that condemn millions of people to lives of despair.

I learned a lot here at Harvard about new ideas in economics and politics. I got great exposure to the advances being made in the sciences.

But humanity's greatest advances are not in its discoveries-but in how those discoveries are applied to reduce inequity. Whether through democracy, strong public education, quality health care, or broad economic opportunity-reducing inequity is the highest human achievement.

I left campus knowing little about the millions of young people cheated out of educational opportunities here in this country. And I knew nothing about the millions of people living in **unspeakable** poverty and disease in developing countries.

It took me decades to find out.

You graduates came to Harvard at a different time. You know more about the world's inequities than the classes that came before. In your years here, I hope you've had a chance to think about how-in this age of accelerating technology-we can finally take on these inequities, and we can solve them.

Imagine, just for the sake of discussion, that you had a few hours a week and a few dollars a month to donate to a cause-and you wanted to spend that time and money where it would have the greatest impact in saving and improving lives. Where would you spend it?

For Melinda and for me, the challenge is the same: how can we do the most good for the greatest number with the resources we have.

During our discussions on this question, Melinda and I read an article about the millions of children who were dying every year in poor countries from diseases that we had long ago made harmless in this country. **Measles, malaria, pneumonia, hepatitis B, yellow fever.** One disease I had never even heard of, **rotavirus**, was killing half a million kids each year-none of them in the United States.

We were shocked. We had just assumed that if millions of children were dying and they could be saved, the world would make it a **priority** to discover and deliver the medicines to save them. But it did not. For under a dollar, there were **interventions** that could save lives that just weren't being delivered.

If you believe that every life has equal value, it's revolting to learn that some lives are seen as worth saving and others are not. We said to ourselves: "This can't be true. But if it is true, it deserves to be the priority of our giving."

So we began our work in the same way anyone here would begin it. We asked: "How could the world let these children die?"

The answer is simple, and harsh. The market did not reward saving the lives of these children, and governments did not **subsidize** it. So the children died because their mothers and their fathers had no power in the market and no voice in the system.

But you and I have both.

We can make market forces work better for the poor if we can develop a more creative capitalism-if we can stretch the reach of market forces so that more people can make a profit, or at least make a living, serving people who are suffering from the worst inequities. We also can press governments around the world to spend taxpayer money in ways that better reflect the values of the people who pay the taxes.

If we can find approaches that meet the needs of the poor in ways that generate profits for business and votes for politicians, we will have found a sustainable way to reduce inequity in the world. This task is open-ended. It can never be finished. But a conscious effort to answer this challenge will change the world.

I believe we have more caring than we know what to do with.

The barrier to change is not too little caring; it is too much complexity.

To turn caring into action, we need to see a problem, see a solution, and see the impact. But **complexity** blocks all three steps.

If we can really see a problem, which is the first step, we come to the second step: cutting through the complexity to find a solution.

Finding solutions is essential if we want to make the most of our caring. If we have clear and proven answers anytime an organization or individual asks "How can I help?", then we can get action-and we can make sure that none of the caring in the world is wasted. But complexity makes it hard to mark a path of action for everyone who cares — and that makes it hard for their caring to matter.

The final step-after seeing the problem and finding an approach-is to measure the impact of your work and share your successes and failures so that others learn from your efforts.

You have to have the statistics, of course. You have to be able to show that a program is **vaccinating** millions more children. You have to be able to show a decline in the number of children dying from these diseases. This is essential not just to improve the program, but also to help draw more investment from business and government.

But if you want to inspire people to participate, you have to show more than numbers; you have to convey the human impact of the work-so people can feel what saving a life means to the families affected.

Still, I'm optimistic. Yes, inequity has been with us forever, but the new tools we have to cut through complexity have not been with us forever. They are new-they can help us make the most of our caring-and that's why the future can be different from the past.

The defining and ongoing innovations of this age-biotechnology, the computer, the Internet-give us a chance we've never had before to end extreme poverty and end death from preventable disease.

The emergence of low-cost personal computers gave rise to a powerful network that has transformed opportunities for learning and communicating.

The magical thing about this network is not just that it collapses distance and makes everyone your neighbor. It also dramatically increases the number of brilliant minds we can have working together on the same problem-and that scales up the rate of innovation to a **staggering** degree.

At the same time, for every person in the world who has access to this technology, five people don't. That means many creative minds are left out of this discussion—smart people with practical intelligence and relevant experience who don't have the technology to **hone** their talents or contribute their ideas to the world.

In line with the promise of this age, I want to exhort each of the graduates here to take on an issue-a complex problem, a deep inequity, and become a specialist on it. If you make it the focus of your career, that would be **phenomenal**. But you don't have to do that to make an impact. For a few hours every week, you can use the growing power of the Internet to get informed, find others with the same interests, see the barriers, and find ways to cut through them.

Don't let complexity stop you. Be activists. Take on the big inequities. It will be one of the great experiences of your lives.

A　Author and Background

Bill Gates was born on October 28, 1955 and he is an American business magnate, philanthropist, investor, computer programmer, and inventor. In 1975, Gates co-founded Microsoft, the world's largest PC software company, with Paul Allen. During his career at Microsoft, Gates held the positions of chairman, CEO and chief software architect, and was the largest individual shareholder until May 2014.

Gates started to prepare this June 2007 speech back in December 2006.

He worked on this speech for over six months.

B Vocabulary and Discrimination

B1. New Vocabulary

生词释义

valedictorian *n.* 致告别辞者，告别演说者

exhilarating *adj.* 使人高兴的，令人兴奋的

intimidating *adj.* 令人惊恐的

inequity *n.* 不公平，不公正

appalling *adj.* 骇人听闻的，令人震惊的

disparity *n.* 悬殊

unspeakable *adj.* 无法形容的

measles, malaria, pneumonia, hepatitis B, yellow fever
均为疾病名称，依次是麻疹，疟疾、肺炎、乙型肝炎、黄热病，

rotavirus *n.* 轮状病毒(一种致婴儿或新生畜胃肠炎的病毒)

priority *n.* 优先，优先权

intervention *n.* 介入，干涉，干预

subsidize *v.* 以津贴补助

complexity *n.* 复杂性，错综复杂的状态

vaccinate *v.* 给……接种疫苗

staggering *adj.* 难以置信的，令人震惊的

hone *v.* 完善

exhort *v.* 勉励

phenomenal *adj.* 显著的

B2. Difficult Sentences

长难句译注

1. I left Harvard with no real awareness of the awful inequities in the world-

the appalling disparities of health, and wealth, and opportunity that condemn millions of people to lives of despair.

我离开哈佛的时候，根本没有意识到这个世界是多么地不平等。人类在健康、财富和机遇上的不平等大得可怕，它们使得无数的人们被迫生活在绝望之中。

2. For under a dollar, there were interventions that could save lives that just weren't being delivered.

那些价格还不到一美元的救命的药剂，并没有送到他们的手中。

3. If we can find approaches that meet the needs of the poor in ways that generate profits for business and votes for politicians, we will have found a sustainable way to reduce inequity in the world. This task is open-ended. It can never be finished. But a conscious effort to answer this challenge will change the world.

如果我们能够找到这样的方法，既可以帮穷人，又可以为商人带来利润，为政治家带来选票，那么我们就找到了一种减少世界性不平等的可持续的发展道路。这个任务是无止境的。它不可能被完成，但是任何自觉地解决这个问题的尝试，都将会改变这个世界。

4. But complexity makes it hard to mark a path of action for everyone who cares — and that makes it hard for their caring to matter.

但是，世界的复杂性使得很难找到对全世界每一个有爱心的人都有效的行动方法，因此人类对他人的关心往往很难产生实际效果。

5. The magical thing about this network is not just that it collapses distance and makes everyone your neighbor. It also dramatically increases the number of brilliant minds we can have working together on the same problem-and that scales up the rate of innovation to a staggering degree.

网络的神奇之处，不仅仅是它缩短了物理距离，使得天涯若比邻。它还极大地增加了怀有共同想法的人们聚集在一起的机会，我们可以为了解决同一个问题共同工作。这就大大加快了革新的进程，发展速度简直快得让人震惊。

B3. Essential Words

在例句中选出和文本中画线词汇同义的句子。

1. But humanity's greatest advances are not in its discoveries-but in how those discoveries are applied to reduce inequity.
   A. She applied for a job with the local newspaper.
   B. Stephen would do well if only he applied himself.
   C. It is said that the same rules are applied to part-time workers.
2. Imagine, just for the sake of discussion, that you had a few hours a week and a few dollars a month to donate to a cause...
   A. You can get fit, and at the same time raise money for a worthy cause.
   B. Breast cancer is the leading cause of death for American women in their 40s.
   C. U. S. officials expect other western governments to make common cause with them over the arrests.
3. You have to be able to show a decline in the number of children dying from these diseases.
   A. The first signs of economic decline became visible.
   B. Mary declined a hot drink and went to her room.
   C. They held a belief that educational standards are in decline.
4. It also dramatically increases the number of brilliant minds we can have working together on the same problem
   A. He tipped his head to one side and sighed dramatically.
   B. At speeds above 50 mph, serious injuries dramatically increase.
   C. She bowed dramatically. "Anastasia Krupnik, at your service," she said.

C Understanding and Thinking

C1. Understanding the Text

根据文章内容回答下列问题。

1. What once made the couple shocked?

2. What are the three steps to change the world? Is it easy to fulfill the change?
3. Why is Bill Gates still optimistic about the situation?

C2. Critical Thinking Based on the Text

根据文章内容思考下列问题。

1. Bill Gates mentioned complexity made it hard to change, how do you understand the complexity here in his speech?
2. What actually did Bill Gates want to convey in his speech at the graduation ceremony? If you were the graduate, what would you feel and what would choose to do after that?

D Extension and Usage

D1. Language in Use

阅读下列材料，在空白处填入适当的内容(一个单词)或括号内单词的适当形式。

You graduates are coming of age in an amazing time. As you leave Harvard, you have technology that __1__ (member) of my class never had. You have awareness of global inequity, which we did not have. And with that awareness, you likely also have an informed conscience that will torment you if you abandon these people __2__ lives you could change with very little effort. You have more than we had; you must start __3__ (soon), and carry on longer. __4__ (know) what you know, how could you not? And I hope you will __5__ (come) back here to Harvard 30 years from now and reflect __6__ what you have done with your talent and your energy. I hope you will judge __7__ (you) not on your professional accomplishments alone, __8__ also on how well you have addressed the world's deepest inequities... on how well you treated people a world away who __9__ nothing in common with you but __10__ (they) humanity.

D2. Literary Bank

用括号里所给的单词或者短语翻译下列句子。

1. 身体受烈日暴晒会造成伤害。(exposure)

2. 没有任何别的组织有能力或愿意承担此项工作。(take on)

3. 幸福就是有能力充分享受你拥有的一切。(make the most of)

4. 这种手段可能产生一个有意义的探索领域。(give rise to)

5. 这些设施已经改造过以方便轮椅使用者进入。(access to)

◎ 参考答案

Lesson 1

B3. CBAC

C1. 1. Her mind was full of disagreeable thoughts about her dislikes and sour opinions of people and her determination not to be pleased by or interested in anything, which made her yellow-faced and sickly.

2. When new beautiful thoughts got into his mind, life began to come back to him, his blood ran healthily through his veins and strength poured into him like a flood.
3. No, he didn't. He traveled far and wide to forget and desert his home and duties.
4. It's the power of nature— the stream, hundreds of little blue blossoms that awaken him.

C2. 1. The first paragraph functions as the top paragraph which indicates the theme of the passage, that is, the power of thought. It is as good for one as sunlight is, or as bad for one as poison. (Any reasonable answer is acceptable)

2. Nature changes one's thought, and then thought changes one's lifestyle.

This reading part is just like key to understanding the novel, and it well illustrates the power of nature and one's thought. Meanwhile "the secret garden" is just the secret to changing the three main characters of the novel-Miss Mary, Colin and Mr. Craven. (Any reasonable answer is acceptable)

D1. slept　2. but　3. rushing　4. were　5. to lift　6. into　7. days　8. that　8. begun　9. better　10. him

D2. 1. 那是一条清澈的小溪，潺潺流水在狭窄的石槽间欢快地穿越过青翠滋润的沼泽地。有时溪水撞击与绕过圆石块，便会发出像是低低浅笑那样的咕噜声。他看到时不时会有鸟儿飞来往水里一冲，将头浸进去喝水，然后又振翅离去。小溪像是也有生命的，它发出的微弱声却使周遭的寂静变得更加深邃。这山谷真是静极了呢……

2. 有一丛可爱的勿忘我生长在靠水那么近的地方，以致叶子都给打湿了，这景象他多年前亦曾见过。他确实是在柔情地思忖，这花儿多么可爱，这成百朵小花简直能算是蓝色的奇迹了。

Lesson 2

B3. 1. delicate 2. emphasize 3. remarkable 4. stretch
5. Concentration 6. circumstances 7. Review 8. appreciate
9. gentle 10. thrilling

C1. 1. Such an attitude would **emphasize** sharply the values of life.
2. Most of us take life for granted and take a listless attitude towards life.
3. The author finds the interesting things in different seasons through mere touch.

C2. 1. This essay is intended to remind people of the value of life. (Any reasonable answer is acceptable.)
2. Many people with perfect sight often take life for granted and don't value what they have owned. I think we should get more close to nature and learn to value our life. (Any reasonable answer is acceptable.)

D1 1. add 2. seeing 3. given 4. to work 5. darkness 6. spend
7. my 8. become 9. that 10. into

D2. 1. His new theory is worthy of note.
2. You can shop online through mere touch.
3. The sun streams through the windows.
4. I am delighted to know that you have been admitted into the football club.
5. She went into the kitchen in search of a drink

Lesson 3

B3. CAAA

C1. 1. The boys had such transient ambitions as clowns, singers, or pirate, but the ambition to be a steamboatman always remained.

2. When the steamboat was coming, all in a twinkling the dead town was alive and moving.

3. She is long and sharp and trim and pretty; she has two tall, fancy-topped chimneys, a fanciful pilot-house, the boiler deck, the hurricane deck, and the texas deck are fenced and ornamented with clean white railings; there is a flag gallantly flying from the jack-staff; the furnace doors are open and the fires glaring bravely; the upper decks are black with passengers...

C2. 1. From the contrast and comparison, we can find the important role of the Mississippi River and the boat in American people's life. Mark Twain further informs us that the river is different from other rivers and how trades along the river develop with the development of steamboat enterprise. (Any reasonable answer is acceptable)

2. "I" probably ran away from home, and tried to find a job on the boat. "I" managed to get a position, and learned how to be a good steamboatman. (Any reasonable answer is acceptable)

D1. 1. would come　2. it　3. aboard　4. lay　5. humbly　6. for
7. cold　8. comforting　9. pilot　10. them

D2. 1. I couldn't help thinking about the past.

2. She speaks as if she knew everything about the issue.

3. Although she didn't mention any names, everyone knew who she was referring to.

4. Occasions are quite rare when I have the time to spend a day with my kids.

5. He doesn't have much knowledge of American history.

Lesson 4

B3：ABCAC

C1：1. Pigsty means looking upon ease and happiness as ends in themselves.

2. Because he has no direct contact with other human beings and human communities.

3. Because only with a sense of curiosity can you find the true art and true science. Those who no longer have the curiosity are as good as dead.

C2：1. Human beings are advanced creatures and we came into being because of evolution. In order to survive and live a better life, we have to work hard.（Any reasonable answer is acceptable.）

2. Because our acts are not only under external control but also subjected to inner necessity.

D1：1. watching　2. to get　3. Inside　4. curiosity　5. not to play
6. slightly　7. that　8. be answered　9. future　10. last

D2：1. You are under no compulsion to pay immediately.

2. We acted in accordance with my parents' wishes.

3. She showed great courage in the face of danger.

4. They take their responsibilities seriously.

5. He loves reading books, science fiction in particular.

Lesson 5

B3. CACB

C1. 1. Melinda and I read an article about the millions of children who were dying every year in poor countries from diseases that we had long ago made harmless in this country.

2. The three steps to change the world are that we need to see a problem, find a solution, and measure the impact. It's not easy to fulfill the change because complexity blocks the three steps.

3. Because the new tools we have, like biotechnology, the computer, the Internet can help us make the most of our caring, then the future can be different from the past.

C2. 1. Complexity lies in many aspects, such as the policy of the government, inequity, people's bias against the poor, people's unawareness of the situation and action they can take... (Any reasonable answer is acceptable)

2. Bill Gates wanted to arouse the awareness of the graduates of the situation of inequity in the world and turn their caring to action, making the most of the modern tools.

If I was the graduate, I would be shocked at the inequity in the world. I would take an active part in surmounting the barriers to help the poor. (Any reasonable answer is acceptable)

D1. members 2. whose 3. sooner 4. knowing 5. come 6. on 7. yourselves 8. but 9. have 10. their

D2. 1. Exposure of the body to strong sunlight can be harmful.

2. No other organization was able or willing to take on the job.

3. Happiness is the ability to make the most of what you have.

4. Such an approach may giveriseto a research field of interest.

5. The facilities have been adapted to give access to wheelchair users.

◎ 本章小节

本章是前两轮实验的总结和提升，主题围绕于英美名篇的高中英语文学阅读提升读写综合素养这一主题，从童话导读、文学阅读与学科核心素养、整本书阅读、实践具体案例等方面展开。

童话契合儿童的心理，童话导读通过唤醒儿童的体验，激发儿童的想象，建立审美意蕴，引领儿童成长，从而提高儿童的阅读鉴赏能力和终身阅读能力。

中学英语教学中引进文学名著作为阅读教学的补充内容有利于提升

学科核心素养，具体的途径有：细读鉴赏、学用结合，培养语言能力；自主探究、合作分享，养成学习能力；分析推断、批判创新，提升思维品质；潜移默化、理解共情，培养文化意识。

在中学英语教学中采用整本英文原著的实践。其阅读主要有三个阶段：初读和理解、细读和分享、研读和表达，并就整本书阅读实践进行了反思，认为整本英文原著的阅读有助于提升学生的阅读素养。

最后部分以作者在教学中开发的文学阅读材料为举例，所选材料注重经典性、教育性、时代性，这些文学阅读材料对开拓学生的视野、提高学生的人文素质，培养健全的人格、提升综合语言运用能力具有无与伦比的功用，希望所选材料和针对材料编写的练习能起到抛砖引玉的作用。